WORDS OF PRAISE FOR

NO MORE DRAMA

A chapter into the book I immediately I thought of a hundred people to send it to. Any woman struggling with disempowerment will benefit from reading *No More Drama* because the power of truth and honesty, so rarely seen in a book, rings through loud and clear.

– Marva Allen, owner, Hueman Bookstore

In *No More Drama*, Sil Lai Abrams shows how she was able to transform from a spiritually bankrupt survivor to a truly empowered contender. These nine simple principles can help you take back your power and stop surviving!

– Florence Anthony, syndicated radio host and author

In *No More Drama*, Sil Lai Abrams in raw and vivid detail uses her own story to show how you don't have to continue to play out the script of your life written by society, abusive relationships, addiction or any breed of pain.

– Michaela angela Davis, fashion and media expert

No More Drama encourages and inspires you to look within and discover your own truth. Through the simple sharing of her story, Sil Lai Abrams demonstrates the importance of trading in your self-defeating behaviors for a truly empowering life.

– Sakina Spruell, Editor at Large, Black Enterprise magazine

No More Drama

*Nine Simple Steps to Transforming a
Breakdown Into a Breakthrough*

Sil Lai Abrams

A SEPIA Book
SEPIA Press Publishing, New York

FIRST EDITION PUBLISHED IN 2007.

Cover design by Jen Huppert Design

Library of Congress Control Number: 2007903500

ISBN 13: 978-0-615-14632-4
ISBN 10: 0-615-14632-5

Printed in the United States of America

ACKNOWLEDGEMENTS

THANK YOU, Christian and Amanda, for
giving me the freedom to pursue my dream.

THANK YOU, Carol Ingram, for your friendship and for
standing by my side through almost twenty years of drama.

THANK YOU, Gwen Clayton and Quay Whitlock,
for your sisterhood and friendship.

THANK YOU, John Pasmore, for giving me the
idea to turn my life into story.

THANK YOU, Wilson Christopher, for your
continuous help reshaping this book.

THANK YOU, Nile Rodgers, for believing in me.

THANK YOU, Andrew Morrison, for showing me
how to transform my dream into a reality.

THANK YOU, Jeff Kaplan, for your faith and support.

THANK YOU, Angela Lyons, Anthanette Fields, Antonio "LA" Reid,
Ayo Roach, Brett Wright, Brian Keith Jackson, Dara Roach, Deborah Gregory,
Dirk Winkler, Donna Bagdasarian, Flo Anthony, Gigi Pierre, Ian Kleinert,
Joyce Wale, Jonathan Edwards, Keith Boykin, Kendal Hart, Leonard E. Burnett, Jr.,
Lesly Zamor, Matthew Jordan Smith, Michael Liburd, Miguel Herrera,
Paula Austin, Pam Pickens, Dr. Pierre Arty, Reverend Conrad Tillard,
Ryan Smith, Sandie Smith, and W. Brian Maillian, for your encouragement.

THANK YOU, Scott Anderson, for the wonderful edit of
my manuscript.

THANK YOU, Jen Huppert, Lisa Henington, and Marc Baptiste,
for your creative genius.

SPECIAL THANKS TO THE FOLLOWING;
WITHOUT THEIR SUPPORT THIS BOOK
WOULD NOT HAVE BEEN POSSIBLE:

*Adaku Okpi, Andrew Morrison, Angela & Lesly Zamor,
Bobbito Garcia, Carol Ingram, Diana Petras, Don Cogsville,
Eric Woods, Jaylaan Llewellyn, Jennifer Brown, Jim Beeks,
Jonathan P. Edwards, Julie Emmons, Julio Castaing,
Justin Guinup, Kobi Carter, Lionel Ridenour, Michael Williams,
Dr. Pierre Arty, Quay Whitlock, Ryan Smith, Thomas Lytle,
Tony Shellman, Trent Tucker, and W. Brian Maillian*

This book is dedicated in loving memory of

May Lai Baber, my sister
1972-1998

Marian Michaels, my mentor
1953-2006

CONTENTS

INTRODUCTION

We have all heard the expression, "Never judge a book by its cover," and this saying not only applies to books but to people as well. We often can't tell what someone is like just from looking at them. Sometimes our first impressions of a person are negative, but once we get to know them we discover that our initial perceptions were without merit. And sometimes it works the other way around and we meet someone who looks like they have it all together, only to find out later that their cover hides a darker story.

For example, if you were to meet me you would encounter a seemingly confident and outgoing mid thirty-something black female who could still wear the same size clothing that she wore as a model several years before. We would probably discuss topics like our careers and families, which for me includes entertainment industry related event planning, and two healthy and educationally gifted children respectively. But as is often the case, things are not always as they seem. If you were to look past my cover, a grimmer story would emerge.

The story of my life could well have been pulled from the script of an over-the-top Hollywood film, a sort of cross between "The Joy Luck Club" and "Leaving Las Vegas." I grew up never knowing the identity of my biological father, the product of an overseas affair held during the Vietnam War between a married black serviceman and a nineteen year old Chinese girl. At the age of four I was abandoned by my mother and subsequently

1

raised in a white family who hid my ethnic background from me until I was fourteen years old.

By fifteen I was an alcoholic runaway who had been expelled from high school and at nineteen, became pregnant with my first child and was living on welfare. After giving birth to my son, I became embroiled in a three-year child support battle with his father, a successful music producer some twenty years older than me.

At twenty things finally seemed to get better when I was able to leave public assistance and become a receptionist, and by twenty-two I was even earning a decent living as a fashion model. This work seemed in many ways a dream come true, but my career was sidelined after I was raped by a long-time friend after a night of hard drinking. The morning after the assault I was admitted to the psychiatric ward of a local hospital following an attempted suicide. When released five days later, I gave up drinking for good, but immediately rekindled a relationship with an abusive ex-boyfriend who would eventually father my second child. Two emergency room visits and countless verbal attacks later, that relationship ended too, but any sense of relief was destroyed when my only sister died from a heroin overdose the same year.

Still reeling from my sister's death, I hastily wed a man I had been dating for less than a year, a safe (albeit incompatible) bet chosen in response to the chaos in my life. During this time I made the transition from office secretary to event planner and was soon working with some of the biggest names in entertainment. After pursuing a career at breakneck speed for several years, my marriage disintegrated, but instead of emotionally processing the divorce I jumped into yet another relationship. And this was when my world really began to fall apart.

Now in my early thirties, I was for all intents and purposes a confirmed workaholic whose limited interaction with my kids took second place to my career. I couldn't sleep at night without the aid of a sleeping pill, and my friendships had withered from a lack of attention. To top it off, I was constantly irritable and suffering from a crippling depression which surfaced following the collapse of my latest relationship. I had become a complete emotional wreck.

Although my personal history is traumatic, it is by no means exceptional. While the circumstances are often not as extreme, there are many women who have lived lives just as full of dysfunction as mine. They too appear to be perfectly normal until we get to know them a little better and are able to see them for who they really are: Women addicted to drama.

Drama can be enjoyable when it's on a movie screen, but it's another thing entirely to live with in real life. In small doses it can be exhilarating and exciting, breaking up the monotony of a routine existence. In larger amounts it can lead to feelings of confusion and panic. Once drama becomes a regular part of our lifestyle it becomes frighteningly destructive.

We all have drama in our lives to varying degrees, but some people seem to be drawn to it like a magnet. People who attract large levels of drama into their lives are commonly referred to as "drama queens" and I'm not referring to the over-the-top personalities we often see on television and in movies.

Are you a drama queen? It may be difficult to answer this question, for most of us tend to downplay our less attractive personality traits; some of us will even go so far as to hide it from ourselves! One clue to help you find the answer is your own personal history. Is your past littered with "issues" and "challenging circumstances?" Have you struggled for years to "keep it all together?"

A real life drama queen leads a roller coaster existence filled with challenging events that send them careening from one end of the emotional spectrum to the other. They seem to have an unexplainable attraction to unhealthy circumstances, coupled with a lack of awareness of how to stop their behavior.

Drama queens tend to end up in situations in which they are in some way cast in the role of victim. A 'victim' can be defined as "an unfortunate person who suffers from some adverse circumstance" or "a person who is tricked or swindled." One important facet of a victim's mindset is the belief that other people or circumstances are the cause of their unhappiness. If other people are the cause of their unhappiness, then it stands to reason that other people possess the power to make them happy. This is why victims often try to make other people responsible for their level of personal fulfillment.

Aside from the obvious wreckage of their past, a victim's speech pattern will easily give them away. Rather than actively working to change a situation they are uncomfortable with, a victim instead tends to blame, justify, or complain. An example of this kind of speech is illustrated below. When asked the question "Why aren't you married?" a victim would likely answer in one of the following ways:

Blame: "I would have been married by now if my parents hadn't disapproved of my boyfriend!"

Justify: "I haven't been able to find a husband because all of the good men are taken! All of the ones left are either gay, in jail or just plain crazy!"

Complain: "Why would I ever want to get married? Men are nothing but dogs!"

Everyone blames, justifies, or complains from time to time… drama queens just happen to make it into an art form!

Most people believe that drama queens are hopeless emotional basket cases doomed to a lifetime of suffering. *This is not true.*

All of us are capable of altering the way we approach life if we truly desire to change. I know this to be true because I have done it! And if this lifetime card carrying member of the Drama Queen Club can eliminate the drama from her life, *anyone can.*

I was able to manifest an incredible amount of change in a very short time through the use of the nine spiritual principles outlined in this book. This solution, called Self Empowerment Principles In Action, or SEPIA for short, began to take shape when I finally started to get some help after spending months in bed depressed following that crucial breakup. I started off using all the usual means. I went to therapy and took antidepressants. I read self-help books, took up yoga, read the Bible, and started studying Buddhist and Hindu philosophy. I tried almost everything, but I still wasn't getting much better. I was surviving…not truly living.

After a few months of this searching something became very clear to me. I realized that everything, and I mean *everything*, in my life was of my own creation. Granted, many of my motivations were completely unconscious, but I realized that I chose who I got in a relationship with…I chose the type of work I performed…I chose how much food I ate or money I spent, and I chose how I viewed the world. Most importantly, I came to understand that the solution to my lifetime of drama would take more than psychiatry and extensive reading. It had to include a spiritual solution. Thus, the Self Empowerment Principles In Action process was born.

Once I started to regularly use these spiritual principles, change began to happen swiftly. Over the course of the next several months I worked diligently to reshape my life according to these principles and the result has been a life beyond my wildest dreams…a life in which fear, self-loathing, and depression no longer have a resting place. Today I still plan special events, but primarily work on those which have a charitable purpose. Instead of simply being celebrity driven, these events create awareness and support for those in need. This new career focus brings me a sense of personal satisfaction no amount of money or prestige has ever done in the past. It has been over twelve years since my last drink and I no longer need to take medication to fall asleep at night. My relationships with my children and friends are more authentic and joyful than ever before and although my dating life is less active than before, it can best be described in the words of Ms. Mary J. Blige: "No more drama!"

The method I use to illustrate how SEPIA can work for you is to recount examples from my own experiences with drama. These personal stories are shared as a way to help you identify your own self-defeating behavioral patterns and to see how these nine principles can be applied to your circumstances. What differentiates *No More Drama* from many of the other self-help books currently on the market is that in addition to giving you knowledge, this book shows you a practical way manifest change in your life *today*. Not tomorrow, not next year, not by spending thousands of dollars on therapy and seminars. Right now. The only thing you will need in order to create a life that you have always dreamed of is a burning desire to live in a way that is a true reflection of your spirit, and the willingness to do whatever it takes to leave the drama behind.

I don't claim to be a spiritual leader, nor do I think I have all the answers to life. I have fallen, gotten back up, and fallen again, just as much as the next person. The only thing which differentiates me from those still struggling with constant drama is that I have found a simple process to become aligned with my personal power. These nine spiritual principles have freed me from years of paralyzing fear and self doubt and helped me to gain greater self-acceptance and inner peace. With regular practice, these principles can help you to uncover the beautiful truth of who you are and use that as the basis for your existence, not the bleak memory of your negative experiences.

Change of this magnitude won't be easy to achieve by any stretch of the imagination, but you have no idea the kind of freedom waiting for you once you begin your process. I know I didn't!

CHAPTER 1

*A*RE YOU A DRAMA QUEEN?

"To see your drama clearly is to be liberated from it."

~ Ken S. Keyes, Jr.

If you were to ask a hundred people what they wanted most in this world, the chances are many would answer, "I just want to be happy." Contrary to this popular response, I believe that what we are really searching for is *self-empowerment*. Self-empowerment is the state of being we possess when our level of awareness shifts to allow us to live in a manner that accurately reflects our authentic selves. By definition, we are self-empowered when we can live authentically and create a life that we find personally fulfilling.

The reason I believe that we are really seeking self-empowerment and not simply "happiness" is because happiness is an impermanent emotion. It is simply impossible for us to be brimming with happy feelings twenty-four hours a day. Self-empowerment is not a permanent state of being either; it is a provisional state of grace that we attain when we actively participate in the solution to the challenges we face. *Happiness is in fact a natural byproduct of self-empowerment*, for if we are self-empowered we can be happy, but we cannot truly be happy if we are not self-empowered.

A self-empowered woman is one who has made a conscious choice to evaluate her life and restructured it to best suit her personal needs. Each of us has different needs in our life, so each of us will differ in terms of what is required to become self-empowered.

A woman is defined as a victim, or disempowered, when she is living a life that is not reflective of her authentic self. Instead of actively participating in creating her reality, she tends to live unconsciously and simply reacts to whatever comes her way. A victim can be hard to recognize because disempowerment is a state of mind rather than an outward appearance, but if we look at her circumstances, we can see how her mindset has had a destructive impact on her life.

The Mask

We have all met people who are the life of the party in public, but quite reserved in private. What we have observed in public is their *persona*. The famous psychoanalyst Carl Jung used the term 'persona' (which is the Latin word for mask) to describe the manufactured personality we present to the world in place of our authentic selves. Personas are used to hide the less socially acceptable parts of our personality and help us blend into social settings.

Difficulties arise if we begin to confuse our personas with our authentic selves. It is very easy to lose touch with who we truly are if we're unwilling to evaluate whether our life is based upon our authentic self or on our persona. Those of us who are willing to take an honest look at ourselves are way ahead of most. This willingness is the first step towards an empowered and authentic life. But before we discuss how to begin the journey towards self-empowerment, let's explore some of the symptoms of a disempowered life.

Are You Disempowered?

- Are you constantly angry or irritable for no apparent reason?
- Do you loathe your job but are afraid to make a change?

- Are your close relationships fraught with chaos?
- Do your friends accuse you of being a "drama queen"?
- Do you substitute food, alcohol, drugs, or work for joyful social interactions?
- Do you fantasize about running away from your life?
- Do you procrastinate about starting long range goals like going back to school, opening a new business, or saving money?
- Do you find yourself wishing you could live the life of someone else?
- Do you have a hard time being alone? Or do you always have to be "in the mix"?

If you have answered 'yes' to any of the questions listed above, you are most likely struggling with disempowerment.

Five Mindsets of Disempowerment

As mentioned earlier, victims possess a mindset which leads to the perpetuation of self-defeating behavior. The following list describes five mindsets which can reinforce a sense of powerlessness:

- Negotiable Moral Code
- Fear of Failure
- Lack of Personal Purpose
- Materially Based Value System
- Spiritual Bankruptcy

Negotiable Moral Code

A moral code is an internalized set of behavior defining principles. When a person says they have "strong morals" they are essentially saying that they have a non-negotiable personal ethical code that dictates the moral boundaries of their actions. A person is said to have "good" morals when they live by a standard of honorable behavior that they are unwilling to compromise under any circumstances. Although many of us consider ourselves to have a strong moral code, we often have no idea how strong it really is until it is tested by a situation in which compromising our integrity seems to be the easier option.

Our moral code is only as effective as the actions we take to live by it. Staying committed to it is not always easy to do, but it's ultimately the *only* thing to do if we want to be self-empowered. Taking the easy way out may appear to solve whatever problem we happen to be dealing with at the time, but this behavior usually ends up creating a whole new set of issues to face.

A self-empowered woman chooses to remain committed to her morals despite the initial discomfort this may appear to cause. This consistent reliance upon her moral code helps to build her sense of honor and personal power. Victims, on the other hand, tend to search for the easy way out of challenging situations. Unfortunately, the easy way is often the one which compromises her integrity, and as a result of this behavior she tends to find herself dealing with new drama created by her "easy" choice. In short, the self-empowered woman's main desire is to uphold her moral code, while a victim's main desire is to avoid the temporary discomfort they may feel as a result of standing by it. Refusing to compromise our moral code is not always easy, but is ultimately always incredibly empowering.

Fear of Failure

Learning to accept that failure is a part of living is not easy because the society we live in places a huge emphasis on winning. As a result, many women feel there is no room in their life for failure. In fact, we can become so hung up on not achieving our goals that we won't even try to go after what we desire because of our fear of not succeeding.

Fear of failure is a stranger to no one...*everyone* has experienced it. Failure is a necessary and vital part of living for it is only through our failures that we learn what aspects of ourselves need growth and development.

How we deal with our fear is what determines whether we are victims or self-empowered. One of the main differences between a victim and a self-empowered woman is that the self-empowered woman takes action in *spite* of her fear, whereas a victim tends to allow their fear to dictate their behavior. As with their moral code, this difference in perspective is what leads a victim to take the easy way out to avoid the possibility of failure, while the self-empowered woman refuses to avoid the possibility of success.

Lack of Purpose

It was the German philosopher Friedrich Nietzsche who said "He who has a why to live for can bear with almost any *how*." When we don't know the purpose of our existence, we can easily become discouraged. Some of us may even give up trying to better our lives. Life can be pretty overwhelming for those of us who don't know or won't search for our personal purpose, for the only thing these people can do is to react to whatever life hands them. This is not a comfortable way to live, because reactive people are fearful people.

We all have very specific talents we can cultivate and use to better ourselves and the world around us. These talents are not always evident, but given enough time and energy we can find them and incorporate them into a profession and way of life which brings us a great sense of fulfillment. For some, this discovery happens very early in life...for others it may take much longer. There is no need to worry about the amount of time it takes to discover our personal purpose, for the joy of discovering our personal purpose doesn't lie entirely within the purpose itself, but also in the search. There is great pleasure to be found in our journey to uncover a sense of meaning, and a life spent searching for a sense of purpose will have a very different level of fulfillment than one spent merely accepting whatever happens.

We can always find excuses to rationalize why we can't put the time and energy into a search for our personal purpose. The thought of burying our head in the sand can be very tempting indeed when dealing with the more immediate demands of work or family, but nothing in life will have any real meaning if we don't have a sense of personal purpose.

Our personal purpose never just magically appears. Discovering it requires dedication coupled with a passionate desire to find it. Self-empowered women are proactive in seeking their life purpose. Victims wait to see what life brings them. Victims are reactive; self-empowered women are proactive.

Materially Based Lifestyle

The vast majority of people in our culture believe that a materially based existence is a good existence. At some point most of us bought into the myth that our level of happiness is directly related to the amount of "stuff" we possess. Because of this distorted value system we now have a nation floundering in both "stuff" and debt, with many trying desperately to keep up with the Jones' yet still feeling unfulfilled.

Millions live with the harmful belief that they can buy happiness, but if we were to ask anyone with material wealth if their "stuff" was what made them happy, most would answer with a resounding *no*! Designer clothes won't cure a broken heart. A six-figure income doesn't guarantee career satisfaction, and a flashy car will not permanently boost a sagging ego. Money may bring a certain amount of financial security, but it will not bring true contentment.

It is very common to be discontented with the things that we own, for we have learned to always want *more*. As soon as we buy one handbag, we want another more expensive one; as soon as we purchase the expensive car we have coveted for the last eight years, we set our sights on a newer, better one. Trying to find our happiness through the ownership of possessions is simply trying to fulfill our insides from the outside.

A self-empowered woman focuses on fulfilling herself from the inside out. She does not define herself by her material possessions, but by who she is inside. Victims tend to define themselves by what they own rather than who they are. Because of this they often spend their lives lamenting their lack of "stuff," miserly trying to keep what they have, or scheming about how to get more.

Spiritual Bankruptcy

Spiritual bankruptcy is essentially the combination of the four prior mindsets. It is the feeling of apathy and disillusionment that develops in the absence of a strong spiritual foundation in our lives. We simply cannot compromise our morals, fear failure, wrap ourselves in materialism, and have no sense of personal purpose without ending up feeling lost and confused. A lack of connection with our spirit is what leads so many of us to embark on lives filled with longing and pain. Our spirit connects us to the source of all love...our spirit helps direct us on our path in life. Self-empowered people know this and embrace a spiritually based lifestyle from within. Victims think the answer to their feelings of dissatisfaction will come from the outside, and spend their lives searching for redemption through other people, places, and things.

What is a Survivor?

When a person has lived a disempowered life for any length of time, a curious thing begins to happen. Trouble seems to follow them like a scent. Another crisis is always in the wings waiting to pounce once the current one subsides. It seems almost as if they are consciously attracting problems.

A person struggling with disempowerment feels life is something to endure, not enjoy. Eventually the resulting emotional pain becomes so difficult to deal with that the person undergoes a very subtle, but profoundly important, shift in consciousness: They stop *living* and begin *surviving*. They become a survivor.

Survivors are those who have undergone traumatic experiences and lived through them. We have all survived *something*. We all carry the scars of life's injustices. That doesn't necessarily mean we are healed or content…it simply means we have taken a lickin' and kept on tickin'. In today's world the word survivor conjures up a positive image. Songs like Gloria Gaynor's "I Will Survive," and Destiny's Child's "Survivor" speak to millions of women who have taken the punches life has thrown them and lived to tell the tale. But just because you have survived something doesn't mean that you have come out on top. It simply means that you have found a way to live with the aftermath of whatever it is you went through.

I'm not a big fan of the term 'survivor' because the word implies that we are victims. We have all faced painful and difficult circumstances, but that doesn't mean we have all been victimized. Most of us will find if we are really honest with ourselves, that a lot of the negative situations we have faced could have been prevented had we just been willing to open our eyes to the truth of those circumstances. Upon reflection, we see that in many cases we were in some way complicit in the catastrophes that befell us, and our unwillingness to pay attention to the warning signs around us is what placed us in the situations which led to our undoing.

Of course there are exceptions to the rule, as in the case of victims of violence, sickness, and natural disasters. In no way am I suggesting that anyone is responsible for the sick and twisted actions of another human being or for a cruel trick of nature. Sometimes things just happen that we have no possible way of avoiding. But there are many, many women in this world who are consistently acting against their best interest by repeatedly placing themselves in harm's way.

Survivor or Contender?

Instead of the word "survivor," I prefer to use the word "contender" to describe those who have overcome difficult life experiences. Contender is a word which evokes the thought of winners, or at the very least people who put up a good fight. Contenders step into the ring of life, get knocked down, and get back up again. One of the important differences between a survivor and a contender is that a survivor has chosen to identify herself based upon the trauma she has survived, whereas a contender will acknowledge that she has undergone a specific trauma, but refuses to define herself by it.

Understandably, it sounds silly to say "I'm a rape contender," or "I'm a contender of cancer." I'm not suggesting the term be used as a total substitution for the term survivor. What I am suggesting is that we change the overall way we define ourselves.

You may be thinking, "What difference does it make how I refer to myself?" Well, it matters a lot! The way that we view ourselves determines the way we navigate our existence. As long as we think of ourselves as survivors that is exactly what we will do: survive.

Signs You Are Ready to Change

You may realize that you've been living in a disempowered state, but remain unsure if you're ready to take action. Fortunately there are a few signs that indicate your readiness, even though they may not seem like it at first. When you are ready to change, your outlook will undergo an important shift in perception. Below are a few indications that you're ready for a change:

- You grow so tired of your cycle of unsatisfying relationships that you start to believe you may be better off alone.

- You begin to seriously contemplate leaving your current job, even without a clear plan of action.

- You become bored with many of your current friendships and begin to question whether or not you still share the same interests.

- Activities that used to bring you much pleasure, like shopping, traveling, and dating, begin to leave you feeling unsatisfied.

- You begin to question the overall meaning of your life.

If you can identify with any of the above statements, you're ready to take the necessary steps to stop surviving and start living an empowered life!

Taking the First Step

We have explored how a lack of personal power is the cause for much of our unhappiness. The remedy to this problem is to take our power back... to become self-empowered. But the question remains: How exactly *do* we become self-empowered?

The most common way is to survive enough drama that we get to a point where we can't take anymore. We finally say "Enough!" and make the changes we've been avoiding for years. The downside to this approach is that because we have been learning by trial and error, we'll have to suffer longer in order to learn how to fearlessly step into our power.

Fortunately, there are other ways to achieve this goal...ways which don't require us to lead a survivor's life of trial and error. One of these methods is named *Self Empowerment Principles In Action*, or *SEPIA*, and is outlined in this book. SEPIA is a step by step approach to using nine spiritual principles that will help you empower yourself. SEPIA is not intended to be a substitute for your personal religious or psychological pursuits, but when used in conjunction with other resources, SEPIA can teach you how to stop living as a survivor and become a contender.

In the next chapter we'll discuss how to become self-empowered by implementing these nine spiritual principles in our day-to-day lives. All that you need to get started is a wish to stop the way you have been living and a burning desire to change.

Let's explore this process now.

$\mathcal{T}$HE NINE SELF EMPOWERMENT PRINCIPLES IN ACTION

"Power can be taken, but not given. The process of the taking is empowerment in itself."

~ *Gloria Steinem*

In the previous chapter we discovered some of the ways a disempowered mindset can negatively impact your life, but as we all know, knowledge alone is never enough to initiate change. Once it is established that we're tired of living as a victim, we need to take action to move towards self-empowerment. One of the simplest ways to do this is through the use of the nine spiritual principles in this book.

Self Empowerment Principles In Action (SEPIA) is made up of nine timeless spiritual principles. It is a simple method of self-inquiry that enables you to challenge your disempowering beliefs and radically change your perspective on life, yourself, and others *for good*. The first five principles are used by asking yourself specific questions. The last four can be demonstrated as either affirmations or specific actions, depending upon your circumstances. SEPIA cuts through the lies we may be living and sets us firmly into a process of change. Its practical use of philosophy, psychology, and spirituality teaches us how to get in touch with our spirits and how to stop living as victims. In order to apply SEPIA, it's necessary to utilize each principle sequentially.

This is the only way these principles can be used to maximum benefit. Let's take a look at these nine principles now.

Self Empowerment Principles In Action

1. *Truth: that which is considered to have the ultimate meaning and value of existence.*

2. *Acceptance: the mental and emotional attitude that something is believable and should be accepted as true.*

3. *Action: organized activity designed to accomplish an objective.*

4. *Commitment: the state of being emotionally or intellectually bound to another person or persons, or to a course of action.*

5. *Focus: close or narrow attention; concentration.*

6. *Faith: a state of belief that does not rest on logical proof or material evidence.*

7. *Love: a deep and tender feeling of affection, attachment, and vulnerability towards others.*

8. *Humility: expressing behavior marked by meekness or modesty in attitude or spirit.*

9. *Charity: benevolence or generosity toward others.*

The SEPIA principles are actually quite easy to remember. The trick to recalling this process is to think about how the cycle of change occurs. Whenever we decide to initiate a change to our life, we have to first search and discover the *truth* of the situation and our part in it. After seeking out the truth, we next have to find a way to achieve *acceptance* of what we have learned and then commence to take *action* with the information we discover. Next, we make a *commitment* to our actions, for without a commitment we will stop doing what needs to be done in order for us to change. Once we are committed, we need to *focus* on our goals and not the inevitable distractions that come our way. After we are focused and committed to a specific action, it's very common for doubt to creep in, so it's imperative in this process to develop and maintain a positive *faith* that we are on the right path, and that all of our needs will be met. Taking these six prior steps continuously challenges and expands our concept of *love*, which allows us to actively show love ourselves and others. If we have taken the previous seven steps, we will undoubtedly be experiencing wonderful results, so it is then that we have to use *humility* to stay humble and grateful. Without humility we may become arrogant and ungrateful; behaviors which will undermine all of our previous efforts. Finally, as we transform our perspective by the use of the previous eight principles, we must practice *charity*, for it is only through the selfless giving of ourselves to others that we can express the highest nature of our being and create a mindset of abundance.

What About the Small Stuff?

Although primarily conceived to address the larger spiritual issues in life, SEPIA can also be applied to solving the typical problems faced in our daily existence. For example, there have been times while driving that I have been cut off by another driver in an impatient rush to get to their destination. In the past my most likely reaction would have been to aggressively let them know that their actions were not appreciated by following them and furiously honking my horn. On a few occasions I have even gotten out of my vehicle to confront them about their driving!

By allowing anger to take precedence over common sense I have, in the past, often placed myself in some incredibly dangerous situations. Now, by using the SEPIA process, when dealing with this same issue I can approach it consciously. Instead of immediately confronting a driver who has cut me off, the first thing I do is to think of what just happened in as objective a mindset as possible. The first thoughts to go through my mind are: *"That guy just cut me off! What a jerk!"* But instead of yielding to these surface thoughts, I then probe my emotions at a deeper level. What is *really* bothering me? In this case, my real concern is that the driver has not only threatened my safety but the safety of himself and those around him by driving so recklessly. That is my truth. I have just taken myself through SEPIA's first step and discovered the *truth* of the situation. The next step I take is to use the principle of *acceptance* and admit that although I have no control over how this man drives, I do have control over my reaction to his driving.

After going through the first two steps I then quickly take *action* to protect my safety by removing myself from his immediate area. Next, I make a *commitment* to stay as far away from him and other drivers like him while I am on the road. Once these actions are taken, I am still likely to feel at least mildly irritated, so I focus my energy away from the irritation by playing soothing music or by saying a prayer of acceptance. The last few things I do is affirm my *faith* by acknowledging that I made the right decision in choosing a non-confrontational approach to the situation and trust that my course of action has shown *love* to myself, and *humility* and *charity* to the other driver.

The above use of the SEPIA process takes place almost instantly, but learning the process well enough to internalize it to this degree will take some time. It won't be mastered overnight, but with practice it will come quite naturally. Perhaps the most important thing to learn from the situation described above is how difficult it is to get sucked into drama when we apply SEPIA to the situations that challenge us. Using SEPIA forces us to think *before* we take action, and gives us armor against succumbing to dramatic behavior.

An Example of How You Can Use the SEPIA Process

The following is an example of how you can use the SEPIA process to work through common life issues. To start the process, select an issue in your life that you would like to change. It can be anything at all: work, weight, finance, relationships. Then write out all of your thoughts on this issue. Write for as long as you like, but try to use short, direct sentences.

Let's use the issue of marital dissatisfaction for the purpose of illustration:

1. Truth

The principle of Truth allows you to identify the issues in your life.

To begin, write out your problem:

I hate the way my husband doesn't listen to me.

I hate that he ignores my needs and places his first.

I wish he treated me better.

The first thing that usually comes up when you write it down isn't the truth, but your feelings. After you have written the first thoughts that came into your mind about the subject, take it one step further and write down your part:

I want to be heard when I want to be heard.

I have a tendency to whine and complain.

I usually stay stuck in a problem and don't look for solutions.

I expect my husband to take away my pain, and when he doesn't respond the way I want him to, I get more frustrated.

Through this process of writing you have worked through the first SEPIA principle and discovered your Truth.

2. Acceptance

The principle of Acceptance allows you to acknowledge your reality as it is.
In this step you will write out your acceptance of the situation:

I accept that my husband doesn't always listen to me.

I accept that he sometimes ignores my needs.

I accept that I often whine and complain.

I accept that I expect my husband to fix my problems.

By acknowledging *what is* on paper you worked through the second SEPIA principle of Acceptance.

3. Action

The principle of Action will lead you out of a victim mindset and into a solution oriented one.
In this step you will ask yourself the question: *What is it that I can do to support what I have just accepted?* Write down what comes to you:

I will stop expecting my husband to fix my problems.

I will stop thinking that there is something wrong with my husband when the problem is within me.

I will stop complaining and start looking for creative ways to solve my issues.

By writing out the actions you can take towards achieving a solution you have completed the third SEPIA principle of Action.

4. Commitment

The principle of Commitment will enable you to support the solution that you have chosen in the third step of Action.

In this step, ask yourself the question: What can I do commit to this course of action? Write it down:

I commit to releasing my husband from the expectation that he can conform to my standard of behavior.

I commit to no longer whining or complaining when discussing my problems.

I commit to use my words to clearly convey my needs.

I commit to taking responsibility for my emotional well being by sharing what I am going through with someone else if my husband isn't available.

By writing out the actions you can take to support your solution you have completed the fourth SEPIA principle of Commitment.

5. Focus

The principle of Focus enables you to keep your attention on the solution.

In this step you'll write down a few of the ways that you can keep yourself focused on your solution:

When I recognize that I am focusing on what my husband isn't doing, I will choose to focus on what I can do instead.

When I begin to think that my husband is responsible for my feelings of dissatisfaction, I will focus my energy on creating a solution to my problems.

When you write down the ways that you can consciously keep your attention on what you can change, you will have completed the fifth SEPIA principle of Focus.

The last four SEPIA Principles can be utilized
as either actions, affirmations or both.

---

6. Faith

The principle of Faith will carry your spirit through moments of doubt.

A very simple way you can use this principle is by saying a prayer. It doesn't matter how long or short the prayer's length, or whether or not you are an atheist or a believer. The purpose of this principle is to assist you in developing the habit of projecting positive thoughts, for we attract to us what we put out in the world. The only thing that is suggested in this prayer is for you to ask that your will be aligned with the Divine will.

Once you have said a simple prayer you will have completed the sixth SEPIA principle of Faith.

7. Love

The principle of Love is used to generate emotional and spiritual growth within yourself and others.

This principle can be used by actively extending yourself spiritually and emotionally to another person or by changing the way you think about yourself or others. For the example given in this outline, you can pray to have anything which limits your ability to love and accept others *for exactly who and what they are in this moment,* to be removed. You can also choose to withhold your criticism of your husband's behavior.

Through the shifting of your thoughts from judgment to acceptance, you have expressed love for yourself and your husband and have completed the seventh SEPIA principle of Love.

8. Humility

The principle of Humility helps us remain teachable and to keep our egos right sized.

This principle can be used actively by manifesting humble behaviors like praying for the removal of specific character defects that you discovered in the principle of Truth. Or it can be used to actively search for the spiritual lesson in the issue you are dealing with. In this particular example, you can pray to learn the purpose of the disagreement with your husband, and/or pray to have your character defects removed. Be specific about what you want taken from you: i.e. emotional neediness, judgmental thinking, etc.

Once you have sought to find the spiritual lesson in the issue you are facing and/or prayed for deliverance from your character defects, you will have completed the eighth SEPIA principle of Humility.

9. Charity
The principle of Charity eliminates our tendency to think in terms of scarcity by showing love to those in need through selfless acts of giving.

This principle can be actively manifested by giving your time, resources, or money to those who need it, or by giving to others what they emotionally need *despite how you may be feeling in the moment.*

In this particular example you can pray for your emotional discomfort to be removed so that you may be of service to your husband. If after praying you are still feeling resentful, write down a gratitude list, which is a line by line account of all the things for which you are grateful for i.e.

I am grateful for:

The air that I breathe

The lesson of acceptance with my husband

The love of my friends

The money that my job brings me

Keep writing until you have a list of at least ten things, and then review. Do you see how blessed you are?

Once you have written down a gratitude list or actively given of yourself to another, you will have completed the ninth SEPIA principle of Charity.

SEPIA is not a way of thinking; it is an *active way of being.* Each principle requires you to not only think about how you will use it, but to actually do the work. This process is not effective without you remaining true to what you discover…so don't forget to continue to do the work!

The Benefits of Using SEPIA

Each of the SEPIA principles addresses a different facet of our lives. The following chart highlights what you can learn from each:

TRUTH	Identify the issues which need to be addressed in our lives.
ACCEPTANCE	Accept ourselves and those around us.
ACTION	Set attainable goals and take the steps needed for lasting change to our overall existence.
COMMITMENT	Make and keep our commitments towards our goals.
FOCUS	Determine what is absolutely necessary and unnecessary in order to attain our goals and begin to determine our personal purpose.
FAITH	Let go of the fears which limit our ability to be most effective.
LOVE	Discover how to open our hearts and place our romantic relationships into proper perspective.
HUMILITY	Learn how to keep our egos in check so we remain teachable.
CHARITY	Become an integral part of making the world a better place by developing a mindset of abundance and giving to others.

How Will You Know If You Are Self-Empowered?

No one can tell us whether we have become self-empowered, because it is an inner manifestation. But if we use the sequential SEPIA principles as a guide, we'll know we are self-empowered when we have acknowledged and accepted the truth of our lives, taken action with this knowledge and committed ourselves to facing it; we are focused on our goals and do not allow ourselves to be distracted from achieving them; we have achieved freedom from fear by walking in faith; we have made the choice to love openly and vulnerably, placing others' spiritual growth before our selfish desires; we seek to be humble and are open to the counsel of others; and finally we express our love and belief in the abundance of life by giving to others.

When we are self-empowered, we will no longer engage in a ceaseless struggle against the challenges of life. Prolonged drama will become a thing of the past. Life will no longer be a difficult and heavy load to be wearily borne and will instead become an exciting and wondrous journey, challenging at times to be sure, but no longer something to fear.

How Long Does This Process Take?

The length of time that it takes to achieve self-empowerment will be different for all of us. The determining factor is quite simply the amount of energy and focus we are willing to put into transforming our life. I was able to reach a comfortable place of self-empowerment in approximately six months, but only after years of struggle to find a path. Once I discovered and began using SEPIA on a regular basis, I was able to transform from living as a Drama Queen who was simply surviving from crisis to crisis, to a self-empowered *contender* in a matter of six months.

SEPIA living requires us to continually work all of the principles in our lives. Of course we will fall off course occasionally along the way. When that happens there is no need to browbeat ourselves. We can use these slips as an opportunity to review our actions and learn from our mistakes. Mistakes are simply opportunities for us to learn more about where we need to grow.

The next section of this book focuses on the nine SEPIA principles. In each chapter we will explore:

- The definition and importance of each principle.

- A further definition of each principle through personal stories of drama.

- How we can practice the principle on a daily basis.

Now let's take a look at Self Empowerment Principles In Action!

CHAPTER 3

$\mathscr{T}$RUTH
Search to Discover Your Own

"We know the truth, not only by the reason, but also by the heart."

~ *Blaise Pascal*

The first SEPIA principle is *truth*, for before we can manifest any sort of change we must seek and discover the facts of our existence. Self-empowered living requires us to strip away all of the false messages we have received over the course of our lives, and learn how to stand in our truth, whatever that truth is. Although the truth can appear at times to be very subjective, it is much more than a perception or personal preference. The truth extends far beyond our personal boundaries and is a guiding force of life.

Discovering our truth is a crucial part of the process of empowering ourselves, for we cannot transcend what we cannot acknowledge because *we cannot change what we won't even admit exists*. In this chapter we'll discuss how to identify our own personal truth and some of the ways we may try to hide from the truth. We will also discuss how to tell the difference between our personal truth and universal truth. Finally, we will see how the absence of this principle in our lives will bring self-destruction and chaos, and how using it will put us on the path to becoming drama-free and self-empowered.

Truth Defined

One of my favorite descriptions of the truth is from the book, "A Course in Miracles": *"Truth is unalterable, eternal, and unambiguous. It can be unrecognized, but it cannot be changed. It applies to everything God created, and only what He created is real. It is beyond learning because it is beyond time and process. It has no opposite; no beginning and no end. It merely is."*

Our personal truth is simply the pure and unadulterated facts of our existence and it can transform our world in a powerful manner once we learn how to harness it. One of the reasons we can have a difficult time determining our truth is because of the tendency we have to confuse truth with opinion. An opinion is simply the personal belief of an individual that may or may not be based on fact. While truth and opinion can often look very similar, the outcomes of decisions based on each are very different. We cannot live an empowered life when we base our decisions on personal opinions, for opinions are subjective and changeable. Any decision made based upon an *opinion recognized as fact* is a setup for disaster. When we are using something other than truth to guide our lives, we are essentially slipping into fantasy-driven behavior.

The truth on the other hand is a tool that can accurately assess who we are and the challenges we must face. Decisions made based on the truth are one of the tools that empower us to change our lives. The self-empowered always base their decisions on fact, not on what they hope or wish those facts to be.

In addition to our personal truths, there are also universal truths. A universal truth is a fact that can be applied broadly toward life. Universal truths are also the foundation of every major religion. A few good examples of universal truths are the Law of Vibration: "everything in life is in motion"; or the Law of Polarity: "there are two sides to everything." The reason we're making a distinction between personal and universal truth is because universal truths can often be used to guide us towards uncovering our personal truths.

One of the challenges we all face is to discover how to use the universal truths to uncover our personal truths. In this chapter we'll focus on the universal truth of the Law of Correspondence, which is "As above, so below. As within, so without." What this law states is that our external environment is often a reflection of our internal thought process. This law is important, for it points out that once we make the changes we need to our inner world, changes to our outer world will almost always follow.

Why Do People Avoid the Truth?

When we are uncomfortable with the truth we may try to manipulate it, but once that occurs we no longer have the truth, but a lie. Any way we slice it, manipulation of the truth will make it a lie. It doesn't matter whether this behavior is based upon good intentions or is simply motivated by selfish desires. The bending and shifting of what is does nothing more than create confusion in our lives and the lives of others.

The vast majority of what we are taught about the truth is how valuable a commodity it is to others. There is a huge emphasis placed in our society on the ability to be honest, but everyone indulges in some form of dishonesty from time to time. And although most of us consider ourselves to be very truthful, it has been my observation and experience that the most destructive lies are the ones we tell to ourselves.

When we lie to someone else, we victimize the other person.

When we lie to ourselves, we victimize ourselves.

Five Reasons Why We Avoid the Truth

Why would anyone choose to live in a world of their own construct when the consequences can be so tragic? It's usually because of our fear. Fear is often the underlying motivation which causes us to ignore the most obvious of facts. Although there are a myriad of fears that explain why people avoid the truth, lets look at the following five most common examples:

- Fear of Self-Evaluation
- Fear of Change
- Learned Behavior
- Attachment
- Denial

Fear of Self-Evaluation

People often fear self-evaluation because taking an honest look at ourselves can be an extraordinarily difficult thing to do. It can be very painful to "look in the mirror" and acknowledge the existence of character traits that are not particularly attractive or helpful. Self-evaluation is a trait not generally cultivated within our culture, and those who *do* spend any substantial amount of time in self-reflection are often labeled self-centered or "complicated."

Because self-evaluation is so challenging, we often find it easier to look outside of ourselves for the cause of our problems. Once a scapegoat is found, we then shift responsibility for our problems by placing the blame on others. Many of us are trained from the time we are small children to find the answers to our problems in the world around us rather than inside ourselves. We tend to approach life from the perspective that if someone offends us, it's because *they* are insensitive…if we lose our job, it's because *the economy* is bad…if our boyfriend or husband isn't meeting our needs, it's because *they* are emotionally unavailable. Again, our external environment is a mirror of what is going on inside of us. If we lost our job, maybe *our* actions helped to make it happen. If someone offends us, maybe it's because *we* offended them. If our boyfriend or husband isn't emotionally available to us, maybe *we* are so consumed with meeting our own needs that we aren't emotionally available for them. We must always be willing to look within to see how we contribute to the events in our lives…and we can't do that if we fear what we may find. This doesn't mean we always have to blame ourselves for everything bad that happens. It simply means we have to be willing to look at ourselves as well.

A survivor will not look in the mirror, for they allow their fear of the truth to keep them from embracing the reality of their lives. Contenders, on the other hand, know that embracing the truth is the *only* way to live. Period.

Fear of Change

Another reason we may avoid the truth is because we fear having to change if we discover something is wrong. It can be painful to make changes to our lives after spending years living in and becoming accustomed to an unhealthy way of life. Even when it's apparent that if we don't change we will be destroyed, we often hold onto our negative behaviors simply because we are unwilling to put the energy into developing new ones. People don't say, "Change is difficult" for no reason!

Survivors are terrified of change and tend to stay locked in dysfunction because they are uncertain of the outcomes of their actions. They are big believers of the saying, "Better the devil I know than the devil I don't." Contenders understand that in order to live life fully one must not fear change, but embrace it. They understand if they don't change, someone or something else will change them instead.

Learned Behavior

Many of us develop our convoluted idea of the truth in our early home environments. Perhaps we grew up being told, "Don't bother Mommy. She has a headache and is resting." Years later we discover Mommy wasn't really resting, she was actually passed out from one too many glasses of chardonnay. Or maybe we are told Daddy couldn't make it home in time for dinner most nights because he was "at the office working very hard to take care of the family." Later on we discover the truth: Daddy wasn't working at the office, he was spending time with his girlfriend.

When we grow up in a home where lying is used as a means to cope with painful emotions, it wreaks havoc on our ability to discern the truth. Almost all of us have been lied to by our parents out of their good intentions. Sometimes they were simply trying to shield us from pain. Other times they weren't shielding us, but shielding themselves from things they would rather not face. This sort of well intentioned and seemingly benevolent behavior teaches children that lying is acceptable and to be expected when things are painful or potentially embarrassing.

Children are inherently honest. They speak their minds without reservation, too young to know the impact of their pointed observations on the world. Through the pained expressions and sharp reproaches of others, they learn that the truth can be something to fear. After enough of these experiences, a child will begin to doubt their own truth and start to accept whatever they are told, regardless of what the facts may be.

Much of our perception of the world is shaped by what we are taught as children, and many of us will live out our adult lives based upon what we learned in early childhood. Survivors feel the need to accept the opinions of others as fact, and this blind acceptance increases their likelihood of being perpetually victimized. Contenders are willing to sift through what they are told and make their assessment of "what is" based upon their understanding of truth. They embrace a truth based upon the facts as they are, not as they are told.

Attachment

Self-empowered living requires us to let go of the parts of our life not aligned with our spirit. Sometimes, however, we can be so afraid of losing what we have that we won't even begin to search for the truth. It is for this reason that the great Eastern religions of Buddhism and Hinduism place such a strong emphasis on the importance of detachment. In the Hindu spiritual text the "Bhagavad Gita," it is written *"When you move amidst the world of sense, free from attachment and aversion alike, there comes the peace in which all sorrows end, and you live in the wisdom of the self."*

Buddhism teaches that in order to achieve peace of mind we must let go of our desire for anything. The second of the Four Noble Truths in Buddhism is *"the origin of suffering is attachment (craving)."* The Buddhist spiritual leader Tenzin Gyatso, better known as the Dalai Lama, wrote in his book "The Art of Happiness," *"The greatest obstacles to inner peace are disturbing emotions such as anger and attachment, fear and suspicion, while love, compassion, and a sense of universal responsibility are the sources of peace and happiness."* If we are having a hard time facing ourselves without negative judgment, we need to ask ourselves the question *"What am I afraid of losing?"*

The greatest attachments in our life are the source of our greatest suffering.

Take the common situation of divorce as an example of how the pain of attachment can manifest itself in our life. Attachment is often the underlying reason behind the decision to stay in a marriage or relationship damaged well beyond repair. Sometimes people stay because of their desire for emotional or material security. Or sometimes they refuse to leave because they have become very attached to a successful image or lifestyle.

One can choose to try to derive their sense of personal security from within the confines of a relationship, and as unwise as this may be, people do it all the time; I know I most certainly have at different times in my life! Unfortunately, when we become extremely attached to our relationships, we can be far too willing to accept unfair treatment from others. Social standing, money, power...attachment to any of these things will create suffering.

Clarifying what we want versus what we need is crucial to letting go of our attachments. Survivors believe their security is derived from what they have. They can never feel at peace because they believe something is always missing from their life, or they live in fear of losing what they already have.

A contender lets go of her attachments by being completely honest with herself about what is necessary for her to live. She doesn't confuse a want with a need.

Denial

A very common method many people use to avoid facing the truth is denial. Denial is a defense mechanism our minds use to protect us from painful emotions. When engaging in denial we may use external things to distract us from how we are really feeling, or simply convince ourselves that whatever is disturbing us doesn't exist.

Survivors will try to cope with their uncomfortable feelings by denying or avoiding the existence of these feelings. Contenders, on the other hand, realize that if they don't deal with their issues in the present, they will end up having much larger problems than the ones they currently face. Contenders understand that denial is a dysfunctional coping mechanism which ultimately leads to self-destruction.

Comparison Between Types

SURVIVOR	CONTENDER
• Refuses to look within because of their fear.	• Is willing to look inside to discover their truth, in spite of their fear.
• Fears change because they don't know what will happen next. Will only change if they are forced to by outside forces.	• Understands that change is a part of life and doesn't fight the process.
• Doesn't question what they hear and accepts the subjectivity of others without reservation.	• Understands that the truth is objective and searches for their own understanding.
• Refuses to search for the truth because they are afraid of what they may lose.	• Searches for the truth because of what they will gain.
• Denies the truth when it is too painful to face.	• Embraces the truth despite its potential for pain.

Denial and Addiction

We have all met people who refuse to acknowledge the existence of situations or behaviors that are clearly damaging to their well-being. It can be very unsettling to watch someone destroy themselves through their refusal to face their problems. This denial or refusal to look at the truth of their lives is one of key components of the addictive mindset.

It has often been said that denial is one of the hallmark traits of addiction. The word "addiction" is most commonly used to describe a person's compulsive use of drugs or alcohol, but in fact we can become addicted to almost anything. Even the avoidance of truth can become an addiction.

An addiction's motivating force is simply the belief that we can outrun our problems by using something or someone else to make us feel better.

Addicts are people who have become stuck in repetitive self-defeating behavior that originally relieved their fear and pain. Over the course of time, this escapist behavior becomes just as terrible to live with as their original painful emotions. Some will use alcohol or drugs. Others will use sex, relationships, work, or food. The forms of escape are different, but all addictions stem from the same faulty premise: the belief that we can successfully deal with our pain by avoiding it.

Human beings are wired to try to avoid pain, so almost everyone has addictive tendencies. This can be pretty terrifying stuff to face, but those who have done so will invariably find that running from their issues was ultimately more difficult than standing and facing them.

The good news is that once the addictive behavior is stopped, the same energy that used to go into fueling it can be transformed into positive action. We can transcend our addictions and become true contenders by facing our truth and refusing to engage in activities which are self-destructive or destructive to those around us.

Almost Too Late

My own struggle with alcoholism is an example of how a refusal to seek the truth can be disastrous. In my case it almost cost me my life. The following story describes how the first SEPIA principle of Truth started me on a journey to sobriety.

The majority of my life was spent living as a survivor. Bad things always seemed to 'just' happen to me and no matter how hard I tried, I could never figure out the reason for my terrible luck. For years I chalked it up to fate and whined about my misfortunes to anyone who would lend me an ear. Over the course of time most of my friends grew tired of listening to the same basic problems, day after day, camouflaged by new and inconsequential details. There were a few who didn't run, and who would listen patiently to my litany of never-ending complaints, but at a certain point even they would say to me, "Girl, you are such a Drama Queen! You just love drama!"

"What are you talking about? I hate the way my life is! Do you really think I want to live this way?" I would ask, incredulously.

As far as I was concerned, they just didn't get it. Everyone was either too blind to see what was really happening or too stupid to understand the unique situations that I faced.

This mindset set the stage for a ten-year struggle with drinking, and for a third of my life (from fourteen to twenty four) I struggled with a deadly addiction to alcohol. After years of not drinking I have come to believe that my descent into alcoholism was inevitable. Not because of genetic predisposition (though that definitely may have been a contributing factor), but because of my propensity for self-deception and my belief that something outside me could make me happy. I had not only inherited my biological parent's physical intolerance for alcohol, but more importantly, I had internalized my adoptive parents' mindset of denial. Year after year I had observed the dysfunctional way in which they handled their issues, which was to avoid them. This is one of the ways I learned how to deny the truth about myself and the world around me.

Like many others, my parents only wanted to know about the things they found easy to handle. And while they placed a huge importance on honesty, there were very specific caveats to this rule. First and foremost, there was but one version of truth, which was theirs'. Second, my siblings and I could lie to them as long as it was for their benefit and could not easily be identified as a lie. Of course, they never sat us down and shared these tenets with us, at least on a formal level. We just absorbed them over time by osmosis.

Our family attitude towards the truth helped me to develop a skewed approach toward facing reality, and I dealt with uncomfortable situations and emotions in the best way I knew how: by pretending they didn't exist. As far as I was concerned, as long as something wasn't acknowledged, it wasn't true, and consequently couldn't affect me.

I essentially ignored this dysfunctional behavior and eventually became a person who could only see what I wanted to see. Although I was pretty honest with others, my capacity for self-deception was monumental. My tendency to romanticize the truth created countless issues over the course of my life, some of which were very minor and others, like alcoholism, which had a catastrophic effect.

Monkey See, Monkey Do

I wasn't the only one in my family who embraced denial and escape as a means to cope with uncomfortable feelings. Our family home was a turbulent one and everyone had different ways of dealing with their pain. For my stepmother, escape was reading Harlequin romances and compulsively cleaning our house. For my father it was drinking beer and working seventy-hour weeks. Mine was reading and eating. Entire weekends would be spent engrossed in a book and by nine or ten years of age I began to compulsively overeat as well. At a certain point I even began to sneak food into my bedroom for late night binges.

These forms of escape were sufficient until my world expanded as I entered the teen years. Suddenly I was presented with lots of new and different opportunities for escape, one of which was drinking. I first tried alcohol at thirteen, and by fourteen was completely submerged in full-blown alcoholism. My addiction, like all others, was borne out of the best of intentions: I had started drinking as a way to handle my severe social anxiety and depression.

As a child I was a painfully shy girl who could barely lift my head to greet a stranger. It actually physically hurt to look into someone's eyes. I would blush and stammer and quickly turn my head away if they looked at my face for more than a few seconds. I knew it was rude not to look someone in the eye when speaking, but I held the irrational fear that they could look straight into my soul and see all of my secrets. This social anxiety seemed to disappear the summer I turned fourteen, for that was when a friend introduced me to alcohol.

Michelle was one of the cool kids I had always looked up to in our neighborhood. Voluptuous, with big, AquaNet lacquered feathered hair, Michelle was confident and outspoken, and even had a driver's license. The car her parents had given her, a battered dark green Chevy Impala station wagon with a leaking oil pan, was nothing to brag about but it was transportation that didn't require pedaling or skating. The possession of a car, any car, guaranteed an elevation of status in our neighborhood.

Michelle was only a year older than me, but much further ahead in terms of physical and social development. Although we had spent time together in the past, she preferred to hang out with older kids. These kids were rebellious girls with frosted and permed hair, who wore heavy turquoise eye shadow and skin tight Gloria Vanderbilt jeans, and boys who smoked Marlboro Red cigarettes and rebuilt car engines while listening to Led Zeppelin. I was nothing like them. A tall, gangly brown child in a white family, I didn't own one pair of designer jeans and certainly didn't smoke cigarettes.

When Michelle approached me that hot summer day and asked if I wanted to take a ride with her to the local Seven Eleven convenience store, *I was thrilled. Maybe,* I thought, *I am finally cool enough for her to hang around.*

"Do you want to go with me to the Sev and get a Big Gulp?" she asked. We always referred to the Seven Eleven as "The Sev."

"Uh, sure. Just let me tell my mom that I'm going to the store with you and I'll meet you at your car."

"Okay, cool! Hurry up though…I've got something to show you."

I found her waiting by her car, a vehicle affectionately nicknamed "The Bomb." We opened up the doors to the station wagon and waited for the overheated air to flow out. The temperature outside the car was 95 degrees with 100% humidity…the type of air which would hover around your body like a stifling, warm blanket. Inside the car it was worse…it must have been at least 120 degrees.

After waiting for a few minutes in the scorching heat, we slid onto the hot avocado green vinyl seats and pulled our seatbelts into place. I turned my head just in time to see Michelle pull a bottle of rum out from under her seat. Its contents sloshed around in the half-empty container, amber liquid glowing in the bright sunlight.

"Is that what I think it is? Where did you get it? Did you get somebody to buy it for you?"

It was a common practice for many of the underage kids we knew to hang out in front of the local liquor store in hopes that a well-meaning adult would buy them the booze they couldn't purchase themselves. These people were usually the same type of grown men who liked to hang around our high school parking lot to ogle at the young girls.

"Nah, no one bought this for me. I stole it from my parent's liquor cabinet! Come on…let's get drunk!"

My parents were very vocal about their wish that I not drink until I was of legal age but I didn't get why they were so hung up on me not drinking. After all, it seemed like every adult did. My stepmother didn't drink much...she said she hated the taste, and I only saw her drink on special occasions. And even then she would only have one glass of wine and nothing more. My father was another story...he invariably had a beer in his hand and our refrigerator always had a case of cold Budweiser in it. The case never went empty either... it just seemed to refill itself like magic.

I was scared and excited at the same time by Michelle's offer. I knew there would be serious trouble if my parents discovered I had broken their rules.

"I don't know if I should do this...my parents will kill me if they ever find out!"

"Don't be such a chicken! They won't know unless you tell them!"

Michelle started to make squawking noises in her throat, doing her best imitation of a chicken.

"Chicken...chicken...Bawk, bawk, bawk!" she screeched.

Her display embarrassed me. I didn't want to risk her telling the other kids in the neighborhood that I was too scared of what my parents might do to get drunk.

I gave in. "Alright, alright! Let's do it!"

We drove off to the Seven Eleven where Michelle bought a Big Gulp of Coca Cola and dumped half its contents onto the black tar roadway. Next, she filled the container halfway to the top with rum. This wasn't a small amount... half a regular Big Gulp is sixteen ounces. We then drove to a remote area of the subdivision where we both lived and she parked the car.

Frankie Goes to Hollywood's *Relax* wafted tinnily from the car radio as I watched her down a quarter of the container in seconds.

Then she offered the drink to me. Grabbing it from her, I took a tentative sip. The liquid burned as it slid down the back of my throat into my gut, slowly radiating its warmth out to the tips of my fingers. Momentarily confused, I was surprised that something so cold could burn so hot in my stomach.

"Wow! I can't even taste the rum," I exclaimed, greedily sucking down half of the contents through the straw.

"Leave some for me!" she said, grabbing the drink out of my hands.

All of my insecurities seemed to fly out the car window along with the strains of the music.

"Relax, don't do it...when you want it come!"

I was relaxed all right. I felt incredibly light and free and *everything was so damn funny*. We laughed hysterically at each other's wisecracks. We screamed out the lyrics to the songs blasting out of the car radio. We were practically rolling on the floorboards of the car with laughter. *"Oh my God!"* I thought. *"This is so much fun!"*

At that moment I thought I had found the solution to my shyness. Drinking was going to be my salvation. I made up my mind then and there never to feel insecure or afraid again.

And voila! Another alcoholic was born.

One Big Party

The rest of my adolescence was spent in an alcohol induced haze. My friends were all heavy drinkers as well. There were a few who got as sloppy as me, but for the most part they knew when to say "when." I, on the other hand, wasn't blessed with an internal off switch that flipped when it was time to quit. My friends could stop at four or five drinks, consuming just enough to loosen up and have a good time. I would keep drinking and drinking until I eventually passed out. I would pass out inside the local teen nightclub. I would pass out on the floor of a friend's bathroom. I would even pass out underneath the naked body of a boyfriend. Blackouts were a measure of how much fun I was having. If I could recall the details from the night before, I considered the evening a waste of time.

Little Girl Lost

At fifteen, my lackluster academic career came to an unceremonious end after I was caught during a raid on the girl's bathroom. A teacher walked in on a group of us smoking in the bathroom and I was arrested after a marijuana pipe was found in my purse. The school administrators had had enough of antics like my propensity to curse at my teachers and showing up for first period bombed out of my mind. I was expelled from school for an incident which, for another less troublesome student, would have resulted in a ten-day suspension.

After receiving my GED that same year I started to work full-time. I flitted from job to job every few weeks, usually quitting right after collecting my first paycheck. Two weeks pay would be blown in a weekend of partying and drinking. I didn't work to live or live to work…I worked to fund my partying. Of course, I always felt justified in quitting my jobs. There were a million and one excuses for leaving…my co-workers weren't pulling their fair share of the load…the boss was a jerk…there was a big party happening that same night which couldn't be missed.

In all honesty, I could have worked for Jesus himself and would still have found an excuse to leave. The truth of the matter was that I hated working. In my opinion, work was a nuisance to be barely tolerated because it impeded my ability to drink. The last thing in the world I was concerned about was college or a career. My only focus was getting to the next big party with my growing group of hard drinking friends. My outlook on life had become entirely turned around: Work was interfering with my drinking.

Spinning Out of Control

As irritating as having to work in order to support myself was, the greater issue I faced was my decreasing tolerance for alcohol. As my alcoholism progressed, I had begun to pass out earlier and earlier in the night and was often knocked out well before a party could even get started. By the age of eighteen, I had slept my way through two New Year's Eve parties, too drunk to stay awake long enough to bring in the New Year. This tendency to pass out early in the night was starting to create a problem in my social life. After all, who wanted to cart around an unconscious girl in the back of their car all night? That was when I began switching the type of alcohol I consumed in a vain attempt to control my drinking.

The first type of alcohol I drank on a regular basis was beer. Weekends were spent with my high school friends at keg parties deep in the woods near our school or at friend's homes whose parents were out of town. Beer was cheap and easily accessible but I eventually gave it up after I learned that self-respecting young women didn't drink beer. Besides, I was starting to develop a "beer belly."

The next attempt to control my drinking was to limit myself exclusively to rum. I loved the way rum tasted, but its high sugar content gave me pounding headaches in addition to all day hangovers. Vodka, Champagne, schnapps, Sambuca…I continuously experimented with every kind of alcohol available and eventually settled on white wine. White wine was easy to pace (which solved the problem with hard liquor's tendency to put me under the table, or worse, dancing on a table) and perfectly represented the image I was trying to present at the time…a sophisticated woman of the world.

In the end it never really made a difference what I drank. I always ended up getting plastered. I just couldn't hold my liquor no matter how many games I played with my consumption of it.

A Brush With Truth

My excessive drinking was causing my life to spin completely out of control. All of my money was spent on my liquid obsession, leaving nothing to pay my bills. I was every roommate's nightmare, moving from apartment to apartment every few months once they tired of my inability to pay my rent on time, if at all. There was no stability in my life whatsoever and I was constantly hung over, depressed, or both.

I had always been a temperamental child, but as I grew older and continued to drink, my mood swings began to careen wildly out of control. It seemed like I was always swaying from elation to misery, and it didn't take much to send me emotionally spinning. To say I suffered from depression would be an understatement. Something as minor as an offhand remark from a total stranger could send me plummeting into the depths of despair. I didn't know if it was my excessive drinking which was causing my depression or if my depression was causing me to drink. What I did know was that the only thing which ever seemed to lift my spirits was booze, and always made sure to consume as much of it as possible.

Deep down in the hidden parts of my soul rarely ventured into, I knew my drinking wasn't normal. And sometimes while feeling really sorry for myself, I would actually consider quitting. It was during one of these moments of crushing self-pity following a particularly hard night of partying that I decided to call information and get the telephone number of a well known alcoholism recovery group.

I had heard about this group through friends of mine who had been forced into rehab by their parents when we were still teens. One of these friends was Michelle, the girl who had introduced me to drinking. She stopped going to meetings as soon as she turned eighteen and the last thing I heard about her was that she had a baby with one of those Marlboro Red smoking boys and was working as a dancer in a strip club after getting hooked on cocaine. Though skeptical about whether or not it would work for me, I was so desperate for relief I was willing to give this group a try.

After getting the address for a meeting from their hotline, I went in search of the location. I spent a few minutes wandering about lost on the street before finding the building I was searching for. Pushing open the heavy metal door, I climbed up some steep stairs before entering a smoke-filled hall. I found myself an empty chair and did a quick once over of the faces in the room before cautiously sitting down in my seat.

Although there were at least fifteen other people in the room, I felt completely alone. They were all middle aged white men, and a few of them actually looked as if they had stumbled out of a homeless shelter.

I arrived just as the speaker for the meeting sat down in a chair at the front of the room. Peering intently at his face, I saw his eyes were red rimmed and he was in the desperate need of a shave.

Ewww! I thought. *What a loser! This oughta be good!*

Clearing his throat, he opened his mouth and loudly said, "Hi. My name is Mike and I'm an alcoholic."

"Hi Mike!" the room answered back.

Mike then began to share his story of drinking, denial, and redemption. He didn't sound at all like I expected him to. Instead of the jumbled ramblings of a broken man, his words were filled with a raw honesty I had never heard before. I listened while he shared his struggle with alcohol and how he had eventually gotten sober by working through the steps of the group's program.

But he could have just as well been speaking in Swahili. I didn't get what he was talking about at all. My heart just wouldn't open up and his message fell on deaf ears.

Look at these guys! I thought. *They are so old! I'm way too young to be an alcoholic!*

Shifting back and forth in my seat, I debated whether or not to stay for the whole meeting.

My impatience grew as Mike continued to share.

How the hell is this going to help me with my problems? What is he talking about?

With the final thoughts of *I'm nothing like them! What a waste of time,* and *How could I not have a glass of champagne with my husband on my wedding night?*, I stood up from my seat and took one last, brief look at the men in the room and walked out into the mid-day sun and into five more years of exquisite emotional suffering and an almost successful suicide attempt.

Piercing Through Denial

One week before my twenty-fourth birthday, after a long day and night of drinking, I was raped by a so-called friend and then hospitalized after attempting suicide by overdosing on sleeping pills. That was when I reached my bottom: sexual assault, the threat of losing custody of my son, and five days in a hospital psychiatric ward. That is what needed to happen in order to shake me out of denial. Only then was I finally ready to seek the truth about my drinking and take the first hesitant steps towards sobriety.

For a long time I wondered why it had taken so long for me to get honest about my alcoholism. After a few years of spiritual exploration and sobriety it came to me. I couldn't face the truth of my addiction prior to being raped and attempting suicide because I had still seen the truth as negotiable. I was willing to suffer through almost anything rather than admit I had a drinking problem.

It was only after embracing the first SEPIA principle of truth that I was able to stop compulsively using alcohol as a means of escape. The most effective tool I used to help reinforce this principle in relation to my drinking was the alcohol support group I had walked out of five years earlier in denial. It was there that I finally began to face the truth of my addiction.

Truth #1: *I was an alcoholic.*

Truth #2: *I had demolished my reputation because of my unpredictable and self-destructive behavior.*

Truth #3: *If I didn't stop drinking I was going to die.*

By openly sharing with others the truth about my drinking I was able to finally break through the denial surrounding my alcoholism.

But facing the truth was only the beginning of the work needed to change my life. After giving up drinking, I needed to build a new existence for myself that didn't revolve around alcohol. The responsibilities of supporting and caring for a family took care of the majority of my time, but that still left weekends and evenings to contend with. An adolescence spent in an intoxicated fog had taught me that the only type of recreation worth having included drinking. I didn't know what to do with myself after the kids were asleep at night and all the chores were done. This lack of direction left me terrified of returning to the bottle.

Now a young woman in my early twenties, I had no idea who I truly was or what I actually liked. I didn't have any real hobbies or interests. I didn't even have any non-drinking friends to spend time with. During my first year of sobriety I stayed close to home, rarely venturing out into the world, too afraid of the temptations that awaited me. Slowly but surely I developed new interests and friendships which weren't based on a mutual love of booze. As the days, months, and then years flew by, I began to create a new life. Not just a pit stop between parties, but an honest to goodness existence that was actually enjoyable most of the time. As hard as it sometimes is to believe, I haven't had a drop of alcohol in almost thirteen years.

Perfection

Part of my unwillingness to admit the truth about my alcoholism stemmed from the desire to be, or at the very least appear to be, perfect. This desire is a common theme in many of our lives and can cause us to deny the truth of our circumstances. We live in a highly competitive culture which pits one against the other, not caring how our success is achieved just as long as we win. Combined with a natural human predisposition towards denial, this warped value system can create the belief that we must appear perfect to those around us. These kinds of thoughts are not only dangerous, but they are also exhausting. It takes an awful lot of energy to keep up appearances!

Everyone has tried to cover up their inadequacies at one time or another. It's very common for people to lie about their actual abilities in order to get a job or to gain the acceptance of peers. What is often at the root of this sort of behavior is the belief that we simply aren't good enough just the way we are. We may eventually gain the acceptance and approval of our peers…we may even get the job we so desperately desire, but these external totems will never fulfill us. It's only through honest and authentic living that we will gain the *self*-acceptance we truly desire.

Pretending to be something we are not will always fail to benefit us in the long run, because the advantages gained are never worth the consequences of contorting our spirit. This sort of persona is created out of a direct result refusal to stand in our personal truth and a fundamental lack of self-acceptance. One of the most loving things we can ever do for ourselves is to eliminate the desire for perfection, for this desire is simply a setup for lifelong misery and personal dissatisfaction.

Human behaviorists say ninety percent of the way we communicate is done through non-verbal means. That alone is enough reason to seriously reconsider why we even bother trying to appear like we have it all together. Even those of us who are masters at camouflage will eventually be found out, for at some point the truth of our spirit will reveal itself. Quite frankly, those who are adept at maintaining an image of perfection are really doing more acting than living.

The overly critical inner voice of perfection can lead us to reject who we truly are. In order for us to fearlessly search for the truth, we must remove any judgments we have about what may be uncovered from our mind. Only then will we feel safe enough to look inward without reservation.

There is <u>nothing</u> so reprehensible about our nature that it cannot be faced!

How to Discover Truth Through Others

The denial of our own behavior and thoughts is one of the ways we can contribute to our disempowerment. Now let's look at how we can contribute to our victimization through the denial of other's truths.

As described earlier in this chapter, the condition of our physical existence is very often a reflection of our internal world. That is to say, any long-term issues we are struggling with are simply indicators of unresolved internal conflicts. Therefore, a great way to determine our truth is to look at the problems in our life which repeat themselves. The following story illustrates how I was able to learn some very important truths about myself through the actions of another.

For many years massive self-denial prevented me from seeing that I was not the woman I imagined myself to be: a woman of great self-respect and power. Low self-esteem held me hostage. In fact, my entire life has been pockmarked with problems directly related to a lack of positive self-esteem. My inability to have a healthy romantic relationship was only one of the ways this issue exhibited itself. That's not to say that I have never been in a relationship based upon mutual love and respect. It just so happened that I always seemed to fall for men least deserving of my affection.

This internal struggle for love and self-acceptance typically manifested itself in uneven relationships burdened with issues of control. But by my early twenties things had moved to a whole new level. I ended up meeting and falling head over heels "in love" with a man who treated me with the same amount of contempt I unconsciously felt I deserved.

Scott was a model in his late twenties that I had met on a modeling assignment in Texas. A strikingly handsome man, his most notable characteristic was his voice, which had a funny pitch to it that made him sound almost like a Looney Tunes cartoon character. This little quirk aside, I found him to be incredibly attractive and was determined to be in a relationship with him.

Scott had a smile that could light up a room and everyone who met him commented on how warm and friendly he was. He didn't appear to have a cruel bone in his body, but underneath his smiling façade, there existed anger and an obsession with control.

All couples have arguments from time to time, but ours were full-on verbal wars. His favorite forms of attack were guerilla tactics like name-calling and threats of abandonment. Scott always threatened to leave me whenever he was frustrated with our relationship, and when really losing ground in an argument he would curse and call me names like "whore," "slut," and "bitch." His words may have cut to my heart but they never stopped me from speaking out. If anything, they inflamed me further.

Crossing the Line

When these other efforts to control me failed, Scott would resort to using physical violence. One of his first physical attacks happened when I was six months pregnant with our daughter. That day, my younger sister May Lai had been invited over to our home for an early dinner and, as usual, she was running a little late. We couldn't afford to buy a dining room table at the time, so we had to sit on the floor and balance our plates on our laps during meals. By the time she showed up, Scott, my son Christian, and I were already eating in the master bedroom. May Lai was in the kitchen fixing a plate of food while we were eating and watching the latest episode of "Melrose Place." I wasn't really paying any attention to the show. Our daughter was going to be born in three months and I was still uncomfortable with the name Scott had chosen for her. Wanting to clear up the issue as soon as possible, I broached the subject with him during one of the commercial breaks.

"Scott? Can I talk to you about the baby's name? Are you dead set on the name Amanda?"

His eyes were glued to the television screen. "What's wrong with the name? Why do you have a problem with it?"

"Scott, I don't know of any sistas' named Amanda, do you? I want a more Afro-centric name…what about the name Kiara? I love that name!"

He laughed out loud. "Come on Sil Lai! What's the big deal? It's just a name! We can tell everyone we named her after Amanda from Melrose Place!"

I was not at all amused.

"Very funny. How do you think that will sound? 'Where did you get your daughter's name from?' 'Oh, we named her after the evil blonde on Melrose Place.' I'm sure that will go over real well!"

Scott listened silently with a bored expression as he waited for me to finish speaking.

I paused for a moment and when he still didn't say anything continued, "Well, what do you think about the name Ashleigh?"

Rolling his eyes he finally replied, "Ashleigh? That sounds too much like ashy knees. Just leave the name Amanda."

"But I hate that name!" I protested, hoping I wasn't sounding like a whiny child.

"Look…you can call her anything you want, but if you put anything down on the birth certificate other than Amanda, I'm not signing the paper!"

Then he turned his head back to the television, signaling that our conversation was over. Angry that he had been so dismissive, I rose off the floor where I had been sitting, strode over to the television set, and quickly switched it off.

Scott looked up at me as if I had lost my mind.

Standing over him with my hands firmly planted on my hips, I looked down and said, "Now are you going to listen to me?"

Nowhere to Run

My son's eyes flickered back and forth on our faces, watching for Scott's reaction to my impudence. In a flash he leapt to his feet and grabbed me by the hair, yanking me down to my knees. As my body hit the parquet floor he jerked my head back and forth violently a few times and then let go. Striding over to the television set, he switched it back on, sat back down, and began calmly eating as if nothing had happened.

We had fought in the past, but up until this point Scott had never been physically violent. I was *definitely* not the kind of woman who would let someone get away with this kind of behavior. There was no way I was going to let Scott get away with it! The last time any man had dared to hit me was when my father slapped and kicked me into the refrigerator when I was a fourteen. I had threatened to call the police if he ever hit me again. He never did.

Who in the hell does he think he is? I thought.

I picked up my plate of half-eaten food, stepped over to him, and raised the plate high above my head. It came down with a crash on his arm, broke into two jagged pieces with a hard crack, and sliced a deep gash into his elbow.

Yellow rice and roasted chicken lay strewn across the floor. A few yellow grains stuck to his arm and mixed with the blood welling out of the wound.

No man's gonna put his hands on me! That'll teach you! I thought triumphantly.

Scott's fury was unleashed. He jumped to his feet and grabbed me by my hair again.

"Let me go!" I screamed.

He was pulling my hair painfully hard, but I was numb to any pain. My son was still in the room and I was too worried about him seeing us fight to feel anything. I tried to turn my head to see where Christian was, but Scott's fingers were so tightly wound through my curls that it was impossible.

May Lai heard my screaming and came running down the hall.

"What's going on?" she yelled out as she entered the bedroom doorway.

Freezing for a moment in disbelief, she shrieked, "What are you doing?"

May Lai only weighed 105 pounds but had the courage of a person twice her size. She ran over to Scott and began pummeling his back and arms with her fists, frantically trying to force him to let go of me.

"Get off of my sister! Let her go!" she screamed.

Scott was wiry and muscular with the build of a lightweight boxer. I knew that he was strong, but I never dreamed he possessed this amount of physical strength. Her fists did nothing to stop him, easily bouncing off his body. While I struggled to escape his grasp, he punched at my sister with his free arm in an attempt to loosen himself from her grip.

Riiiiip!

I watched as May Lai spun across the room, Scott's ripped white t-shirt dangling in her hand. His torso was now bare... shirt torn completely off his body. She rushed back and began to claw at him again as he started to drag me by the hair down the apartment hallway.

What is he doing? Where is he taking me? I frantically wondered.

My hands were gripped tightly around his wrists, attempting to keep my hair from ripping out of my head. I frantically kicked my legs against the walls of the hallway, desperately trying to protect my very pregnant stomach from hitting against them as he dragged me across the floor. My son snapped back into my consciousness as I heard him crying in the background, but there was nothing I could do to help him. I was completely focused on trying to escape Scott's grasp.

Once he reached the living room Scott let go of my hair and dropped me in a heap on the floor. His eyes were filled with loathing, but his demeanor was remarkably calm. The only indication of his true emotional state lay in his ragged breathing and fiercely blazing eyes.

I was panting and holding my neck, trying to catch my breath. Christian quickly ran to my side.

"What are you looking at?" Scott roared as my four year old son stared at him, eyes open wide.

Christian ducked his head into my chest while I hugged him close. May Lai rushed over as well.

"Are you okay? Are you hurt?" she cried as Scott sat down on the couch across from us, legs sprawled out in front of him.

He glared at us all while dabbing at the cut on his arm with the remnants of his shirt, gingerly wiping up the bright red blood trickling down his dark forearm.

"Do you see what you did to my arm?" he demanded, lips curled back in disgust and anger.

I couldn't believe it. He could have easily made me lose our baby and his only concern was a cut on his arm?

A sudden loud banging on the front door caused us all jump.

"Open the door!" a deep masculine voice called out. "It's the police! I said open up!"

Apparently one of the neighbors had called 911 after hearing the commotion in our apartment. As my sister let them in, I exhaled a huge sigh of relief.

"You need to arrest him," May Lai said, pointing at Scott. "He just attacked my sister for no reason!"

The two officers stood in the middle of our living room, their large bodies dominating the space. They listened attentively to my account of what had happened.

One of the men looked at Scott and said, "Sir is this true? Did you drag her through the apartment by her hair?"

Scott asserted, "I was just defending myself! She hit me with a plate! Look at my arm!"

The Truth

The officers had no way of determining which one of us had started the fight; after all, Scott was the one bleeding. This is when it became clear that I might be headed to jail right alongside him. If I hadn't retaliated against his attack by hitting him with the plate Scott would have been hauled off to jail, no questions asked. Since there wasn't any real evidence of his attack other than my say-so and my sister's corroboration, both Scott and I were now at risk of being arrested. It was his word against mine, and the only way I could avoid going to jail was if we each declined to press charges against the other.

"Do you want to go ahead and file a report?" an officer asked.

There was no way I was going to be arrested for defending myself. Scott and I glared at each other, but we both quickly said no. I then asked one of the officers if they would escort him out of the apartment.

"Can't you make him leave? I don't feel safe with him in here."

"I'm sorry ma'am, but he has just as much a right to be in the apartment as you do. If he won't leave, I'm advising you to do so."

The apartment we shared wasn't even in Scott's name. As a matter of fact, I had been supporting him for the past year…he hadn't paid a bill in months. None of that made a difference to the police. Scott didn't have to leave the apartment and nothing could be done to make him go.

I was going to have to stay at my friend Carol's apartment until things calmed down. Grabbing an overnight bag from my closet, I rushed about the apartment, gathering my son's pajamas and school clothes and hurriedly throwing them inside.

"Ma'am? We hafta leave…?" one of the officers called out.

"Just one more minute…I'm almost done!" I answered frantically, tossing a toothbrush and some deodorant into the canvas bag.

The officers stood out in the hall, waiting for me to leave the apartment before they left the building themselves. In order to exit the apartment, my sister, son, and I had to walk by Scott, who was waiting by the front door. As we passed, he smiled broadly and said, "Have a nice night!" laughing as he shut and locked the door in our faces.

It was now almost midnight as we rode the subway down to lower Manhattan. The white florescent lights of the train were glaringly bright and giving me a headache. I closed my eyes and leaned back on the seat of the train. Physically exhausted and emotionally spent, I replayed what had happened that evening over and over again.

How in the hell did things get so out of control? It was just a damn name!

Sadly, this was the type of madness I lived with for almost five years. Things never made sense whenever we fought. The smallest discussion was always a potential powder keg for Scott's temper tantrums. This wasn't going to be the only time he "put his hands on me" as he preferred to call his attacks, but it was the only time I ever hit him back.

What Is the Real Truth?

The first step that I needed to take in changing my circumstances was to seek to discover the truth of our relationship. After being with Scott for years, I finally came to the realization that my truth was self-destruction. His abuse forced me to acknowledge that for the majority of my life I had been unconsciously moving towards self-annihilation.

Whenever I was told by others that I was trying to destroy myself through this relationship, my response was to tell them that they didn't know what they were talking about.

"But I love him!" I would exclaim. "Can't you see he is changing? He doesn't hit me anymore. He only curses, and it isn't all the time..."

There was no way change would occur until I could admit that I was slowly being destroyed by our relationship. Scott provided a physical expression of my lack of self-love and a way to subconsciously punish myself. I somehow believed I deserved to be demeaned and beaten by him.

People usually deny the truth when they are too afraid to face it. Our fear is at the root of many destructive relationships. Fear of being alone, fear of further abuse if we leave, fear of financial insecurity...for years my fear had kept me attached to Scott. This relationship forced me once and for all to decide whether or not I wanted to live or die. I finally made the decision not to assist anyone in the crushing my spirit, and chose to embrace a new truth of self-love.

Breaking the Cycle

I used every resource available to get the help needed to begin healing. The emotional wounds from my childhood were tended by a therapist who specialized in working with women in abusive relationships. Those sessions led me to understand the origin of my intense self-hatred and why I had tolerated Scott's abuse for so long. It was a big surprise to discover that much of my ability to endure abuse had been taught to me in my early childhood.

Domestic violence experts say a woman is highly likely to become involved in an abusive relationship as an adult if they either witnessed or experienced domestic violence as a child. One of the earliest memories I have is of my father and mother engaged in a vicious physical altercation which ended with the police breaking up their fight and leading my mother to safety. For years I viewed their fight as an isolated incident. After experiencing my own abusive relationship, I discovered there is never just one incident and physical abuse is just the tip of a much deeper iceberg.

If we find ourselves in a dysfunctional relationship, we can look to our childhood for similarities between our parents' or primary caregiver's relationship and the one we are in. We all too often pattern our intimate relationships after the examples we grew up witnessing. In order for us to change, we need to do much more than merely seek the correlations between our childhood and adult lives, but searching for our truth is the beginning.

I also joined a support group for battered women. They were a great source of comfort, and helped break me out of the deep sense of shame and alienation I felt about being abused. It was a relief to know there were people who understood what I was going through and that my experiences could be shared without fear of judgment.

Scott and I got back together within a week of the first attack. There were a dozen rationalizations for my decision, the main one being a fear of giving birth to another child without their father being a part of their life. He tried to stop abusing me, but couldn't get a grip on his temper. After he was arrested for physically attacking me three days after our daughter Amanda was born, he called me collect from jail, crying. He swore he would never hit me again…he said he loved me more than anything in the world. But this time his words didn't have much impact. My "love" for him was beginning to fade; the years of his abuse had left me nearly emotionally dead.

Scott was released from jail and began to pressure me to drop the charges against him. No matter how much he pleaded I refused, knowing the only way he might stop beating me was if there were serious consequences to his behavior. He was convicted of assault and then sentenced to a court ordered batterer's treatment program. A one-year Order of Protection was also instated and the judge sternly warned Scott what the legal ramifications would be if he were to violate the Order.

Even after all that had happened between us I still thought there was a chance he would change. Not wanting to break up our family and terrified of being alone, I made the decision to continue to stay in our relationship, but only under one condition: he would have to remain in individual therapy. I made it very clear that I would leave him if he left counseling. Together we attended a special form of couples counseling designed specifically for people dealing with issues of violence in their relationship. It was only then that I came to understand a new truth about the man I claimed to love so much.

False Hope

Very little in life is written in stone. We all have the ability to manifest change in our lives. The English poet Alexander Pope coined a phrase which summarizes well why I believe so many women choose to stay with their abusers. It was he who wrote *"Hope springs eternal in the human breast,"* and it is an overdeveloped and misguided sense of hope which lies in the heart of so many abused women. We *hope* at some point to discover all of our masochistic sacrifice for love was not done in vain. We *hope* some form of cosmic intervention will cause our beloved to put down the arms that bring so much pain and embrace us permanently with tenderness. We *hope* our men will seek our forgiveness and treat us with the compassion and care we so desperately desire. After another round in the cycle of violence, we sigh and whisper to ourselves, *I hope this is the last time,* praying for the day the violent Dr. Jekyll in our lives will forever transform into a loving Mr. Hyde.

Domination and violence as a means of control is not a pathology created overnight. Men who abuse their women have had many years to develop their twisted view of love and partnership. This truth was what helped me to make the decision to leave Scott for good. For thirty-two years he had been relating to women out of a paradigm of fear. He had essentially been a batterer for his entire adult life.

Too Much Too Little Too Late

It had taken almost two years for Scott to learn how to restrain himself from physically attacking me when he became enraged. He still lurched at me whenever he got very angry or when arguments weren't going his way, catching himself just in time. It was exhausting to walk on eggshells whenever we had arguments, waiting for the other shoe to drop, always keeping one eye on the door in case I had to make a run for safety.

Even though the threat of physical violence had diminished, he was still hyper-controlling, dictating the type of clothing I could wear and who my friends could be. I was a twentieth century slave with my lover serving as my overseer, but there was no emancipation forthcoming from this Master. Scott was simply incapable of letting me live freely.

This truth finally helped me to reach the conclusion that I was not willing to wait and see *if* and *when* he changed. Even though he had done a lot of work to get better in the last year and a half of our relationship, it just wasn't good enough. Sure, maybe over the course of the next five to ten years he could eventually become less controlling, but I was no longer willing to live out my existence with his oppressiveness haunting my every step. I no longer wanted to deal with the suppressed emotional needs which forced him to secretly follow my every move. I was fed up with his abuse and controlling behavior and finally made the decision to terminate our relationship once and for all.

Ending a Lie

I was only able to end my relationship after severing all ties to him. I couldn't talk to him "a little bit," nor spend just one more passionate night in his arms for "old time's sake." After we split up, Scott was able to receive emotional support from his batterer's recovery group. The other members rallied around him as our relationship ended and acted as his emotional base, relentlessly warning him not to retaliate against me.

In the end I told him to seek visitation rights for his daughter through the court system. He wasn't capable of any kind of peaceful negotiation and saw any attempt by me to structure a child support and visitation arrangement as an attempt to control him. I am one of the fortunate women who have been able to get out of an abusive relationship without further violence and I can happily say I have not been involved with any violent men since.

Truth Summarized

Searching for and then embracing the truth is the first step we can take towards empowering ourselves. The reward for this behavior will be measured in the confidence we gain from our willingness to face facts, no matter how difficult they may be to acknowledge. It will be evident in the strength and clarity of purpose we exude. Eventually, we will even find that we instinctively know the difference between fact and fiction. By seeking to discover our truth we will free our spirit and become a true contender instead of remaining a fearful survivor. Our life's purpose will become clear as we embark on the path we have been called on this earth to walk.

In order to manifest positive change to our life we must search out the lies of our physical reality and challenge them by seeking both universal and personal truths. In this way we can begin to uncover the ways in which we have allowed fear to lead us down the path towards self-destruction. Of course, we don't *have* to do this… we don't have to do anything we don't want to do. We can always choose to ignore the truth, but eventually we'll be forced to find it through the life events that reflect our internal crisis. Whether we choose to initiate the changes needed willingly, or are led to them kicking and screaming, is entirely up to us…the choice is ours!

The most courageous thing we can do is turn the spotlight on our soul and seek the truth with all of the force of our being. Only then will we be able to take the next step of accepting what we have learned and begin to break the bonds which are holding us back from self-empowerment.

$\mathscr{A}$CCEPTANCE

You Can't Change Without It

"Confident and free, filled with wonder and ready acceptance, we permit ourselves to be taken over by our unquestioning self."

~Marcus Aurelius

The second step in the SEPIA process is *acceptance*, for it is impossible to change what we do not acknowledge. Now that we have taken the first step to self-empowerment with the SEPIA principle of truth we need to accept our personal truth. It would be wonderful if simply knowing the truth about our issues were enough to empower us, but knowledge alone will not create the life we desire. We cannot become self-empowered unless we are willing to accept our truth, whatever it may be.

A refusal to accept the truth is one of the main factors which can lead us toward unhappiness and depression, but acceptance of ourselves and others can free us from years of pain and suffering.

In this chapter we'll explore why acceptance can be so difficult to practice and how, when taken to the extreme, the lack of this principle can bring us to the brink of emotional destruction. Finally, we'll be shown how the use of acceptance can help us begin to heal our emotional and spiritual wounds.

Acceptance Defined

Acceptance is *"the mental attitude that something is believable and should be accepted as true."* When we accept someone or something, we are simply acknowledging what it is. Nothing more, nothing less.

Acceptance is not the same thing as tolerance. Tolerance is defined as *"the power or capacity of an organism to tolerate unfavorable environmental conditions."* When we tolerate something, we not only acknowledge what something is, we also yield to it. Acceptance, on the other hand, is admitting that something exists, but at the same time realizing that we may have to change the way we deal with it. When we practice acceptance we do not engage in any attempts to change what it is through the use of denial or escape.

We can see the distinction between these two terms in the following example involving sexual harassment. Sexual harassment is the unwelcome sexual advance made by an employer or superior who has the power to cause us to lose our job or a promotion if we don't accept their behavior. If we *tolerate* our supervisor's abuse, we are accepting his behavior but not doing anything about it. Tolerance is acceptance without power.

When we *accept* that our supervisor is a harasser, we are acknowledging his behavior for what it is: abuse. We don't sugarcoat it with rationalizations or excuses. We don't pretend that it isn't happening. We accept it as a truth, with the realization that we retain the power to do something about it.

Acceptance is an empowering mindset. By accepting that we are being harassed, we can empower ourselves by taking action against the abuse. We can file a complaint with our company's human resource department, or we can transfer out of our job. *That* is self-empowered behavior.

There is of course much more to the principle of acceptance than embracing ourselves and others as they are. Acceptance is also the understanding that certain things are going to happen, whether we want them to. or not. It is learning how to live life on life's terms and the letting go of our attachment to the outcome of the situations that occur in life.

Living in an empowered manner requires us to accept everything about our life and who we are today. This is true not only about the good that has happened to us, but also the bad. *Especially* the bad. The principle of acceptance is something we must practice if we are to ever change our circumstances. Those who don't invariably expend an enormous amount of energy trying to deal with the frustration they end up feeling as a consequence of not using the principle.

The Myth of Control

Acceptance is not always an easy principle to practice. Part of what can make it so difficult is the very primary human desire for *control*. People seek control because it gives them a sense of power, and let's face it: almost everyone loves power.

The opposite of acceptance is control.

When we try to control something, we're not accepting it.

A person who is obsessed with control is commonly referred to as a "control freak." Since a control freak has typically set their world up in a way that allows them to exercise as much control as possible, one would think they would be very happy people. The reality is that those with serious control issues are generally miserable much of the time. We may never know this because they are so good at, well, controlling their emotions, but it's impossible to have peace of mind when we are focused on managing everything around us.

The reality is that we are not in control of anything other than ourselves. We only have ability to *influence* others and situations. Anyone who obsessively seeks to control others and situations is bound to be disappointed most of the time.

Attachment to control is futile for, like anything in life, control is at best a fleeting condition. Situations always change…those in power one moment often find themselves not in the next. The idea of control is a very comforting thought for those who may feel powerless and oppressed by the people and situations around them. Given that most of us have experienced some form of oppression at one point or another, we all struggle with control issues to varying degrees.

Those with serious control issues don't limit their behavior to others. Control freaks are notoriously self-critical and place just as much energy into trying to manage themselves as they do other people. Their mindset is focused upon achieving the impossible goal of perfection, a mindset which doesn't allow them to accept themselves as they are.

Acceptance and control cannot co-exist. In order to relinquish the need for control we must let go of our preconceived ideas of how things *should* be. The principle of acceptance eliminates the desire for control and perfection and will make a tremendously positive difference in our outlook.

Three Reasons Why We Can Become Obsessed With Control

If the ability to control is really an illusion, then why do so many people struggle to achieve it? Although the reasons will vary from person to person, three very common ones are:

- Ignorance
- Distorted Perception of Power
- Fear

Ignorance

One reason people lead a control based lifestyle is because of ignorance. Most are taught that control over their environment is possible and to be desired. If we don't know that this goal is impossible, then of course we'll continue to seek it.

Survivors believe that control over others is possible and exert a massive amount of energy trying to do so. A contender has learned that control is a fear-based action and works to eliminate their attachment to it.

Distorted Perception of Power

Another reason why people embrace a control based lifestyle is because they have a distorted perception of power. The ability to control and manipulate others is often mistaken for strength in our society. Take for example the dictator who tries to control every aspect of his people's lives through the use of fear. He can only rule as long as his people fear him. The moment his people no longer fear him, he loses his power.

An example of true power is when others are given the choice to determine how they want to live and then still choose to follow our example. The truly powerful individual is one with *self*-control, and who has an ability to *influence* others. Jesus Christ, Mahatma Gandhi, Mother Theresa, Abraham Lincoln... throughout the history of humankind we find that the most influential and powerful persons have all shared this trait.

A survivor believes the ability to control others is an indication of their power. A contender recognizes the only power she has is over herself, and seeks to influence rather than control others.

Fear

At the core of the desire for control is fear. If we look a little deeper into why people seek control, we'll find that it is not really power they are seeking, but a release from their fears. All control freaks share one common trait: their actions are driven by fear. A survivor believes she can successfully eliminate her fear by controlling their environment. A contender understands that any action motivated by fear is ineffective.

Comparison Between Types

SURVIVOR	CONTENDER
• Tries to control the world around them.	• Understands that control is an illusion.
• Believes their ability to control others is a reflection of their power.	• Knows the only thing they can control is themselves.
• Believes they will be released from their fear by controlling others.	• Realizes one only tries to control what they fear.

Survivors have a difficult time moving forward because they are intently focused on their painful past. In their efforts to make sure that they aren't hurt again, they can become consumed with trying to manage everything around them. Their obsession with trying to ensure that the past doesn't repeat itself often leaves them with any energy left over to change their present.

A contender knows that they cannot change their past. They accept that painful situations are a part of life and don't allow their attention to focus on what *may* happen. Contenders don't put their energy into changing others, since they know the only thing they can truly control is themselves. In short, survivors are focused on the past and future, and contenders are focused on the here and now.

The Importance of Acceptance

The need to control can be a learned trait from our family of origin. The following story shows how control issues can be nurtured and developed in one's childhood.

I'm a recovering control freak. In the past when accused of being one I would puff my chest out and say proudly, "Damn right!" To me the word was a positive term. I truly thought that my ability to bully others was a sign of strength.

Control freak was a role I was groomed for as far back as I can recall. Our family home was a place where a shared struggle to manage our environment was the way we related to one another. Everyone was fixated on one-upping the other. I tried to control my brother, sister and stepsister, and they fought to control each other. Our stepmother was intent on controlling us children and my father was obsessed with controlling the entire family.

The nucleus for this dysfunctional activity was my father, a man who faced the many disappointments in his life with an attitude of resentment and an overwhelming need to dominate. Our family home was decidedly patriarchal and Dad had the final say on anything occurring under *his* roof. My stepmother, a quiet and unassuming woman thirteen years his junior, was no match for his will. We all grew up watching her bend and yield to his dominating personality, but as docile as she outwardly appeared, our stepmother did not escape her own struggles with control. Dad may have been the king of his castle, but while he was out, *she* ruled the home.

My stepmother employed methods much more subtle than his, but they were equally effective. Every aspect of our lives was micromanaged, from the simple things most children endure, like the type of clothing we wore and the time we went to bed, to the profoundly tyrannical, like locking up the household food so we couldn't eat unless given permission.

Four young children running rampant through a small house was more than my stepmother's nerves could usually handle, so the majority of our time we spent banished outdoors. The suburban neighborhood in which we lived was made up of cookie cutter homes neatly lined up on weathered tar-topped streets. There were four models to choose from, each set back exactly forty feet from the street. Every home sat on a quarter acre of land with the only distinguishing characteristic being the occupant's creative use of low-lying shrubbery.

Directly behind our development was a tract of unused land set aside for future development. Partially hidden dirt pathways wound through the brush littered with old beer bottles and rusted soda cans. My sister May Lai and I would ride our bikes on these paths as far as our tires could manage in the shifting soil, and then abandon them to march about on foot, searching for buried treasure in the dirt. Our neighborhood was a child's dream, with wide sidewalks and quiet traffic-free streets perfect for roller skating and running. Swimming was a big part of our lives as well, since we had a small kidney-shaped in-ground pool in our backyard.

All of this daily physical activity gave me a very skinny frame and exceptionally speedy metabolism. Most active and growing children have tremendous appetites and eat all day long. We were only allowed to eat carefully portioned meals at very set times. Random snacking was not an option and if we were late for a meal, we didn't eat at all.

My parents provided three basic meals and a healthy snack each day, but it still wasn't enough food for my growing body. I would fall asleep and awake with hunger every day. Lying in bed at night, the growls from my stomach would echo and rumble. My mind would race as I obsessed about the food in the kitchen, only twenty feet away. My parents' motivation for limiting how much we could eat was to keep the household food budget manageable, but the result of their hyper-vigilance was a very hungry child. Around the age of eleven, I decided to address the issue by eating whenever my parents weren't looking, which would usually be after they were fast asleep. This didn't continue for long. Once my parents found out what was going on, they came up with a creative solution to my food thievery.

Dad operated a small home based business that renovated residential properties. His clients were landlords and homeowners who were putting their properties up for rental and sale. He and a small crew would clean up these homes prior to being listed in order to increase the likelihood of a quick turnover. The work they performed were mainly superficial tasks like interior painting and carpet cleaning.

One perk of his work were the castoffs from other people's homes. Tenants would often leave behind the items that they didn't want to take with them on their move. These leftover pieces made up the majority of the furniture in our family home. Striped rusty-hued sagging sofas, lop-sided lighting fixtures and brass accented wooden tables littered the various rooms.

One early afternoon my father came in from work with an old, slightly yellowed refrigerator that he rescued from the most recent home he was repairing. It was buttressed against the Kenmore washer in the laundry room off to the side of the kitchen, and inside its brightly lit interior my parents kept any food they didn't want us kids (meaning me) to touch. There were blocks of delicious cheeses, sticks of creamy butter, flavorful sandwich meats, and any other items they feared I would consume. Next, my parents promptly placed a lock on the refrigerator. That put an end to me sneaking anything more substantial than saltines and bread once and for all.

When I say that everything was micromanaged in our home, I mean *everything*. As we grew older my stepmother even began rationing out the shampoo for our hair. There were two bathrooms in our home: one in my parent's bedroom and another in the main area of the house. Shampoo was kept locked up in their bathroom until it was time for us to bathe. In order to wash our hair we had to ask our stepmother for the shampoo, and she would carefully squeeze out a small portion of shampoo into a cup for each of us to use. If my stepmother wasn't home when I needed to wash my hair, it didn't get washed at all, so showers had to be timed accordingly.

Survival of the Fittest

I learned very early on that the only way we could survive in our home was by beating my parents at their own game, and with time I became very adept at fighting their oppression. An all out war was waged in our home with me hell bent on getting out from under my parents' control. Running away, skipping school, physical fights….there was nothing I wouldn't do to achieve this goal, but my all-time favorite method was verbal warfare.

Dad was a man who liked to use his voice to make a point. None of us kids ever asked him for anything because his usual response would be to yell at us to leave him alone. My stepmother didn't believe in raising her voice… she just ignored or dismissed us. If we kept at her long enough however, eighty percent of the time she would give in to whatever we asked. In retrospect I see that she was a person willing to rethink her position, but I couldn't see that at the time. The difficulty she had remaining steadfast in her decisions led me to lose respect for her. I openly scorned and rejected her passive-aggressive approach to confrontation, and chose to identify with my father's example of "might is right."

Most of the time my destructive behavior was limited to verbal assaults, but for a short while I resorted to using the threat of physical violence as well. For about a month during my ninth grade year I carried a small butterfly knife that I flashed whenever I wanted to shake things up a bit. I kept it hidden in my jeans pocket and thankfully never used it on anyone. Sometimes I would use a razor to terrorize the people around me. While dissecting frogs in Mr. Pagano's ninth grade science class, I took the dissection razor and sliced open the top of my forearm with light, short cuts. My classmates were understandably freaked out and labeled me crazy. This behavior was extreme, but it achieved its goal: the kids who had terrorized me during my early adolescence left me alone, and my parents eventually threw up their arms in disgust, completely clueless as to how to manage me. Everyone knew I wasn't afraid of physical pain and would do anything to win an argument; things they weren't prepared to do themselves. My mission was accomplished.

This overdeveloped need for control eventually left me unable to accept myself or others as they were. Everything around me had to be molded into my idea of what should be, and over time I became convinced that my perspective was the only one that was true. *Control or be controlled* was my unspoken maxim and for years I used it to survive. And although this outlook made me invulnerable to emotional attack, it also successfully locked away my ability to access my gentler emotions, like empathy or patience.

Despite an increased ability to dominate others, I was still desperately unhappy. I could never accept others for who they were and was always scanning myself, searching for any flaw which could be exposed and used against me. My true self was camouflaged... my persona had completely taken over. I had spent so much time hiding from others that I didn't even know myself. I had become cut off from my true, authentic self.

Judging Books by their Covers

The universal truth of the Law of Correspondence (as above, so below; as within, so without) states that whatever is within us, regardless of whether or not we accept that it exists, will somehow become manifest in our life through another. That is to say, the things we don't accept about ourselves often end up being acted out by the people closest to us. Over the years we often see hints of these hidden parts of our personalities, but are usually completely unaware of their full force until something triggers a release.

Given the fact that I would do almost anything to control the people around me, it was not surprising that I tended to attract others who shared the same sort of need. At one point this need manifested through a boyfriend who would use physical violence to control me. At the age of thirty two, the depth of this problem became clear when I started a relationship with a man who would say anything in order to control the outcome of our interaction.

Birds of a Feather

Co-dependency is loosely defined as a compulsive attachment to one or more addicted persons. The following story highlights through my experience with co-dependency how an obsessive need to control others brought me to the brink of insanity, and how I was able to heal through the use of the second SEPIA principle, Acceptance.

Nick was a successful, good looking and well educated man with a high powered job in the entertainment industry. We were introduced by a mutual friend who thought that because we both "spoke white" and were also in his words "kinda corny," we would hit it off. Those weren't the usual characteristics that I would attract people to each other, but I had recently ended an incompatible relationship and was eager to start dating again.

Our first meeting was an unremarkable brunch at a seafood restaurant in the Soho district of Manhattan. Nick arrived ten minutes late and spent twenty minutes more looking for parking. By the time he strode in the door, I was on the verge of leaving.

We sat down at a cozy table outdoors that allowed us to enjoy the beautiful fall weather. Our mutual friend had said that he was a good looking guy… which he was, but he was also as my friend had said, "corny." When I say corny, I mean he spoke with very proper English and seemed super-square. Needless to say, there was no love connection made on that day. We both came away from the brunch completely unimpressed with the other.

After that uneventful first meeting we continued to stay in touch and would get together every couple of weeks to hang out. Nick had recently come out of a two year long-distance relationship and had told me from the start that he was not ready to get seriously involved with anyone. Of course, this didn't pose a problem for me since I wasn't interested in dating him. Then one night, something changed. It was unexplainable…in an instant my perception of him shifted. One moment I was sliding into the backseat of a car with my friend… the next I was sitting in a car next to a man I found incredibly attractive. Suddenly, this friend was a man I wanted to be with.

Things changed very rapidly between us after that, and despite his initial protestations, we were pulled into a deeply passionate love affair. I felt like I had hit the relationship lottery. Nick was a dream come true; well-educated, successful, good looking, and incredibly driven. I loved the earnestness in which he threw himself into everything in life, especially our relationship. We spoke on the phone ten times a day and saw each other four or five times a week. Our time together was magical…with every moment charged with heightened sexual tension. A passionately confident man, Nick brought me to levels of physical pleasure that I never imagined existed.

Finally, I thought…*I have found the love of my life.*

There were little things along the way which hinted that he wasn't as wonderful as I thought, but for the most part I ignored them. While he was very attentive, he could also be very inconsistent. There were times when he wouldn't call when he said he would. He would never attend a public function with me, always saying that he was too tired or had a conflict on his schedule. He generally didn't call me when he was traveling on business. I just chalked these instances up to him "being a man in the entertainment industry." I foolishly believed that as our relationship continued to develop, he would change.

The Other Woman

After about eight months of dating we finally attended our first event together. It was being held by a mutual friend of ours named Diana, and I was giddy with excitement. This was our coming out event, the first time we were presenting ourselves as a couple to our social world.

Diana lived on the twenty-ninth floor of a high-rise building in the Financial District. The weather was beautifully warm and clear that day, and a barbecue was loaded down with different meats, wafting deliciously pungent smoke up and over the balcony as a glowing yellow sun slowly descended against the backdrop of the Hudson River. Nick and I arrived just as the party was moving into full swing. Grabbing a club soda from the kitchen, I headed out to the terrace to chat with our host.

Diana and I were exchanging pleasantries when out of the corner of my eye I saw Nick speaking with a petite woman with a large Afro. I didn't think anything of it and continued to speak with Diana until she interrupted me to say, "Where is Nick going?"

I turned my head just in time to watch him bolt out of the penthouse with his cell phone glued to his ear.

"I don't know!" I answered, confused.

My cell phone rang. It was Nick.

His voice was edgy as he spoke, "Hey…"

"What happened to you? Why did you take off like that?"

"My stepmother is sick and in the hospital…I have to fly down to Florida and see her!"

"I'm sorry to hear that, but why didn't you tell me at the party? How could you leave me there alone?"

"I panicked, Sil Lai. She is the only mother I have and I wasn't thinking clearly. The only thing on my mind was booking a ticket to Florida as soon as possible."

"This doesn't make sense. There is something very wrong here...I'm coming over to talk."

Hastily apologizing to Diana, I quickly departed and went to his apartment, ready to end our relationship.

Nick let me in the door and I proceeded to give him twenty minutes of my mind. He listened quietly and tried to explain his behavior, but none of his rationalizations made sense. Frustrated, I grabbed my purse and started to head out the door.

Nick grabbed my arm and asked me to stay.

"Nick...I can't take this anymore! I can't do this...your behavior is driving me crazy!"

"Don't go! I have something to tell you...you're going to hate me, but I have to get this off my chest."

"What is it? Tell me! Tell me why you've been acting so crazy. Do you have a mental illness? Is that what's wrong?"

That was the only explanation that I could think of which made sense of his behavior.

He stumbled and stuttered for another three minutes, trying to force the words out his mouth.

Now I was starting to get really worried.

Oh God, is he sick? Is this man gonna tell me he has an STD or something?

My heart was pounding so hard it felt like it was going to come out my chest. "Tell me! Just say it! Whatever it is, I can handle it!"

"It isn't over between me and Toni. She is still my girlfriend."

A wave of relief and anger fell over me like a dark shadow. *Thank God he's not sick...*

"What? Are you kidding? You have been lying to me all this time?"

"I knew you wouldn't date me if I had a girlfriend, so I told you that it was over when it wasn't. I am so sorry...I didn't want to lose you..."

He went on to explain that the reason he had bolted out of the barbecue was because in a random coincidence, Diana had unwittingly invited one of Toni's best friends to the party. His panic over this friend telling Toni about me was what caused him to rush home, not his sick mother.

Part of me wanted to slap him upside his head for lying, and the other half wanted to cry. The fact that he had me fooled for almost a year was humiliating, but I didn't want to let him go. This whole infidelity piece was not a part of my master plan.

So I gave Nick the ultimatum to choose between Toni and me.

"I will end it with her once I see her."

"What do you mean once you see her? How are you going to see her? She lives in London!"

"I can't break up with her over the phone …I owe it to her to do this in person…"

"If you get on a plane to go see her it's over between us! I'm serious Nick! What the hell do you need to see her in person for? Anything you need to say can be done on the phone! Make your choice!"

"Come on Sil Lai! I have known her for four years! She was my best friend! You can't expect me to break up with her over the phone! I owe her the respect of saying this in person!"

"Respect? Your ass shoulda' been respecting me all this time you've been cheating!"

Grasping For Control

Nick didn't get on a plane and ended up breaking up with Toni over the phone. Although he became much more attentive towards me, something still didn't seem to be right. Things remained rocky between us and his behavior continued to be somewhat erratic. Two months later Nick told me that he would be spending Labor Day weekend at a family reunion. It was just three days before the holiday and my children and I were left without any weekend plans. I was livid.

Family reunion? What family? There are only your two sisters and their husbands and kids left…how are you having a family reunion with only seven people? I wondered. The past two months had been hell on our relationship and I wanted to show him that he had regained my trust. I said nothing to him about my doubts, and kept any second-thoughts about the validity of his story under wraps.

The weekend was miserable. Half of the time was spent missing him, and the other half was spent plotting how I was going to end things between us when he got back into town. Any plans I had to terminate our relationship disappeared once he returned of course.

"Hey baby…I missed you! God, it's good to be back. I couldn't wait to see you. Come over here girl…"

He showered me with affection, but despite his attention I still couldn't shake the feeling that something was very wrong. I couldn't quite put my finger on it, but something just wasn't right.

On September 11th at 3:00 a.m. the thing that wasn't right blew the lid right off our relationship.

D-Day

Nick and I were in his apartment fast asleep when the bedroom light suddenly switched on.

"Nick! Nick! Get up! I said get up right now! I want to speak with you!"

A woman's voice with a clipped British accent loudly filled the room. Bolting upright in bed, out of bleary eyes I saw a slim light-skinned woman standing in the middle of his bedroom.

"Nick! I want you to get up right this minute! I said, get up!"

He slid out of the bed, standing in front of her clad only in a t-shirt, head hanging down on his chest like a whipped puppy.

"Who is she?" she asked, gesturing at me.

Never lifting his head to meet her eyes he mumbled, "That's Sil Lai. Sil Lai, this is Toni," he answered.

Nick didn't need to bother with an introduction. I recognized the woman standing in front of me from a photo album he kept on his bookshelf.

I looked at both of them with my eyes and mouth wide open.

"Nick told me that he broke it off with you!"

Toni stood back with her arms folded across her chest, looking at me with barely concealed scorn.

"No, Nicky here has been a very bad boy. We've never broken up!"

"What! Not even in July? He said he broke up with you in July!"

Turning to look Nick dead in the face she answered, "Oh, he told me then that he had cheated on me with you, but it was only because of the sex."

Ouch.

"Did you know he was at my house not ten days ago, holding me and crying in my arms, saying he couldn't imagine living without me?"

Her words hit me in the chest like a tire iron. *So much for the family reunion!*

Now I was staring at Nick, hoping and praying that he would deny her words, but nothing came out of his mouth. He just kept staring at the floor.

Who was this person I had been sleeping with for the last ten months?

What was happening was surreal, like a bad dream. But it wasn't a nightmare. It was really happening.

This isn't happening...This isn't happening...

Toni moved closer to Nick, her voice shaking in rage. "So this is what you've been doing this whole summer? I can't believe I listened to you and all of your lies! All of this time you said you needed more time to work things out for us...that you were going through mental problems..."

This whole scene could have been pulled out of bad reality TV show, but there was no hidden camera. I was sucked right into the middle of this horrific mess.

"Do you have anything to say for yourself?" she shouted. "Do you? Do you? Answer me dammit! That's the least you can do!"

He just looked back at her silently with a remorseful look on his face.

Flinging his house keys at his chest, she shrieked, "I can't believe what a liar you are!"

Slapping him across the face, she turned quickly on her heel and stormed out of the apartment. The front door slammed shut behind her and suddenly everything was very quiet. Silence engulfed the room.

"Sil Lai, I am so sorry..."

I finally broke down. Leaning back on the bedroom wall, the tears began to flood out of my eyes.

"Baby...I'm sorry," he said as he wrapped his arms around my shaking frame. Leading me back into the bed, Nick held me in his arms while my body convulsed with sobs.

"I didn't know what to do…I wasn't in love with her anymore, but I didn't want to lose one of my best friends...I wanted to be with you, not her…"

Now, this doesn't sound like the basis for a healthy relationship, does it?

Those Damn Attachments…

The next day I told my friends what had happened, and while they were aghast at the circumstances, they weren't really surprised. Most of them had warned me all along that Nick was probably cheating on me. I had refused to believe it. I couldn't believe that he could do such a thing. After all, he had said that he loved me…

Nick obviously had issues with honesty and integrity, but I couldn't accept the truth staring me in the face. I had become completely dependent upon him to bolster my self-worth. My attachment to our relationship led me to turn a blind eye to his shady behavior, and as much as it pained me, I chose to continue in the relationship, albeit now completely filled with insecurity and fear.

A Descent into Madness

Not long after the incident with Toni, Nick spoke to me about possibly marrying in the near future. We even went house hunting together. Despite these actions, my heart whispered that Nick was performing a role he never had any intention of actually fulfilling. We struggled through another difficult fourteen months together, constantly fighting about his inconsistent behavior and habitual lying. Most of my waking moments were spent thinking up elaborate ploys to catch him in lies or reading books on how to get him to commit further to our relationship. I would read through his email account and go hunting through his apartment looking for any sort of clue that he was cheating again. I seized every opportunity to search through his pockets for slips of paper with women's telephone numbers on them. Whenever possible I would flip through his cell phone call list to see who he had been talking to, and if there was a telephone number that looked suspicious, I'd call it to see if a woman's voice answered.

Every new day was another opportunity to catch him red handed in a compromising position, but for all my searching he never gave me a justifiable cause to cast him aside, at least as far as other women were concerned. It seemed he had stopped cheating, but the trust could never be rebuilt between us, because his lies didn't stop with Toni. He lied about completely inconsequential things as well, like the place of his birth, who he had dated in the past, or how much something cost.

Benjamin Franklin wisely said, *"The definition of insanity is doing the same thing over and over again expecting different results."* My sanity was coming undone by Nick's constant distortions of the truth and my desperate attempts to control his behavior. I could not accept that he was not capable of telling me the truth. I could not accept that the last two years of my life had been spent with a man who would not become my husband. I was fully entrenched in a vicious and debilitating cycle of denial.

Breaking the Camel's Back

Our last year together was spent in couple's therapy working on "trust building and effective communication skills," until two years of his lying and promises of change finally broke through my denial. On the day of what was to be our final therapy session, I caught Nick again in another lie.

"Why does he keep doing this?" I asked our therapist. Looking at him I said "Nick, why can't you just stop lying?"

"Sil Lai, your anger doesn't help Nick to feel safe enough to be honest with you. You need to change how you respond to what he says if you want him to feel comfortable enough to tell the truth."

I exploded, livid that she would try to put part of his problem on me.

"I don't make him lie! I am not responsible for his behavior!"

My denial about the truth of our relationship was finally stripped away as I embraced the principle of acceptance. Fear is always at the heart of denial and control, and my fear of being alone and losing a two year emotional investment had kept me from accepting the truth about Nick's nature. I accepted that there was always going to be a way for him to justify his lying. I accepted his character for what it was: dishonest and manipulative. I accepted that all of the couple's therapy in the world wouldn't help us to have a healthy relationship. I accepted that it wasn't my responsibility to help this man become an honest person, but it was my responsibility to protect myself from further emotional harm by leaving our relationship. It was only when I had finally accepted these unalterable facts that I could start the painful process of releasing my unhealthy attachment to our relationship.

Willingness to Change

Every challenging situation that we go through with another is an opportunity for us to learn. My relationship with Nick taught me that I cannot control the behavior of another and that I still had value even without a relationship with a man. I realized that for many years I had equated my personal value with the level of external success of the man at my side. I believed if he became my husband I would automatically receive the power and status I so hungrily desired.

By finally accepting the truth of our relationship, I was able to move forward in my truth and take action to heal my spirit.

The Joy of Acceptance

While pain can be a great initiator for us to embrace the principle of acceptance, suffering is not necessary in order for us to embrace the truth. We do not have to understand a situation completely before accepting it. For example, if one were aboard the Titanic while it was sinking, would it be better to accept what was happening and get off the ship, or to stop and analyze the reasons why the ship was going down? Would we stay on the boat as the water rushed over the decks, pondering where the iceberg pierced the hull or at what speed the water was filling the engine room?

Knowing the *why* would not prevent the ship from spiraling down to its inevitable demise with us still aboard. There are certainly cases where one should take some time before deciding if something is a fact, but we should always ask ourselves what is motivating our actions. Are our choices based on fear? Or are they based on truth and acceptance? For many of us, our lives are like the sinking Titanic, and unless we accept this truth we are headed straight to destruction.

Acceptance Summarized

A life in which the principle of acceptance is practiced will be one filled with peace. We will realize that there is nothing we can do to control the behavior of others, and no longer take the actions of another personally. We will truly accept and understand that everyone has their own path to walk in this life, one that is not contingent upon anyone else's approval and blessing.

Once we have embraced acceptance we eliminate our inner critic and begin the process of accepting *all* of who we are. As we become more and more empowered, we come to accept that everything about our life is exactly as it should be...*in this moment.* We will realize that everything that has happened in our life has happened to help us evolve into a higher state of being.

The Moon in all of her beauty has both its shadow and its light. One cannot bask in its glow without accepting both. In this same way we must accept the dark and light sides of ourselves, for only then can we effectively take action and integrate all of our personality into a life which truly reflects our wonderful and beautiful self.

CHAPTER 5

ACTION
Move Swiftly and Without Hesitation

"Ideas without action are worthless."

~ *Helen Keller*

Once we have sought and accepted the truth of our present life, we need to take *action*. Action is a principle which requires us to make an effort to create a positive change in our life with the information we have learned through the use of the first two principles of truth and acceptance. As Napoleon Hill wrote in his inspirational classic, "Think and Grow Rich," *"Knowledge is only potential power. It becomes power only when, and if, it is organized into definite plans of action and directed to a definite end."* When we begin to use the first three SEPIA principles together we are taking an active step towards eliminating the self-defeating behaviors which have helped to create the drama in our life.

In this chapter we'll see how our actions (or the lack thereof) can have a profound impact on our life. We will also see a few of the reasons why a survivor may not take action and how a contender masterfully uses the principle.

Action Defined

Action is a verb, which means it is something that is performed. A very common mistake many make is to believe that *thinking* about taking action is action is the same thing as actually *taking action*. Action requires the exertion of energy to accomplish a goal. It is the act of extending our will through physical or mental activity.

Action is necessary for all who desire to change their lives. Although the word is very commonly used, it is also an extremely spiritual concept. All major religions emphasize the importance of this principle in their doctrines. One of the most popular scriptures in the Bible stresses the importance of action. In the NIV version it is written: "In the same way, faith by itself, if it is not accompanied by action, is dead." (James 2:16-18) A central point in Hindu and Buddhist beliefs is karma, which is a sum of all that an individual has done, is currently doing, and will do. The word 'karma' in the ancient Sanskrit language literally means "deed" or "act."

Our ability or inability to use this principle is one of the basic struggles we all face in life. Perhaps this is why one of the main goals of all religions is to teach us how to live an *actively* spiritually conscious life.

The opposite of action is sloth.
Sloth is the refusal to pursue a virtuous life due to laziness.

Four Common Reasons Why We Do Not Take Action

There are many different reasons why we struggle with this principle, and while they will vary from individual to individual, four of the most common are:

- Procrastination
- Approval Seeking
- Fear of Failure
- Externally Based Motivation

Procrastination

Procrastination is the act of putting off doing something which needs to be taken care of, usually out of carelessness or laziness. When *procrastinating*, a person has allowed excuses or rationalizations to prevent them from taking action. Those who procrastinate often suffer from the feelings of shame and guilt that can be generated from the subconscious when we avoid taking action.

Researchers have found that those who wrestle with procrastination tend to be perfectionists. As we explored in the previous chapter on truth, perfection is an impossible and frustrating goal. A perfectionist's desire to perform the "perfect" action creates high levels of anxiety that they try to alleviate by jumping into either frenetic activity not related to what needs to be addressed or pleasurable escapist activities.

Survivors allow their anxiety to cause them to distract themselves with unrelated work or pleasurable activity. They allow their fears to take over which leads them to procrastinate. Contenders understand that procrastination will create even larger issues in the future. This leads them to take a disciplined approach to what needs to be done in their life *today*.

Approval Seeking

Another reason why people avoid taking action is because of a need for approval from those around them. Enslaved by the fear of what others *may* think about our decisions, we can become paralyzed because of a fear of how others will respond to our actions.

By using the principle of acceptance we can understand that there will always be people who will criticize what we do, no matter how flawlessly an action is performed.

A survivor allows their need for approval to dictate the actions they take. They allow their fear of criticism to prevent them from taking action with their truth. A contender does not base her actions on the need for approval from others. She uses the principle of truth as a guide for her behavior. A need for approval is often linked to a third reason for inaction, the fear of failure.

Fear of Failure

Fear of failure is a common reason why we may fail to take action. Failure does not define who we are…it is about behavior, outcomes, and results.

As Napoleon Hill wrote in "Think and Grow Rich," *"every adversity, every failure, and every heartache carries with it the seed of an equivalent or a greater benefit."* Every failure is simply an opportunity for us to learn more about whom we are and where we need to grow.

A crucial self-empowerment tool is the universal truth of the Law of Mentalism, which is popularly referred to as the Law of Attraction. In a nutshell, the Law of Mentalism states that everything we think will manifest in our life. When applied to a fear of failure, if we believe we will fail, we will.

We affect our reality, positively or negatively, based upon our thoughts. It's natural to believe we won't be able to achieve an objective, especially if attempts made in the past have failed. If we tried our best and didn't achieve a goal, it was not because there was something inherently wrong with us…it just means there was something wrong with our plan.

Survivors allow their fear of failure to grow to the point that they don't take any action at all. They tend to lives filled with regrets and excuses for why they don't take action. Contenders understand that while it can be very painful to fail, the alternative of not trying is far worse. They see the challenges they face as opportunities to succeed, not fail.

Externally Based Motivation

Externally motivated people need the behavior of people or circumstances outside themselves to stimulate them into action. When a person is externally motivated they wait until someone or something else forces them to respond. Their lives tend to be chaotic and disordered, because the impetus for their activity comes from a place which is always changing: the world around them.

A survivor's motivation comes from outside, and a contender's motivation to action comes from within.

For every reason our fear may tell us that we will fail,
there is an opposing reason why we can succeed.

Comparison Between Types

SURVIVOR	CONTENDER
• Procrastinates due to fear.	• Takes action in spite of fear.
• Is overly concerned with what others may think.	• Does not allow what others may think to determine their actions.
• Allows fear of failure to prevent them from taking action.	• Focuses on the reasons why they will succeed.
• Is motivated to take action by people or circumstances outside of themselves.	• Is motivated to action from within.

At the heart of the four listed causes of inaction is *fear.* Fear is an emotion that can be conquered. In fact, we can take action *in spite of our fear.* Courage is the ability to take action in spite of our fear, uncertainty, pain, or danger. All of us possess the ability to confront our demons. Just the fact alone that we have survived the challenges of our lives and are still willing to do the work to empower ourselves is a testimony to our courage. No matter what we think or feel, we can still take action. That's not to say it will be easy to do, but it can be done.

Survivors are masters of coulda, woulda, shoulda. They can always tell us the reasons why they can't do something, and tend to ignore the reasons why they can. A contender, on the other hand, can acknowledge that she is afraid and still take action. She won't focus her energy on the reasons she can't do something, but instead actively seeks out the ways she *can* reach her goals.

The Importance of Action

Although not apparent at the time, my unhealthy relationship with Nick would become a catalyst for me with the third SEPIA principle of Action. The following story illustrates how I was able to get to the bottom of a life long attraction to drama by taking action with the truth that I had accepted about myself.

One day not long after Nick and I broke up, I crawled into my bed and didn't get out for three months. My personal hygiene fell by the wayside, and I stopped cleaning my apartment...the only chore I performed with some regularity was washing my bed sheets every few weeks, and that was only when I could no longer stand the feel of the clammy fabric against my skin. The only meal I ate was in the early evening, and that was usually made up of the leftovers from whatever I had ordered in for my children's dinner. The rest of the day I ate dry Lucky Charms and drank Diet Coke.

My son and daughter could do nothing more than stand by and watch while their mother disintegrated before their eyes. As the days dragged by, they did all they could to try and maintain a semblance of normalcy in the home...as normal as a child's home can be when one's mother is lying in bed crying all day long. They dutifully handled the basic household chores to the best of their ability...Amanda would tidy up the apartment as best she could, washing dishes and cleaning the bathroom, and Christian would take out the garbage and periodically go to the local grocery store to pick up food staples like bread, eggs, and milk.

I have always taken great pride in nurturing friendships and associations... success in my industry depended on my ability to stay socially connected. But as my depression deepened, I lost my desire to work and completely withdrew from the outside world. With no income at all, my finances fell into complete disarray. Instead of getting out of my house and hustling for new contracts, I lay in bed watching reruns of Law & Order on TNT all day long. Once the cable was shut off for non-payment, I started watching anything on television...anything that could distract me from the black cloud that had settled upon my consciousness.

Day after day went by as my main activities became weeping and crying or catatonically sitting alone in silence for hours. The very thought of Nick would make my eyes tear up and cause me to catch my breath sharply. My heart felt like it was slowly being squeezed in the grip of a cold metal vise, with a knife stuck straight through the center of it. My daily schedule fell into a static routine, varying only between the days I would drag myself to the bathroom to bathe and the days I didn't bother. Nothing could break my descent into depression. Not the guilt of knowing my children were essentially orphaned and living in a home with a ghost mother, not impending economic disaster, not even the threat of losing my home.

Friends who had known me through many years of emotional ups and downs realized that something was very wrong. When I called them to console me, they gently chided me with words of encouragement while sympathetically listening to my tears and complaints.

"Sil Lai, can you *please* just let it go? Don't let that man do this to you! He ain't worth it!"

My response to them would be more weeping and Lucky Charms.

A Light in the Darkness

Of course none of my friends could help. I was seeking what they could never grant me: emotional peace. One by one, they stopped picking up the phone. Pathetic messages left on their voicemails remained unreturned and their daily check-ins began to stop. By the sixth week of my depression there were only four people left in my life who would still take my calls: My oldest and dearest friend Carol, a newer friend named Gwen, my former employer, Lesly, and my mentor Marian. With Carol I would whine, with Gwen, analyze, Lesly, vent, and Marian, question the reasons why Nick had done me wrong. Day after day, they listened to my pain while everyone else dropped away.

The days were just as bad as the nights; while the city slept my mind would race. Nick's absence was hard to handle as the evening slipped by...his empty space in my bed glaring back at me. Carol, Gwen, and Lesly would console me during the day, in between their work schedules, and since Marian lived in Los Angeles and was three hours behind New York's time zone, she ended up taking on the "night shift."

Marian was a wisecracking professional astrologer I had met five years before through a mutual friend. Our relationship with the mutual friend had withered, but we ended up becoming quite close. Marian was a lifelong student of philosophy, holistic medicine, theology, and of course astrology, and she possessed a wealth of knowledge and experience. She differed greatly from my friends and acquaintances in the entertainment industry for she was completely unmotivated by money or fame. The only thing that mattered to her was raising her teenage son and living her life in a manner that was creative and uncompromising.

Over the course of our friendship, Marian had seen me go through two dysfunctional relationships and several aborted first and second dates. She would listen for hours while I complained about the men in my life...patiently, sympathetically, and without judgment.

One night, about twenty minutes into one of my tirades, she abruptly cut me off.

"Sil Lai, can't you see what's happening? All of your relationships are exactly the same...nothing is changing except for the players. You have some real issues about your self-worth that are going to have to be addressed before you can even begin to think about having a healthy relationship with a man. Until you work through your unresolved emotional issues, you are going to keep attracting the same type of men into your life."

This wasn't the first time that she had said something to this effect to me. In fact, Marian had been repeating this statement consistently over the last five years.

"What am I supposed to do? Stop dating completely?" I asked.

"Yes, that's what you need to do. What's the point of continuing to date if you are just going to keep getting yourself into dysfunctional relationships that cause you pain? Unless you face whatever it is that is driving you into these relationships, you are going to keep getting the same negative results."

"Well, how long do I have to abstain from relationships? How will I know if I'm healthy enough to make better choices?"

"For as long as it takes. I have no idea how long that will be, but when you are ready you will know."

On one hand, I knew that it was high-time for me to take action and deal with my unresolved emotional issues. On the other, I was scared to death of being alone. My entire adult life had been spent leapfrogging from one relationship to the next, but by now I was so desperate for emotional relief that I actually took her advice.

For the first time in almost twenty years I refused to buoy my emotions from the breakup of a previous relationship by running into another. And although I thought things couldn't get any worse, they did. Without a new love interest to distract me from my pain I was finally forced to face a lifetime of disappointment. The numbing sadness which had enveloped me after Nick and I broke up spiraled into a shock that splintered the remains of my soul and I fell into a dark chasm of sorrow and self-pity.

Hitting Bottom

Of course what Marian said made total sense…it would be impossible for anyone to have gone through the experiences I have and not have some serious emotional issues. After three months of lying on my back in bed, even I had to admit that there was more to my depression than the end of a relationship. Of course, this wasn't the first time I had faced a major depression…depression had haunted me from the time I was a young child. There was no rhyme nor reason to explain when or why it would hit…sometimes a depression would slowly wrap itself around my mind after a traumatic incident; other times one would blast out of nowhere and knock me on my back for no apparent reason at all.

These mood swings weren't easy for those close to me to deal with, but friends and loved ones did their best to deal with my temperamental nature. There were times when my moodiness would really turn someone off and I would lose a friend, but instead of facing the truth of my behavior I would rationalize it away.

So I have a hard time managing my temper, big deal…lots of people do!

People just need to learn to stay out of my way when I'm angry!

So what if I get depressed sometimes? Everyone else does too!

I needed to do something…the bills were piling up… creditors were sending notices…my children needed their mother. It had become very clear that if I didn't do something to address my emotional health I stood a real risk of losing everything. Ninety-three days after first crawling into bed, I took Marian's advice and sought the help of a psychotherapist.

Beyond Appearances

This wasn't the first time I had used the services of a mental health professional. At various points over the course of my life I had sought help for my periods of anxiety and depression, either by sporadically seeing a therapist or taking antidepressant medication. Neither of them did much long term good for me. Therapy wasn't really effective because my sessions were mainly used as opportunities to vent about whichever man I was currently dating. I spent so much time complaining about my boyfriends that I never got around to actually talking about how I was feeling. Antidepressants worked to a certain extent, and I went off and on many different ones over the years, stopping treatment as soon as my symptoms faded.

Instead of committing myself to treatment I had always opted to devour enormous amounts of psychiatric literature in an attempt to heal my emotional problems. Many of these books were standard pop psychology fare, and a few were actual college textbooks. It was while reading one of the textbooks that I came across a mental illness named Borderline Personality Disorder, also referred to as 'BPD' for short. As I read the words on the page my heart skipped a beat. The symptoms were frighteningly familiar. My breath hung suspended while its symptoms jumped out at me. Closing the book, I panicked.

What if I have BPD?

My mind was racing.

I can't have a mental illness...no way!

I stuffed what I had read into the back of my mind, where it would remain buried at the edges of my memory for over ten years. Denial was easy when I had twelve hour work days, two children, and an active social life to keep me so busy that I didn't stop to see my truth. And the entertainment business was a perfect place for me to blend in and hide. Crazy work schedules and outrageous behavior were the norm. Very few people in the business are actually interested in getting to know others beyond a title or appearance, so I was safely hidden away in a world that insulated me from the reality of my emotional landscape. To the world I looked normal, but the reality was that everything was not okay. Life went on and I continued to keep my demons at bay for another ten years until the breakup with Nick knocked me off my feet.

Baring It All

On the advice of Marian, and after doing some online research on various types of therapy, I chose to work with a psychotherapist who specialized in treating people with addiction issues. A sassy and direct woman in her late forties, Susan had a completely no-nonsense approach to therapy. She never let me use our sessions as gripe fests. Whenever I started to bring Nick into the conversation, she would interrupt me with a pointed question.

"What are you trying to avoid, Sil Lai?"

"I'm not trying to avoid anything! Why isn't he relevant?"

"Have you noticed that you always bring him up whenever we are talking about you? What is so frightening about your feelings?"

"There's nothing frightening about how I am feeling…if it wasn't for Nick, I wouldn't be feeling this way!"

Despite the frustration I felt over Susan's refusal to indulge my fascination with what was wrong with my ex-boyfriend, I continued to seek treatment from her. About a month or so in to our sessions I finally got what she was talking about. She was right…I have always used men as a way to avoid dealing with what is going on inside of me. Once that became clear, I stopped talking about Nick and started to keep the focus on me.

Into the Light

Two months went by and I wasn't feeling better at all. If anything, I was feeling worse. It was like I had a warped cassette tape stuck in my brain that kept looping the same thoughts over and over and over.

You shoulda known better…

You shoulda seen this coming…

You shoulda done something earlier…

Nothing could make the tape stop…it kept on playing and playing, and I kept getting more and more despondent. Susan was concerned about the severity of my depression and suggested that I consider going on antidepressant medication. Although I was ambivalent about taking any drugs, I hesitantly agreed to visit a psychiatrist for a second opinion.

Opening up the massive insurance directory, I randomly selected a psychiatrist whose location was reasonably convenient to the subway and called to set up a session for the following week.

The office was easy to find and I ended up arriving a little early for my appointment. Dr. Jesker shared an office with a podiatrist who never seemed to be in. The waiting room was a hodge podge of cozy armchairs and medical's equipment. Along with typical office reading materials like ancient Sports Illustrated and nine year old Reader's Digest magazines, there were pharmaceutical company pamphlets on Wellbutrin and Effexor interspersed with reading material on the latest and most effective treatment of bunions and hammer toes.

Eying my surroundings, I was not impressed.

Oh Lord...I hope this guy knows what he's doing...

The door to the psychiatrist's office opened and a gray haired older man clad from head to toe in varying shades of blue polyester entered the waiting room.

Nodding his head at me, he said "See Lai? I'm Dr. Jesker. Come in."

His office was a small ten by twelve space which housed a wide wooden desk cluttered with notes, pharmaceutical company giveaways, old pens, and stacks of patient files. The linoleum floor was dulled by scuff marks and one wall was adorned with two prominently placed diplomas written in Russian, and a certificate from Columbia University. An uncovered window about six feet off the floor immediately behind my chair allowed passersby on the sidewalk to see right into our sessions from the street.

Dr. Jesker was in his late fifties with a shock of grey hair rimming his skull and a very aloof manner. He had emigrated from the Ukraine some twenty years earlier but still spoke with a heavy Russian accent. Rooting around in his desk for a pen, he grabbed a notepad and turned to face me.

"So, vat brings you here today?"

Sitting in a narrow metal chair next to his disorganized desk, I haltingly repeated the convoluted story of my life. The initial intake was only supposed to take a half-hour, but because of my extensive history of trauma, it ended up being spread out over two full fifty minute sessions. As I spoke, I became painfully aware of exactly how filled with drama my life had been. For the most part there hadn't been a year that had gone by which didn't contain some serious form of chaos. Many of these memories had been submerged long before and were only now being painfully revisited for the first time in years. It was embarrassing to share so much with a complete stranger so quickly. I felt naked and exposed.

As we neared the end of our second session, the information on BPD I had read years earlier came to mind.

"Doctor, can I asked you a question?"

"Vat is it, See Lai?"

"This depression hasn't just happened this one time. This has been going on and off for years."

"Yes, zat is pretty clear from your history..."

"It's not like am trying to do your job for you, but...," my voice trailed off for a moment, then continued stronger. "I'm a bit of a bookworm you know, and after doing some research I think I have something more serious than depression."

His slate blue eyes peered at me intently through the glasses perched on the end of his long nose.

I nervously swallowed, then continued speaking.

"Do you think I have Borderline Personality Disorder?" The sentence blurted out of my mouth, the words flying off of my tongue.

My words continued to rush forward, "You don't have to worry about telling me. I won't freak out. It's just that it would be really helpful for me to know exactly what I'm dealing with."

He blinked slowly twice, and then spoke in very measured tones.

"Vell See Lai, I vood not say that you qualify for a full diagnosis of the disorder." He continued, "You exhibit some Borderline traits, but function too vell overall to have full-blown BPD."

As we continued to discuss my history it became clear that I had been struggling with varying degrees of the disorder since early adolescence. The difference between those who receive an "official" diagnosis of the illness and those who only have "borderline traits" depends on how successfully a person can function in the world. Those who can sustain employment and for the most part take care of themselves are termed "high-functioning," while those who can't are described as "low-functioning." Although I had been fairly "high-functioning" since I quit drinking, the stress of my dysfunctional relationship with Nick and subsequent breakup had triggered a huge flare up of symptoms.

The Beginning of the End

A symphony of emotions washed over me as I left Dr. Jesker's office that day. Pondering his diagnosis, different thoughts flooded my mind:

What will everyone think if they find out?

Does this mean that I am crazy?

Will anyone ever love me if I truly do have a mental illness?

Temper tantrums, chaotic relationships, and constantly shifting mood swings…things about my behavior which had always baffled me and my family started to make so much sense. While the diagnosis was comforting on a certain level, it was overwhelmingly frightening as well. After all, it's one thing to think that an illness might be a possibility, but an entirely different matter altogether to confirm it.

The days between my appointment with Dr. Jesker and the upcoming one with Susan couldn't pass fast enough. By the time our next session arrived, I was brimming with excitement over what I had discovered. Sinking into the soft cushions of the beige sofa in her office, we started the session.

"Hello Sil Lai! How was your appointment with the psychiatrist…?"

"It was okay. He was a bit dry, but it's not his job to amuse me, right?"

She briefly smiled and answered, "Did he prescribe any medication for you?"

"Yes. He put me on Effexor, so we'll see how it goes for the next couple of weeks. Hopefully it will kick in and I won't be feeling so awful."

"I'm glad to hear that you followed through…"

Interrupting her sentence, I blurted out the news to her, "You know what else? I asked Dr. Jesker if he thought I had Borderline Personality Disorder and he said that he thought I only have traits. What do you think?"

Susan leaned back in her chair and exhaled slowly.

"Why do you find it so important to label yourself?"

"I don't know…I guess I feel like knowledge is power. Are you afraid I'm gonna freak out if I find out I have a mental illness?"

"No, it's not that…I just think that people place too much emphasis on labels. Labels can trap a person…but to answer your question, yes, I agree that you have Borderline traits…perhaps even the disorder, but I don't think you should be focused on a diagnosis. What we need to focus on is how you are going to get better."

As my treatment continued, I gathered as much information as possible on the disorder. What I was surprised to discover was that almost *everyone* has a few BPD traits. Its main symptoms include black and white thinking, frantic attempts to avoid abandonment, volatile mood swings, and turbulent interpersonal relationships. Two well known individuals believed to have had the disorder include Princess Diana and Marilyn Monroe. Although just as many people in this country have Borderline Personality Disorder as Bi-Polar Disorder (which by medical estimates is about five million), the limited public information is shrouded in outdated data and Hollywood myth.

The perspective on BPD within the medical community has changed greatly since it was first officially included in the DSM (Diagnostic and Statistical Manual) in 1980. At the time the disorder was believed to be incurable, but over the years it has been discovered that BPD is in fact highly treatable. It's a chronic illness, like arthritis or high-blood pressure, but with proper treatment, people can and do lead healthy and productive lives.

Taking Action with the Truth

One tool which helped me get better was a specialized form of group therapy named Dialectical Behavioral Therapy, or DBT for short. For three months I attended individual and group therapy sessions every week, and these taught me how to use the tools of mindfulness to gain self-acceptance and reliance upon inner wisdom.

The darkness and fear which had followed me for so much of my life was rolled away as I learned how to manage my emotions. I finally understood that in order to truly change my life…and not just a surface change, like switching jobs, losing weight, or getting a new man…a deep and profound change, I would have to become completely willing to accept the truth of my life and take action to change what I could.

This was a revolutionary new way of thinking. It was as if I had been trapped in a darkened room for years and then someone suddenly opened the door and switched on the light. For the first time in years I felt there was truly a chance for me to live a drama-less life.

Within a month of starting DBT, I experienced a tremendously positive shift in mood and perception. My emotions had stabilized and I no longer suffered from obsessive thoughts or depression. For the following ten months I regularly attended individual therapy, and around the one year mark my body began to reject the antidepressants. Apparently because I was no longer clinically depressed, the drugs had stopped being of benefit. With the blessing and assistance of Dr. Jesker, I went off of the antidepressants completely.

The level of healing I had experienced was not just on an emotional and spiritual level, but on a physical level as well. One year after going through one of the darkest times in my life, my life had stabilized on all fronts. I was no longer working in dysfunctional environments and I had stopped engaging in co-dependent relationships. For the first time in years I was experiencing internal peace.

Susan had noticed the shift and shared this with me in one of our last sessions.

"Sil Lai, I think I was too quick to label you as having Borderline Personality Disorder. I am going to revise your diagnosis to Borderline Personality Disorder traits."

Less than one year after making the choice to take action and face my truth, I no longer qualified for an "official" diagnosis of a mental illness!

Out of the Dark

There are branches of the psychiatric community which believe that many common psychiatric illnesses are manifestations of a lack of connectedness to one's spirit. The ancient philosopher Plato said: *"As you ought not attempt to cure the eyes without treating the heart, or the head without treating the body as a whole, so you should not treat the body without treating the soul..."* Some within the psychiatric community don't believe there is a need to address the spirit, while others believe that without treating the soul one cannot ever achieve any sort of emotional health. But for me, it was only after embracing a spiritually based lifestyle and undergoing psychiatric treatment that I was able to achieve any real measure of emotional healing. Years of conventional therapy on its own had done nothing to heal me. My personal experience with this matter has led me to believe that there really is something to what Plato said almost 2,500 years ago.

It would be irresponsible to claim that a spiritually based treatment approach is for everyone. Any biochemically based mental illness, such as schizophrenia, bipolar disorder or even some forms of depression, requires a very different approach to treatment. From my personal experience however, I do believe that many forms of emotional illnesses can be successfully treated through a combination of psychiatry and the consistent application of spiritual principles in one's life.

The stigma surrounding mental illness has lessened in recent years, but we still have a long way to go. Shame can lead us to avoid taking action with the truth, but without action we will end up with the same result. Point blank: If we *think* we have a problem in any area of our life, we just might. We *can* trust our instincts and get the help we need in order to take action to heal our body, mind, and spirit.

Issues Do Not Define Who We Are

Once we start taking positive action with the truth we will have to arm ourselves against the possibility of slipping back into self-defeating behaviors out of habit. This can be done by replacing our old dysfunctional behaviors with new, healthy ones.

When we have lived as a victim or survivor for any length of time it can be frightening to give up our self-image. It can be scary to lose our identity, even if it is a negative one. Many victims have lifestyles which are centered on the problems in their lives. In essence, what they have done is allowed their personal identity to be defined by their lifestyle.

If we find ourselves facing this issue, it's time to redefine our interests. We can do this by expanding our world beyond our immediate circle of friends and acquaintances. Other ways we can do this is by getting actively involved in our local communities, or by helping others. Or, we can join a group of people with whom we share the same hobbies. Whatever it is, we need to get active and stay active.

Action Summarized

As with anything, the principle of action begins in the mind, in cultivating an ability to control the direction of our thoughts. We all face many challenges, but we must always remember that our present challenges do not define our worth and our history does not have to define our future. The truth will start us on a journey to self-empowerment, acceptance will guide us to charting a course, and action will move us towards our goal. The greatest stumbling block to staying in action will be our fear, but we can always counter fear with truth, acceptance, and action.

Action within the SEPIA process requires us to use the principles in sequential order when dealing with an issue. If we do not seek the truth before we respond, we are simply reacting. If we discover the truth but do not fully accept what we have learned, we can slip into denial. With enough practice, these three principles will eventually become our first response to any given situation that we face.

The key to this principle is as the well known Nike campaign says, "Just do it!" Taking action with our truth is a difficult step, but it is one that makes all the difference.

$\mathcal{C}$OMMITMENT

Commit to Your Objectives

"You need to make a commitment, and once you make it, then life will give you some answers."

~ Les Brown

An integral part of being self-empowered is learning how to maintain the fourth SEPIA principle of *commitment*. The ability to make and keep a commitment is one of the great hallmarks of spiritual and emotional maturity. Though much of what we hear about this principle surrounds the importance of being able to make a commitment to another, *the first and most important commitment we must ever make is to ourselves.* The ability to keep our commitments to others springs out of our capacity to successfully perform this one simple task.

In the previous chapters we discussed how we cannot change our life unless we first seek the truth of our reality, then accept what we discover about ourselves, and finally take action with the information we have learned. In this chapter we'll explore how the principle of commitment can help us achieve our goals and take us to an entirely different level of freedom from fear. We will also see how the absence of this principle can wreak havoc on our ability to interact with others and accomplish our goals. In addition, we'll discover how the use of this principle can change our relationship with ourselves and the world around us.

Commitment Defined

Commitment is defined as the act of binding ourselves to a course of action. When we make a commitment to someone or something, we do it with the understanding that we will do everything within our power to honor our word or mindset.

The principle of commitment forces us to ask ourselves, "What do I really want? What am I willing to do to get it?" An inability to commit will invariably lead to a life filled with broken promises and dreams never actualized. Our ability to successfully achieve our goals comes from being able to make a commitment and develop loyalties to people, places, and causes. Most of us have struggled with this particular principle to varying degrees at one time or another in our lives. Some will struggle with surrendering to this principle for their entire lives.

Taking a Stand

As is often the case, many times we learn to fear commitment through our early experiences. Perhaps we were told that we were loved by our parents, but it was not backed up by any sort of action. Or maybe our parents were too busy with their careers or problems to truly make a commitment to being in our lives.

I know I said that I would come see you play, but I can't make it to your game because I have to finish working on taxes...

Honey, I know I promised to take you to the movies with your friends, but I just didn't think there would be so much housework...

This is just one of the ways that children learn that commitment is only a word. Over time a child's heart will defend itself against disappointment by rationalizing their parent's irresponsible behavior. Eventually they will incorporate the following message into their subconscious: *Saying* that we will do something is just as good as actually doing something, and keeping our word is simply an option.

The Myth of Self-Esteem

There is a direct link between our ability to honor our commitments and our level of self-esteem. Dr. Antonia Martinez, a holistic life coach and author of "The Self-Fulfillment Workbook: 50 Exercises and Secret Truths for a Powerful Radiant Life" states, *"commitment builds esteem faster than esteem builds commitment."* One of the simplest actions we can take to build our self-esteem is making and keeping a commitment to our word.

Remember, no one is just born with great self-esteem!
We are either gifted with it as a child or we earn
it by consistently honoring our word.

Deeper Than We May Think

In 1987 Steven Carter & Julia Sokol, in their first book on the subject of commitment, "Men Who Can't Love," coined the term *"commitmentphobia"* to describe the irrational fear that some people have of making commitments. They examined the link between a person's ability to commit romantically and their ability to make and keep commitments in other aspects of their lives. What they found is that people who struggle with making and keeping romantic commitments often have difficulty making commitments in *all* areas of their life. In their second book, "He's Scared, She's Scared: Understanding the Hidden Fears That Sabotage Our Relationships" they wrote: *"People who struggle with commitment have a tough time deciding on anything permanent... Wary of making the wrong choice, worried about getting trapped or stuck, nervous about losing their freedom and their choices, they can never comfortably close off any options...Commitment anxiety can surface anytime a decision has to be made. That's because there is no such thing as the perfect choice."*

When a person can't make a commitment to saying yes to something or someone, they also have just as difficult a time saying no. This is because saying no requires us to commit to a course of action as well. People who struggle with commitment have a disempowered mentality that affects everything around them, for this mindset is not only upsetting to those who possess it, but also to the people who care about them. In the absence of commitment between two parties there can only be emotional distance and/or mistrust.

Why Do People Tend to Avoid Commitment?

The ability to make and keep our commitments is an important part of living an empowered life, but many people avoid making commitments because of their fears. While there are at least a dozen possible fear-based reasons for why people struggle with commitment, the following are four that we will explore in this book:

- Fear of a Loss of Control
- Fear of Letting Go of Our Fantasies
- Fear of Not Being Able to Keep a Commitment
- Fear of Losing Freedom

Fear of a Loss of Control

A very common reason why people have difficulty honoring their commitments is because of a fear of losing control. This particular fear is often expressed in a passive aggressive manner like forgetting to call when we say we will or habitually showing up late for appointments. Behavior of this sort is simply a manifestation of an internal struggle for control over our environment. As we have explored in a previous chapter, control over others is a futile exercise with an outcome that is usually just resentment.

Survivors fear making commitments because of their need for control. They often refuse to commit even when to do so would be to their benefit because their need for control is greater than their desire to be self-empowered.

Contenders know they have no control over anything but themselves, and understand that they are the only ones who can compel them to make a commitment. Confident in their own power, they willingly make the commitments needed to live in their truth.

Fear of Letting Go of Our Fantasies

Sometimes we shy away from making commitments because we want to hold on to specific fantasies. These fantasies are potent because they tap into the universal human desire for immediate gratification. Take for instance the timeless "Prince Charming" fantasy: Why bother to commit to changing our life when Prince Charming (whose only purpose on this Earth is to rescue us from our problems) is just around the corner? Another popular fantasy is the "All We Need Is a Dollar and a Dream" fantasy. Why make the commitment to save our hard earned money for retirement when we can buy lottery tickets or gamble to gain "instant" financial security today?

Survivors will hold on to their fantasies despite mounds of evidence that point to their futility. They will indefinitely hold off committing to an action plan because they believe someone or something will magically rescue them from their painful reality.

A contender realizes that by making a commitment to a course of action she is choosing to live in the present, not the future. She understands that commitments are not about giving up her dreams, but making the choice to pursue her dreams actively and with a sense of purpose.

Fear of Not Being Able to Keep a Commitment

People often put off making commitments because they fear they will not be able to keep them. This fear is often based upon a desire to not let others down, but ironically, their refusal to make a commitment ends up disappointing others nevertheless. Another reason they don't make commitments is because they are afraid that they will be perceived as "flaky" if they don't keep them, but people who avoid making commitments tend to be perceived as "flaky" anyway.

Survivors will allow their fear of failure to dictate their actions. They are so afraid of disappointing others that they will not make a commitment. Contenders also struggle with the same fears but handle them differently. Contenders do everything they can to keep their commitments.

Fear of Losing Freedom

Finally, people avoid commitment because they fear losing their freedom. The idea of having limitless options can be a seductive fantasy, and this mindset can keep us hooked into keeping open as many options as possible. When we keep our options boundlessly open however, it can be difficult to truly move forward.

Keeping our options completely open is a sort of "limbo." Limbo is the slightly uncomfortable place we place ourselves in when we are pondering whether or not to make a commitment. The word 'slightly' is an important part of its description. Limbo is not quite uncomfortable enough to spur us into action, and yet not quite comfortable enough to make us want to stay put.

There are many people who feel very uncomfortable when they are not taking a decisive stand on an issue, but for the person struggling with commitment, the truly uncomfortable feelings begin only *after* they make a decision. Just the idea of losing a degree of freedom is enough to throw them into a panic. Heart palpitations, nervousness, anxiety...these are all physical symptoms of the potential loss of freedom.

Survivors are so used to living in uncertainty that they actually prefer the uneasy feeling of being noncommittal over the fear they experience making a choice they see as limiting to their freedom. They often choose to ride the fence rather than make a choice. They justify their behavior by focusing on the opportunities they *may* lose by making a commitment.

A contender will focus on what she will gain from a commitment. She knows that everything in life requires a certain amount of sacrifice and that nothing worth having can be gained by half-measures.

Birds of a Feather

In addition to damaging our self-esteem, another negative outcome of commitmentphobia can be found in the quality of our relationships. Remember the Law of Correspondence discussed in the chapter on Truth? "As within, so without?" When we have personal issues with commitment, we tend to attract people with the same problem into our life. People who are afraid of commitment often feel most comfortable around others who share the same issue. Perhaps this is because they know that these relationships will rarely require them to face their own issues with commitment.

While we may maintain "freedom" through these sorts of relationships, we are also greatly limiting ourselves. We are limited in our ability to deeply connect with another, for intimacy and trust require a commitment.

We are limited in our ability to endure, for endurance is impossible without commitment. We are also limited in our ability to truly love, for love requires us to commit to a relationship. Thankfully, once we begin to address our issues with commitment, the people we will attract into our lives will tend to have an ability to honor their commitments as well. Birds of a feather *do* tend to flock together.

Commitment is a state of mind and a voluntary action. An inability to practice this principle is not insurmountable. All states of mind can be controlled, so commitmentphobia is not something we have to live with if we *choose* not to. We can begin to embrace commitment by changing our perception concerning the exact nature of the principle. It is important that we realize that commitments are choices that only we can make. *No one* else can force us to make a commitment.

Comparison Between Types

SURVIVOR	CONTENDER
• Fears that making a commitment will cause them to lose the ability to control their own decisions.	• Realizes that the only person that can control their behavior is themselves and that no one else can force them to make a commitment.
• Believes that a fantasy of how their life "could be" is preferable to making a commitment to living in the present.	• Understands that commitments empower them in making their dreams a reality.
• Allows their concerns about their ability to commit to stop them from actually making a commitment.	• Understands that it is natural to question their ability to commit and doesn't allow these concerns to stop them from making commitments.
• Focuses on the freedom they will lose by making a commitment.	• Focuses on the opportunities they will gain by making a commitment.

The Importance of Commitment

Now that we have explored some of the fears that can lead us to avoid commitment, let's take a look at these fears in action. The following story highlights how the fourth SEPIA principle of Commitment eluded me for most of my life. It also shows how by changing my perspective on this principle, I was able to maintain a new, authentic way of living.

Commitment is an issue that has plagued me most of my life. While on the surface it appeared as if it didn't, that was just another elaborate mask. It was true that I had made a commitment to parenthood by giving birth to two children and raising them. And yes, I had worked in one profession for almost ten years; I had even made the monumental commitment of marriage. The reality was, however, that although I *had* made many commitments, the majority of them were not kept. Although I have worked in the events industry for almost a decade, I changed jobs every two years. My marriage ended in a divorce I initiated, and while I had taken care of my children physically I had been so caught up in my own problems that I couldn't be truly present to meet their emotional needs. Every commitment I made was conditional except the decision to not drink, and my commitment to sobriety was mainly kept because the insanity of active alcoholism was something that I *never* wanted to experience again.

The Game of What If

Resolutely determined to live by rules of my own making, I rushed into major life decisions without fully considering the ramifications of these choices. It was always very easy to make an initial commitment to someone or something…it was just the follow through that was the challenging part. Once the reality of my decision became clear, I would start to panic.

What if I made the wrong choice?

What will happen if I don't keep my word?

What if something better comes along? What do I do then?

These thoughts would start spinning in my mind until I would come to the only possible solution to the constant swirl of doubt in my head: break my word. This was the only action that ever seemed to eliminate my overwhelming feelings of anxiety. Immediately after extricating myself from a decision a huge wave of relief would wash over me; there were times when I actually felt physically lighter. Once the weight of my commitment was lifted I no longer felt constricted or confined...I would revel in my freedom! But almost as soon as this happened however, *another* tape would start playing in my mind.

What if I made a mistake?

I am so weak...I can't keep my word for anything.

Maybe I should have tried harder...

Two repercussions from my inability to keep a commitment were the specters of shame and guilt. The way they typically manifested was as follows: If I made a commitment to myself and didn't keep it, I would become burdened with shame. Upon failing to keep a commitment to someone else, I would become overwhelmed with guilt. Since coping with uncomfortable emotions was never one of my strong suits, my solution was to deal with them by, you guessed it: avoidance.

In retrospect, over the course of time I made the completely unconscious decision to make as few commitments as possible. This, I believed, was the only option which seemed to solve my problem. My train of thought was essentially that if I don't make any commitments, then I have no reason to let anyone down or beat myself up. Of course, the alternative solution of actually *keeping* a commitment never entered into my mind. That solution would have required me to make changes to my behavior. Stuck in my victim-based mentality, the idea that I was free to choose my actions was never considered.

The funny thing was that this solution had nothing to do with the real issue I struggled with, which was fear. My reason for making most commitments didn't stem from the belief that my choice was the right one for the circumstance. The commitments I had made were all based upon what my emotional frame of mind was at the time. If I felt like making a commitment to help someone move out of an apartment because in that moment I felt like helping another, then I would commit to doing it. If the morning of the move I woke up feeling like I didn't want to do it, then I wouldn't. All of the choices I made were driven by the state of mind I had in the moment and had nothing to do with whether or not I was actually capable of fulfilling them.

Upon occasion I would be called out on my actions, but instead of owning my behavior I would defend it by rationalizing all of the reasons why I couldn't commit. As a lifelong victim there were always circumstances or individuals to blame for why I couldn't keep my word. It took until I was well into my thirties for me to truly understand and accept that this particular chronologically adult woman didn't have a clue about what it was to make and keep a commitment.

Fear Made Conscious

Living in an empowered manner has been a constant test of my ability to use the principle of Commitment. Although every day is an opportunity to commit to taking actions which are consistent with self-empowerment, we never know when a situation will occur that can be a catalyst for life-altering change. Two years after dedicating myself to this lifestyle I found myself facing a situation that brought many of my hidden anxieties into the bright light of consciousness. It forced me to face fears which I thought had been resolved over the past few years: fear of judgment, fear of vulnerability, fear of losing control, fear of economic insecurity, and fear of failure. There was no way I could have known that one month after completing one of the largest projects of my career I would unwittingly be plunged headfirst into a situation which would require me to answer the question: How much am I willing to endure in order to maintain a commitment to self-empowerment?

This Is Only a Test

For nearly ten years I have worked in the special events industry in some capacity. Over the years my work has evolved from booking small dinner parties at restaurants to conceptualizing and executing dinner galas for hundreds of guests. My career, while never wildly lucrative, has provided a fairly decent means to care for myself and my two children.

One of the most challenging projects I ever took on was for a small community-based non-profit that worked with a wide range of disadvantaged clients. My primary responsibility for this client was to plan and execute their annual fundraising dinner, an event which was responsible for raising almost a fifth of its annual operating budget. The event was the first time I was charged with organizing every aspect of a fundraising event…soliciting benefit committee members, creating invitations and mailers, solidifying celebrity hosts and entertainment, and managing the actual event night with whatever time I had left over.

One of the celebrities I recruited to speak at this event was a well-known personality with a large following in the entertainment community. Ray was a very well-spoken B-list celebrity who was known for playing as hard as he worked. We were introduced by a mutual friend I was dating at the time named Eric. Eric was a benefit committee member for the fundraiser and a long-time acquaintance of Ray's. During one of our conversations, I had shared with Eric the problem I was having solidifying presenters for the event, and he volunteered to try to bring Ray on board.

After making a few quick phone calls, it was all set up and within an hour we were on our way to meet Ray at a small downtown Manhattan boutique hotel for drinks. Eric left his car with the valet and we walked up a small flight of dramatically lit glass and steel stairs before settling into a small sitting area on the second floor of the hotel, a location where large groups of downtown scenesters gathered nightly to sip creative cocktails and nibble on remarkably overpriced and undersized plates of food.

The last warm rays of daylight cast long shadows across Eric and I as we playfully snuggled into our sofa. After ordering a few appetizers (along with a cocktail for him and some sparkling water for me), we continued to flirt with each other and chat about the events of our day. Some forty minutes later, our conversation had shifted from the usual industry gossip to how long we were willing to wait for Ray to show up. As the last few bites of our appetizers passed our lips, Ray slowly sauntered up to the table.

"Yo! What took you so long? We've been waiting here forever." Eric pointedly asked.

"Sorry man. The traffic in the tunnel was crazy." Ray answered, settling onto a low ottoman across from us.

"I need a drink. What are you guys having?" Ray asked.

Raising his hand, he summoned the cocktail waitress and placed his order.

The waitress had barely finished writing it down when Eric hit Ray up for the favor.

"My friend Sil Lai here is putting together a fundraiser. I told her that you love to support charities…why don't you get involved?"

"Aww, man…just give me a second to relax. I just got here!"

"Come on…I ain't askin' you to do this for me…I'm askin' you to do it for the charity! Just do it!" Eric cajoled.

After hemming and hawing for a moment, Ray grudgingly agreed to participate.

"You hear that Sil Lai? Yo Ray, give her your contact information so she can send you information on the event."

Ray passed me his business card and our conversation moved on to more social things. I was surprised by how outwardly personable he was. A girlfriend of mine had told me a horrible story about Ray trying to take advantage of a drunken girl in a club a few years back, but the man I met that night seemed genuinely open and friendly. Well, maybe a little *too* friendly.

A newlywed of just over a year, Ray bombarded me with compliments on my appearance and repeatedly asked me to go out with him for drinks. He shamelessly fawned over me for the duration of our meeting…despite the fact that I was obviously dating his friend. The intensity of his interest was extremely off-putting to say the least, and I found his behavior to be disrespectful, a point which I didn't hesitate to mention to Eric after we left the meeting.

"What's the deal with your boy? Doesn't he realize that we're seeing each other?"

"He knows…that's just the way he is, Sil Lai. He does dum-dum moves like that sometimes, but don't worry about it. He's a good guy, trust me."

I didn't agree with Eric's assessment of his friend's character; after all, how nice can a person be if they hit on their friend's date?

For The Greater Good

Under any other circumstances I would have quickly given Ray the brush off. Unfortunately, the fundraiser was just over two months away and I needed his help. Despite my initial misgivings, I decided to ignore my discomfort with Ray's flirtations and to try and tolerate his behavior until the night of the event. I had no control over his behavior, but decided to accept it for the greater good of the charity. After the fundraiser was complete, I reasoned, there would be no reason for me to deal with him at all.

To be fair, Ray threw himself thoroughly into his role once he committed to participating in the event. When I shared with him that we were still in need of additional presenters for the night, he immediately went into action, securing the participation of several of his well-known friends. By the time the fundraiser rolled around we had a very solid roster of local and national celebrity participants, replete with corporate and media sponsorships. The actual event went off without a hitch and raised almost $200,000.00 dollars. The night was a bona fide success.

As is customary, immediately after the event I sent all of the participants a handwritten note of thanks, and Ray followed up on his note with a phone call. During our conversation he asked what my career plans were now that the event was over. I shared with him my dream of creating a non-profit organization that would teach young women how to empower themselves. Much to my surprise, he was very interested in the concept and asked to see the book I had been writing upon which the program would be based.

Ray was very helpful and gave me solid advice on the steps needed to establish the organization…he even volunteered to introduce me to some of his connections as potential board members. This conversation was the beginning of what was to become a weekly conversation on the status of the non-profit.

Questions as to why Ray would be helping me start my program crossed my mind, so I asked him why he was willing to take time out of his hectic schedule to counsel me on my venture. His response seemed quite reasonable: he had always had an interest in helping young people and was touched by what seemed to be my genuine desire to help others. Thus, despite the rocky start to our relationship, I started to believe that we could develop a simple friendship based upon a mutual desire to help others.

Establishing Boundaries

Ray and I continued to communicate fairly regularly over the phone and our discussions were for the most part very project oriented. From time to time however, he would try to shift the focus of our conversations by bringing up the topic of sex but I was not interested in engaging in that sort of conversation with him.

"What do you like to do in bed?"

"What do you mean, what do I like to do in bed? That's none of your business!"

"What's wrong? Can't friends talk openly about things?"

"Yes, friends can talk openly, but I don't talk about sex with people I am not sleeping with."

"Come on…what's wrong with talking about sex?"

"Let me ask you a question Ray. Do you think your wife would be happy to know you were talking to me like this? Seriously. What do you think she would say if she was listening in on this conversation?"

"She wouldn't have a problem with this."

Laughingly I replied, "Oh really? You're so full of it! No woman in her right mind would feel comfortable with her man talking to another woman about sex. Next subject please."

I accepted Ray's occasional testing of boundaries as part of the price of working with him. Although his behavior could be annoying at times, I chose to focus on his willingness to assist with my project instead of his inappropriate boundary testing.

Bad Timing

By the time the holiday season fell upon us Eric and I had stopped dating, but Ray and I continued to stay in contact because of the non-profit. The day after Christmas I spent in the city with one of my closest girlfriends at the movies. After the movie ended I said goodbye to my friend and called Ray. He was scheduled to go out of town with his wife for the New Year and I wanted to catch up with him before he left. Coincidentally, he was in the city as well, so we decided to grab a quick drink before each of us went back to our respective homes. After a few hours of socializing, I told him that I needed to get back to my kids.

"You sure you don't want to hang out just a little longer? I have a friend I want you to meet!"

"No, I've got to get home. It's getting late and I'm getting tired..."

"Come on...it'll be fun!"

"I said no, Ray. I wanna go home."

"Okay, okay...I'll give you a ride."

"I don't want to stop you from seeing your friend..." I protested.

"It's cool...I'll just drop you off real quick and then get right back into the city to meet him afterward."

"Great...thanks."

The ride home was a welcome treat...it was freezing outside and the idea of riding the train at 11:30 at night wasn't particularly appealing. You could never be sure if the trains were running on schedule and I wasn't about to spend money on a cab. I was still trying to catch up on my bills from the recent holidays.

Ray slid the soundtrack to a recent hit movie into the CD player and pressed play. A deep, soulful voice filled the interior of the car.

"God, I love this song...turn it up, would you?" I asked.

My head bopped from side to side to the music, feet tapping against the floorboards as my hands slapped against my lap to the beat of the song.

"Isn't this song amazing?" I asked.

"Do you see what you do to me?" he asked.

Turning my head in his direction, I froze in shock at the sight of Ray proudly brandishing his manhood before me. I blinked...incredulous at what I was seeing. It was so ridiculous; it would have been comical if it wasn't so offensive.

Jeesus, what the hell is he doing? What do I say? What do I do?

The first thing that came to mind was something I had read years ago in one of my abnormal psychology books, some fact about the mental makeup of a person who exposes themselves. This book said that the "exposer" was simply looking for some sort of strong emotional response from a victim and that the way to make sure a "flasher" doesn't get any satisfaction was to ignore them.

Rolling my eyes, I turned my head away and said, "That's very impressive Ray, but I have no interest in seeing that. Why don't you do us both a favor and put that away?"

He ignored me and kept driving, fly still unzipped, member still exposed.

"You see how much you turn me on?" he asked, reaching towards me. Before I realized what was happening, he had placed my hand on his lap.

I quickly yanked away.

As the light turned yellow we veered onto the Manhattan Bridge. The music was still loudly playing in the car, the stifling heat from the vents in front of my face blasting hot air from the dashboard. The combination of effects was overwhelming.

Oh jeesus, what do I do now?

It was freezing outside and close to midnight.

Maybe I should get out of the car? I thought, but then I remembered I only had $3.00 in cash on me. Besides, we were speeding along at close to forty miles per hour, so jumping out the car wasn't really an option.

*I can get out at the light...*was the next thought that crossed my mind, but then I remembered that if I got out of the car at the light, I'd be left standing on the street with $3.00 in my pocket in a dicey area of town.

Seven minutes...that's all, just seven more minutes and I'll be out of this car and away from him.

I decided to take my chances and continue with the ride. After all, we knew the same people and I figured he wouldn't push things too far with me.

"Do me a favor Ray, just quit it, okay? We're friends...don't do this."

He stared at me for a moment and then looked away. Out of the corner of my eye I saw that he was no longer outside his pants.

After what seemed to be an eternity, we finally turned onto my street. Ray pulled into an open spot directly across from my brownstone. Breathing an audible sigh of relief, I grabbed my purse off the floorboard as Ray put the car in park. Leaning back, I quickly went to retrieve a second bag from the rear seat of the car, but as soon as my left arm was extended behind me, Ray lunged and started aggressively kissing my neck.

"Ray, stop...I said stop it! I gotta go..."

Lifting his face up he raspily whispered, "Kiss me….come on, kiss me," before planting his lips firmly on mine.

Temporarily caught off guard, my momentary lack of resistance must have been interpreted as a sign of consent, for he then forcibly shoved his tongue into my mouth. His breath smelled faintly of red wine. I was repulsed.

Pushing him away, I hissed, "Let go…I said let me go…" as he started groping my right breast.

My heart was racing…all I wanted was to grab my purse and bag and get out of the car. But he wasn't having any of that.

"Touch it…," he said hoarsely, exposing himself again.

"This is so wrong…just stop…" I pleaded.

He then tried to push my head down into his lap, but I wrested myself away.

"Just touch it…," he begged again, grabbing my hand and returning it to his rigid member.

I gave up. Our struggle had been going on for close to six minutes and I figured he would leave me alone if I just let him do what he wanted. Ray continued to stroke himself for another minute until he climaxed, all over my hand and his. Reaching across me, he opened the glove compartment and pulled out a stack of napkins.

"Here you go," he said, handing me several. I quickly wiped his mess off of my hands and then gave the used napkins back to him.

"Well, you need to make sure that you get the outline together for the program soon…" Ray began.

My head was throbbing and I couldn't hear what he was saying. Only one thing was spinning around in my mind and it wasn't going to stop until I said it.

"You know what Ray? I don't want to chit chat. What I really want to know is why you just did that?"

He recoiled in his seat, averting his eyes from mine.

I continued, "That was such bad karma! Do you have any idea how bad that was?"

"Sil Lai, you didn't do anything wrong…I did. I'm sorry…I don't know why I did that…I guess you just really had me worked up."

Was that supposed to make me feel better?

Shaking my head, I grabbed my bag and purse again and put my hand on the door handle.

"Now can I go?" I asked, voice loaded with sadness.

Without waiting for his response, I climbed out of the car and stood for a moment in the doorway.

He smiled at me and eagerly said, "Do me a favor, will you? Call me to let me know that you got upstairs okay, alright?"

Oh, now you're interested in my well-being, huh? I thought. *You weren't five minutes ago when you were mauling me.*

I simply shut the door in his face without a response and headed towards my brownstone. Turning my key in the lock of my building, I bounded up the narrow stairs two steps at a time. As soon as I was in my apartment, I locked the front door behind me, dropped my bags on the hallway floor, and headed straight into the bathroom.

The only thing I wanted to do was to get any trace of him off of me. Looking into the mirror, the bright light over the vanity highlighted the tired look on my face. *Ugh.* Turning the water on as hot as I could take it, I pumped several streams of antibacterial soap into my palms. The lather bubbled over my hands, streamed over my fingers, then slithered down into the drain. Drying my hands on the towel hanging on the rack behind the door, I left the bathroom and plodded back down the hall towards my bedroom.

Bringggg-bringgg! Bringggg-bringgg!

Picking my cell phone off of the bureau, I saw the name on the caller ID and exhaled. It was Ray.

Damn. What the hell does he want?

Flipping the handset open, I answered coldly, "Yes?"

"Hey…you didn't answer me when you got out of the car. How you gonna treat me like that? I just wanted to make sure you got in okay."

"Since when did you become concerned about my well being, Ray? You definitely weren't in the car!"

"Listen, I'm really sorry, Sil Lai. I screwed up."

"Yeah, you did. You never answered me, though. Why did you do it? Can you tell me that?"

"I just had a little too much to drink and got carried away…"

So that's how he's gonna play it...the "I was so drunk I didn't know what I was doing" game.

"I gotta go." I said.

"Okay," he said, pausing for a minute. "Hey..."

"Yes?"

"I'm really, really sorry."

"Good night, Ray." was my terse response.

After I hung up the phone I collapsed on my bed and pulled the covers tightly around me. My emotions were completely numb...I couldn't even process what had just happened in his car. Sometimes when I'm really overwhelmed, I just need to sleep. So I slept.

Shock and Betrayal

The next morning I awoke and went through my regular early morning routine. I did my best to push what had happened out of my mind, but felt so dirty, so weak. Somehow I couldn't shake the feeling that I could have prevented what had happened by doing something differently. If I had just made a different choice, like not getting into his car, or punching him in the face. Anything in fact, but what I did do, which was to freeze up.

The night kept replaying in my mind over and over and over again, images flashing, pausing just long enough to draw a bit of blood, and then flitting out of sight. I didn't want to think about *him*, but I couldn't stop. Every minute of the attack was revisited as I tried to figure out how and why something like this happened. Catastrophe doesn't discriminate and bad things happen to decent people all the time. I just couldn't believe that something like this could have happened to me *now*, not after all of the work I had been doing to heal myself. The same questions kept revolving in my head, ripping at my soul with relentless constancy.

Why didn't I just get out of the car?

Because I'm too attached to my material things. I valued my purse over my dignity.

Why didn't I fight back harder?

Because I am weak.

Why didn't I scream?

Because I was more concerned about what my neighbors might think if they heard the noise than my own safety.

Why did this happen?

I chose to ignore Ray's character flaws because I really wanted his help. My ambition did me in…again.

Fifty more versions of these questions and answers lay siege to my mind as I went through the motions of work. As the day progressed I became increasingly agitated. In the past I would have just ordered in some takeout food for the kids and then climbed into bed to lick my wounds, but to do that would have been giving him too much power. By now I knew that I could *choose* my response to this situation, so once my children came home, I greeted them as usual and immediately started preparing their dinner. I was adamantly opposed to letting Ray affect my life anymore than necessary.

At 9:00 p.m. the kids went off to the living room to play video games and I was left alone in my bedroom, a room which was usually so comforting to me in times of trouble, but tonight felt achingly empty. I felt so isolated…trapped in my head without any sense of reprieve from the noise in sight. Body coiled around my pillow, the tears finally began to stream down my face.

Why did this have to happen to me, now? Everything was going so great in my life. Why did Ray do what he did?

Around 1:00 a.m., I finally fell asleep, exhausted and determined to find some sort of solution to the looping echoes in my head.

In Spite of Myself

The first thing I did in the morning after awaking was to look online for the phone number to a rape crisis center. I didn't really feel like taking any action at all to help myself, but past experience has shown that just because I didn't feel like doing something, it didn't mean I wasn't *supposed* to do something. I eventually got a counselor on the phone and set up an appointment to meet her at the beginning of the following week.

The days leading up to the appointment went by in a blur as I counted down the hours until I could speak to someone who might be able to help with the feelings threatening to overwhelm me. Although I had shared what had happened with a few close friends, I was frightened of burdening them further.

My last experience with a serious crisis had taught me to be careful of how much I shared my problems with other people.

As much as I fought it, another depression seemed to be looming on the horizon, but unlike before, it didn't knock me down without warning. Instead, I began to feel the rumblings in the depths of my stomach. The difference now was that I was much more attuned to the physical symptoms of my true emotional state.

Today an impending depression is easily recognizable, since I have experienced it off and on for most of my life. One of its first signs is difficulty in focusing. No matter how hard I tried, I could not seem to focus on anything after Ray's assault. The second and third signs are a change in my sleeping pattern, followed by an increasing desire to isolate from my friends. Constant butterflies in the pit of my stomach are a sign of anxiety and depression, and I found myself bracing against what seemed to be another full-blown depressive episode.

By the time my appointment rolled around, I was stuck in my head and ridden with guilt and anger over what had happened. On more than one occasion I have read that that depression is anger turned inward. It was no surprise therefore that I was feeling depressed. I *was* angry. I was furious. The truth was that I had been sexually assaulted and more importantly I felt I hadn't done anything to fight my attacker.

The tape inside my head kept telling me that I was somehow responsible for Ray's behavior, but I knew that was a lie. That was simply my ego's way of trying to convince itself that I had control over what happened to me, when that really wasn't the case. It was my ego telling me that I was not powerless over Ray's actions, when in fact I was. Once I accepted that I had been a victim of a sexual assault, I needed to take the next step, which was to take action with the truth I had learned. Action in this case would mean getting counseling and reporting Ray to the police. In my heart I knew that the only way I could maintain my commitment to self-empowerment was by taking action with the truth, but I didn't want to file a report with the police because I was afraid of what might happen. Somehow my old disempowered mindset had crept back in after what had happened and that old enemy, Fear, was now running the show.

With that in mind, I had to confront my fears so I could understand what was holding me back from honoring the truth. One primary fear was that I was afraid that the story of what happened to me would end up in the New York Post. Ray was, after all, a fairly recognizable personality and I have seen the media go to town over less well-known individuals. The second fear was of not being believed. My past was riddled with self-destructive behavior and Ray had a rough copy of my book I knew he would try and use against me as a way to discredit my integrity with the police and court.

Looking at these two fears, I realized that too much of my decision to go to the police hinged on what Ray, the press, or the police would do. My decision was not empowering. It was based upon fear, and in my experience, decisions based on fear were generally not sound ones. Even with this knowledge I still couldn't take action. Once I realized that I didn't want to file a report because of my fear, I decided to try and work through my feelings with a rape crisis counselor.

While these therapeutic sessions provided a safe forum for me to discuss my feelings about the attack, they weren't succeeding in lifting my anxiety. After praying about what to do for several days I realized that what I had perceived as depression was really just my spirit telling me to honor my commitment to self-empowerment. It became clear to me that my soul was not going to let me rest as long as I didn't do something about what Ray had done.

One of my favorite authors, the late psychiatrist M. Scott Peck, wrote in his classic book on modern psychology, "The Road Less Traveled," *"This tendency to avoid problems and the emotional suffering inherent in them is the primary basis of all human mental illness."* Dr. Peck also wrote in the same book, *"Mental health is an ongoing process of dedication to reality at all costs."*

The reality was that my spirit was crying out to be acknowledged, that the truth needed to be heard. It was true that I had made a choice to live an empowered and authentic lifestyle, but in the midst of grave emotional pain I had reverted to the old, disempowering behaviors that had served me so poorly for most of my life. The incident with Ray had forced me to remember a very basic truth about the nature of self-empowerment, one that can be very easy to forget when things are going well for us: self-empowerment is not a permanent state of being. We don't make a decision to empower ourselves and then pat ourselves on the back, content that we are "fixed." Empowerment is a provisional state of grace we are given when we actively participate in the solution to the challenges of our existence. We cannot keep it if we aren't willing to practice it, in every aspect of our life.

The Road Less Traveled

The path that I had walked for much of my life was one in which I *could* rationalize away my responsibility to myself and my truth. To stay committed to a new path would require me to step outside of my comfort zone and face the fears that have haunted me my entire existence...again. I could choose to pretend that what had happened never did, but to do so would be at the expense of my self-respect and dignity. If I chose not to report what had happened with Ray to the police I would gain peace from the fear of what might happen if I took the action. On the other hand, I already knew what the effect would be on my emotional well-being if I didn't report it, for I had been down that path before, twelve years prior, when I was raped by a man I had considered my friend.

At that time, as a twenty-four year old active alcoholic, I chose to not report the attack because of my fears. I was afraid that no one would believe me because I was drunk at the time of the assault...I was afraid that no one would believe me because the man who had done it was a former lover...I was afraid that no one would listen to me because I had swallowed a bottle of sleeping pills and ended up in a psych ward after it had happened. I was afraid that because he was famous and had millions of dollars at his disposal that I wouldn't stand a chance in court. Twelve years ago I had allowed my fear and shame to dictate my actions, but today I knew that it didn't matter what my history was, how many people I had slept with in my life or how much money I had. I was armed with the most important thing of all: the truth. This knowledge led me to finally accept that the only way I was going to stay empowered was by committing to take action with the truth.

Commitment is a Choice

On a cold, bleary winter Sunday, nineteen days after the attack, I walked into the local police precinct and reported what had happened to me. And although I knew that by taking the action I was opening myself up to a potentially vicious court battle, I placed my desire for comfort aside in order to honor my commitment to my spiritual well-being.

It was embarrassing to repeat my story to one police officer and two detectives, but I pushed through my feelings, confident that I was taking action which was consistent with the empowered woman I wanted to remain. My story had to be repeated again to two Assistant District Attorneys. The story didn't get easier to repeat as I continued to relay the facts to the people involved in the prosecution, but I kept going despite my discomfort. During one of the interviews with the ADA assigned to the case I was asked what I wanted to happen to Ray. My honest answer was "Nothing." It didn't matter what happened to Ray, because this situation wasn't about Ray at all. It was about me and my ability to keep a commitment despite my fears and discomfort. My part was done. I had done my part to use my voice and take a stand against a crime which had occurred to me. What happened next was entirely up to God.

Within one week of reporting what had happened to me to the police, my depression lifted.

Every day is an opportunity to recommit ourselves to living in our truth!

The Truth About Pressure

The shortest route between two points is not always the best. We are often called to take a more winding path, one that is sometimes longer and more challenging. This can be hard to accept at times, so whenever a challenge arises that leads me to question a commitment, I remember the element of carbon.

Carbon is the sixth most common occurring element in nature. There are three naturally occurring forms of carbon: amorphous, graphite, and diamond. What distinguishes each of these forms of the same element from the other is the amount of pressure that each can withstand. Amorphous carbon and graphite are some of the softest materials known to us and are very inexpensive. Diamonds are created when carbon is heated and compressed over thousands of years in the earth's crust. Over the course of time this pressure and heat creates a substance that is one of the strongest natural elements in the world.

(Incidentally, diamonds are deemed to represent purity and commitment, hence their use in engagement rings).

The process of creating a diamond does not occur overnight. It takes time, heat, and extreme pressure. Likewise, self-empowerment does not instantly occur. It is a process that takes a lot of work and commitment. We all have the potential to become a diamond if we are willing to withstand the pressure in our lives and honor our commitments in the best way we can.

Commitment Summarized

There is something about the process of acknowledging the truth that empowers us to honor our commitments. When we no longer look at commitment as an option, we are able to move forward in our journey to self-empowerment. When we use the principle of commitment on a daily basis, we will see some immediate changes to our world. Some of our relationships will fall away, unable to stand in the light of our new conviction to honor our word. At times we will have to stand in the face of great adversity, but we should never despair. When we make a decision to live an empowered lifestyle, we will be tested. And the test won't be easy; otherwise it would not be a test, it would just be a minor inconvenience. One of my most fervent beliefs is that all that occurs in our lives is an opportunity for us to grow into a more loving and conscious person. It is whether or not we have the willingness to bear the frustration and pain that determines our ability to keep our commitment to our overall well-being.

There is a saying that it's always darkest before the dawn. Remember that the sun is just below the horizon, and it will eventually rise if we just hang in there a little while longer. Make a commitment to your goals and then stand by them!

$\mathscr{F}$ OCUS

Be Single Minded in Your Purpose

"I find hope in the darkest of days, and focus in the brightest."

~ *Dalai Lama*

Through the use of the SEPIA principles of truth, acceptance, action and commitment we will be able to determine the areas in need of change in our lives, accept what we discover, take constructive steps to change our disempowering behaviors, and maintain our continued growth and development. The fifth SEPIA principle of *focus* teaches us to take everything that we have learned through the use of the first four principles and zero in on what it is that we want to achieve. Focus is essential to anyone who wishes to transform their life, for without this principle our energy will be diffused on irrelevant activities or on thoughts not related to our goals. By making a conscious choice to use this principle we will be able to move steadily towards self-empowerment with as little distraction as possible.

In this chapter we'll explore how the principle of focus can be a tremendously empowering tool to help us achieve our goals. We will also learn how a misdirected focus can prevent us from effectively managing our time and prioritizing our activities. Finally, we'll see how the absence of this principle can lead us down a path of frustration and dreams never actualized.

Focus Defined

Focus is defined as *"the ability to hone our attention in on a specific task or goal."* It is an active principle that requires us to exercise the self-discipline of pulling ourselves away from anything that distracts us from what we need to concentrate on. When we are able to gather our thoughts and energy and focus them on our goal, it is virtually impossible for anything to stand in our way.

Why Do We Avoid Focus?

Focus is an active principle which can be cultivated in many different ways, some of which will be discussed later in this chapter. Before we take a look at these methods, let's first explore some of the reasons we may not be practicing this principle now. The reasons may vary from person to person, but the three predominant reasons I have seen over and over again are:

- Negative Interpretation of Principle
- Lack of Purpose
- Inability to Prioritize

Negative Interpretation of Principle

As with many other behaviors, one of the reasons for not using this principle can come from our childhood experiences. A common area that this issue presents itself is in school. Most parents and teachers have the expectation that children should be able to study and do their homework. Studying requires focus, but a child's natural rambunctious energy can be highly incompatible with prolonged periods of concentration. As a result, children are often berated for their seeming inability to focus on their studies. After being consistently reminded and reprimanded for not concentrating hard enough on their work, they begin to develop negative emotions around the idea of prolonged concentration and focus. Concentration becomes associated with disappointment and frustration, and many children make the decision to avoid focus except when they have no other choice.

Focus can be enjoyable if it's approached with the proper perspective. The application of this principle can generate joy, optimism, and understanding of the great possibilities that exist with its use when we are able to realize that the reason for its application is to help us achieve our goals, not torture us. If we focus on all the things we can gain from learning how to hone our attention, we won't spend time lamenting the fact that at times it doesn't feel enjoyable.

A survivor will use the fact that they don't find it enjoyable to focus as an excuse to not practice this principle. They will allow the feelings generated by the act of focusing to dictate their actions, and this in turn results in inconsistent behavior.

A contender understands that focus is necessary and vital to the achievement of any goal. A contender doesn't waste energy bemoaning the fact that focus can be challenging at times to practice, and keeps her focus on the end result she seeks.

Lack of Purpose

In order to stay focused, we must have something that burns inside us, something that stimulates us to make the effort to focus our attention. This "something" is a sense of purpose. It is very challenging to sustain focus without a sense of purpose for *prolonged focus is impossible to maintain without passion.*

If at this stage you don't know what your purpose is, try using the passion you have for transforming your life. A passion for transformation is often the first step towards discovering our purpose. The act of picking this book up today is a step towards self-empowerment. If you weren't seeking a way to improve the quality of your life, another action or inaction could have been taken instead. You could have plunked down in front of the television for hours upon hours, or picked up the phone to call an ex-boyfriend who didn't treat you too well when you were together. Or you could have poured yourself a glass of wine and fantasized about all of the ways that you wished life were different.

But you didn't.

The choice to read this book instead is a testimony to a passion for transforming your life. As long as we make up our mind to discover our purpose, we will eventually discover it. This a universal truth based upon the Law of Attraction. T. Harv Eker, a master motivator, wrote in his book, "Secrets of the Millionaire

Mind," *"Whatever you focus on expands...your field of focus determines what you find in life. Focus on opportunities and that's what you find. Focus on obstacles and that's what you find."* You will always attract the predominant thoughts in your mind, so guard your thoughts.

Unwillingness to Prioritize

To prioritize means to arrange and then deal with our issues in the order of their importance. It is an invaluable tool, and it greatly increases the effectiveness of our actions. The Pareto Principle is a business philosophy which reinforces the importance of prioritization. Leadership guru John Maxwell wrote in his book, "The 21 Irrefutable Laws of Leadership," *"If you focus your attention on the activities that rank in the top 20 percent in terms of importance, you will have an 80 percent return on your effort...If your to-do list has ten items on it, the two most important ones will give you an 80 percent return on your time."* The Pareto Principle is a good illustration of the practical benefits of prioritizing what we do.

Many of us choose *not* to put our energy into prioritizing, because this requires us to take the time and effort to actually think before taking action, but it's not difficult to do if we approach the process in steps. The first thing we need to do is figure out if something requires our urgent attention, and if it is determined to be urgent, then we need to decide if it is important. If we believe that it is important, then we need to decide whether or not it contributes to our goal. If it doesn't, then we need to determine whether or not it absolutely has to be done in that moment. If it doesn't have to be done at that moment, then we need to focus on taking care of the things that will move us towards our goals. Prioritizing is not hard to do once we understand why we are doing it. The only thing we need in order to do it is the willingness to put in the work and set aside the time.

A survivor will not take the time to prioritize, because they are unwilling to put in the effort. Survivors spend their days putting out fires and reacting to whatever comes their way. A contender will prioritize what needs to be focused on, based upon whether or not something is absolutely necessary in order to achieve their goals. They are *proactive* in the creation of their schedule, not *reactive*.

More on Focus

One of the most important truths that we can learn is that *we cannot change another person…no matter how much we may try.*

Since survivors tend to blame others for the problems in their lives, the first thing they do when they are unhappy is try to figure out which external person or factor is bothering them. Once they make that determination they then try to change it. They focus their time and energy on futilely trying to make others comply with their idea of how things should be, but their efforts never produce anything more than frustration in themselves and others. No matter how much we may try, the one and only thing we can truly change is ourselves.

An empowered woman keeps the focus on herself and her issues, for she knows this is the only way that she can truly manifest change in her life. Instead of spending her time focusing on how she can change others, she focuses her attention on discovering the truth about herself and then taking constructive action on the things which limit her ability to be effective in her life.

How to Develop Focus

It is very common to think to ourselves, "I just need more time" or "I need to learn how to manage my time." This thought implies that the reason why we have difficulty focusing our attention comes from outside of us. The truth is that we don't need to manage our time. What we need is to manage ourselves, and in order to manage ourselves we need to discipline our thoughts and actions. We must learn to focus.

Admittedly, focus can be a challenging principle to utilize at times, particularly if we are not accustomed to doing it with any frequency. Focus of the mind can be developed just like the muscles of the body. Unlike things in life that are limited by our natural ability (such as intelligence), focus can be learned if we're willing to put in the effort. Focus can be developed exactly like a muscle. It requires perseverance and training, but with enough discipline even the most scattered individual can become highly focused.

We all have the ability to increase our ability to focus if we desire to do so.

Developing the ability to focus is in itself an exercise in self-empowerment.

One of the most profound tools we can use to develop our focus is meditation. Meditation is defined as *"an engagement in contemplation, especially of a spiritual or devotional nature...an attempt to concentrate the mind on a single form or an idea or an aspect of divinity at the exclusion of all other forms and ideas."* In addition to its healing properties to the mind (which include an increased ability to focus), meditation calms the body and helps it repair itself and prevent new damage from the physical effects of stress.

The act of meditating involves little more than sitting in a relaxed position and clearing our mind by focusing on a sound or image in our head. It requires practice and a little patience, but the investment in time and effort is well worth the benefits. Many find it difficult to get into at first, but with practice it becomes easier to do.

(For more information on meditation, go online and research local meditation classes and centers in your city. Classes are often either free or require a nominal donation.)

Comparison Between Types

SURVIVOR	CONTENDER
• Doesn't pay attention to what they will gain from practicing focus, and uses irritation and resentment as an excuse not to focus.	• Keeps their attention on what they will gain from practicing, and stays focused despite how they may be feeling in the moment.
• Allows a lack of defined life purpose to limit their ability to focus their time and energy.	• Uses their passion for transforming their life as a motivator to stay focused even when they don't have a concrete goal to achieve.
• Is unwilling to put their time and energy into prioritizing what they need to do.	• Understands that they limit their effectiveness if they do not prioritize their actions.

The Folly of Envy

Anyone who has ever spent any time comparing or wishing for what other people have, experiences something called envy. Envy is a force so destructive that it is considered one of the Seven Deadly Sins in Christianity. The Oxford American Dictionary defines envy as *"a feeling of discontented or resentful longing aroused by someone else's possessions, qualities, or luck."* Envy is so harmful because it takes the focus off ourselves and places it on those around us. It is very hard to be effective in our own life when we are busy taking stock of the lives of others.

Misdirected Attention

One of the ways we prevent ourselves from keeping the focus on ourselves is by comparing ourselves to others. The following story highlights how my misdirected use of the fifth SEPIA principle of Focus led me to spend years defining myself through someone else's reality.

For many, many years I treated my sister May Lai's life as the baseline for what should be happening in my own. In retrospect this was a ridiculous thing to do, for comparing the two of us was akin to comparing a dolphin to a transistor radio. While we shared the same biological mother, we had different fathers, and this difference in genetics did more than just create a discrepancy in our physical appearance. The variation in our genetic code also created a huge disparity in our temperaments and personalities as well.

May Lai could best be described as dreamy and feminine. Her name in Cantonese means "double beauty," and by any standards she was a beauty. Petite with a reed-like build, she had large, warm brown and expressive almond shaped eyes framed with high, sculpted cheekbones and a shower of long, straight black hair. She was our family's princess, the fortuitous sum of the best of her parent's genetic material. A relatively simple soul, she tended to speak in quiet tones and had an upbeat, don't-take-anything-too-seriously approach to the world.

I, on the other had, was neither delicate nor feminine, and the most notable feature of my temperament was my outspoken nature and frenetic drive. Vast reserves of abundant energy lay coiled within my body, ready to spring forth at the slightest provocation. This energy proved helpful in sports, but was ruefully inappropriate in my interactions with others. My tendency to aggressively give unsolicited opinions didn't endear me to family members or friends. Years of physical exercise had helped me to develop into a strong and agile young woman with a face as round as an apple and outlined with a shock of unruly, fluffy black hair which couldn't decide if it was curly or fuzzy. May Lai and I were never mistaken as each other's twin.

Despite these differences in our temperaments we shared a very close bond, especially as little girls. Only twenty months apart in age, we were each other's constant playmates. May Lai didn't seem to care that I was loud or that I tried to hog the spotlight. She always treated me with the respect and awe that only a younger sibling can show for her elder sister.

The Favored One

Of course, May Lai's kindness did not endear her to me at the time. It only served to highlight the glaring differences in our personalities and magnify my obnoxious behavior. Worse yet, May Lai seemed to breeze past the awkward stage of adolescence and emerge a stunningly beautiful young woman in a matter of months. I wasn't so lucky. My face grew chubbier and my hair began to change texture. It seemed to go from flyaway and fluffy one week to tightly coiled and curly the next. My parents didn't know what to do with hair like mine, and I grew tired of always wearing it pulled back.

Ponytails weren't a popular hairstyle in 1984. The favorite styles of the day were jheri curls, teased and frosted spikes accented with large bows or sleek asymmetrical cuts stopping at the jaw line. I so desperately wanted to be cool that in a moment of rebellious frustration I shaved all of my hair off except for the crown. Although I was never really overweight, my weight began to wildly fluctuate because of alcohol and food binges, and standing next to the waiflike build of my sister I felt positively obese.

Maybe it was because she was my adoptive parent's biological child, or maybe it was because of my obnoxious personality, but there seemed always to be an undercurrent of favoritism in our home…an almost imperceptible shift in energy whenever my sister walked into the same room as me. By the time we were teenagers I knew better than to bring up the difference in how they treated us. They simply denied that the favoritism existed anyway, and that only served to produce more frustration and resentment in me.

What does she have that I don't? What's so special about May Lai? Why don't they like me the way they like her? What's wrong with me?

Dark Resentment

As we grew older my anger at our parents crystallized into a monstrous resentment that I proceeded to take out on the easiest, most vulnerable target: May Lai. It wasn't her fault that my parents favored her, but she became the lightening rod for my frustration and rage. She was completely banned from hanging around with me and my friends, and if she did come around I would mercilessly tease her until she ran away in tears. Our stepmother tried to intervene on her behalf, but her interference only served to prove that May Lai was her favorite, fueling more anger and resentment on my part. I kept up this behavior until we eventually became completely polarized and ended up living completely separate lives.

At seventeen years old I began modeling with a local agency in Orlando, and by twenty two (after a short derail because of my first pregnancy), I was pursuing a full-time career as a fashion model. During the interim May Lai also became a model who, to my dismay, was much more successful than me. I was an average catalog model whose looks veered toward the commercial. My career mainly consisted of traveling to smaller markets, such as Miami and Dallas, and doing catalog work for decidedly unglamorous retail companies like JC Penney's and Sears. May Lai was what the industry termed a "beauty" model. Beauty modeling consists of work in editorial shoots, cosmetics, and advertising campaigns. In one year alone she shot ads for three different blue jean companies and was featured in dozens of magazines around the globe.

Ironically, she didn't even care if she got the bookings when she went to an audition, or go-see, as they are called in the business. Modeling was just an easy source of cash for her and she didn't take the business all that seriously. Without any real effort, she developed a career that took her all around the world. By twenty one she was engaged to a very wealthy older French pop star and split her time between a mansion in Beverly Hills and an apartment overlooking the Eiffel Tower in Paris. She was leading the sort of life the rest of us see on the old television show, *Lifestyles of the Rich and Famous.*

I should have been happy for her, but her success infuriated me. It wasn't enough that I was a twenty-three year old earning $1,500.00 a day standing in front of a camera. I wanted what *she* had. My bookers tried to steer me into a successful catalog career, but I rejected their direction. If they told me to shoot natural pictures and add them to my portfolio, I would do it my way instead…the supermodel way. I would convince the hair and makeup artists to go overboard, and end up with photographs that were essentially worthless. Too much makeup, not enough clothing, a baby faced woman playing dress up in someone else's clothes. I couldn't accept the fact that I was never going to be on the cover of a magazine.

If May Lai can get an editorial campaign, so can I!

If May Lai ever picked up on my jealousy, she never mentioned it.

The Innocent

My only focus was how I could develop my career into one that rivaled my sister's career. I *had* to know how her career was going so I could give myself one more reason to be discontented with my own. The first thing I would do whenever we got together was ask to see her portfolio, and every single time I opened it up I would be greeted with beautiful images of her staring back at me from some exotic location, the visual proof of her latest magazine shoot or fashion campaign. She never mentioned these jobs to me unless I asked, but I on the other hand would jump on the phone to boast about it to her every time I got a booking for a job. These phone calls would always start out under the pretense of me just phoning to say hello, but would quickly steer towards what I had been doing.

"Hey May Lai! Whaddya up to?"

"Nothing much. Just hanging out with Elena…We're getting ready to go out."

"That sounds like fun. Hey…did you know that Hechts was in town shooting?"

"Yeah, I heard. I went to their casting the other day."

"I went to the casting too, and guess what? They booked me for three days! It's only paying $1,500.00 a day, but that beats nothing, right?" I would say, laughing.

"That's great Sil Lai! Good for you!" she'd say with complete sincerity.

In time I even got myself a wealthy European boyfriend, an IBM or Italian Business Man, as we models referred to them, from a prominent Milanese family. During this time my son was being cared for first by my ex-boyfriend's mother and later by my best friend while I pursued my career in Europe. For the first time in my life I had the financial and physical freedom to do whatever I wanted. We spent the summer of 1994 traveling up and down the Amalfi coast of Italy in his Cigarette speedboat, hopping from yacht to yacht and swimming in the lapis blue seas off the rugged shores of remote islands. I moved into his home, a beautiful converted carriage house on his father's estate with a maid and a cook. None of this made a difference to me…I was still frustrated and resentful. *May Lai's* boyfriend was wealthier. *May Lai's* bookings were more prestigious. *May Lai* had homes in two different cities. I didn't want what I had…I wanted what she had.

The Truth

Instead of focusing my attention on developing my career as a catalog model, I focused on trying to transform my life into that of my sister's. But underneath all of this competition and envy lay a simple truth: I hated the fashion industry and all that it represented. Aside from the money, the work really held little appeal to me. It was too fickle an industry in which one's level of intelligence came second to one's ability to strike a fierce pose. For me, fashion was like an arrogant and elusive boyfriend who did nothing but feed all of my insecurities about my appearance, yet I continued to pursue it with reckless abandon because of my envy of my sister. Of course I had no conscious notion that I was envious…that would have been too much for me to admit to myself at the time. Instead, I wrapped up my envy in the cloak of ambition and chose to invest five years of my life pursuing a career that I didn't even like.

Needless to say, focusing on my sister's career did nothing to help mine. The Law of Correspondence states that whatever is within will manifest outside and within my heart was jealousy and envy, emotions which did not lead me to focus on building my career, but did manage to manifest in a competitive and negative personality which turned everyone off, including my bookers. They eventually stopped sending me out to castings, and my career came to a halt. Disillusioned and frustrated, I broke up with my IBM and returned home to New York, immediately reuniting with and becoming pregnant by Scott, the man I had left behind to pursue my career in Italy. Scott, the man who became the father to my second child, and who would eventually send me to the emergency room twice.

It is virtually impossible to build a successful modeling career with two small children, unless one has either a full time nanny or the willingness to have someone else raise them. In New York, I had neither, so my career was finished. At the time of my unceremonious departure from fashion I was at a financial bottom I hadn't seen in years. Scott was fanning the last glowing embers of his own dying modeling career, trying to coax a few more dollars out an industry that had lost interest in him. He worked infrequently with long stretches of unemployment, filling his time seated in front of the television, SEGA controller in hand. With no other means of support in sight, I took a job as a temporary secretary to pay our bills. I spent long days filing and typing for a steady paycheck of around $400 every Friday. This new financial experience was in sharp contrast to the extravagance I had experienced just a few short months earlier.

Fortunately, the amount of time needed to navigate through my many responsibilities at that point in my life didn't allow me to focus on anyone else. There was too much to be done… the raising of young children, juggling bills, and coping with a dysfunctional relationship. Envy was a luxury I could not afford. Instead, I kept myself focused for years on the busy work of struggling to support and care for a family.

Once I left the fashion industry, much of the envy I had for my sister dissipated and I was finally free from the obsession to outperform her on her turf. Without the pressure of competition and envy, I now had the freedom to finally put my attention on developing what should have been my focus all along: myself.

Discovering Our Passion

Sustained focus requires us to have a goal or sense of purpose. Napoleon Hill devoted an entire chapter in his book on the achievement of success, "Think and Grow Rich," to the absolute necessity of having a sense of purpose. In the book he lists thirty one reasons for failure, and the second reason on his list (following deficiency in brain power) was a lack of a well-defined purpose in life. He wrote, *"There is no hope of success for the person who does not have a central purpose, or definite goal at which to aim. Ninety-eight out of every hundred of those whom I have analyzed had no such aim. Perhaps this was the major cause of their failure."*

Our purpose often changes as we evolve and mature. Things which inspire us today may or may not inspire us ten years from now. Life is a journey full of discovery. If and when the time comes for us to alter our purpose, we will simply shift our focus and begin moving in another direction. It will be a natural process in which we will be led by our spirit. Until then, we should embrace what inspires us today, fully and completely.

One of the ways I was able to discover my purpose was to ask myself the following questions:

1. What are the things that I do well?

Everyone has certain things that they do very, very well. Our gifts always have two sides. When used with discipline, they can be our greatest asset, and when used unscientiously can be our greatest weakness.

2. What are the things that make me laugh?

3. What are the things that move me to tears?

4. What are the things that make me angry?

Whatever it is that we are called to do will incorporate all of our answers to the above questions, for the answers will give us a snapshot of the things that inspire passion in our spirit. Our true purpose will be the net result of our most marked characteristics. If we focus our attention on determining what our purpose is, it *will* come to us. This is yet another fact of the Law of Attraction.

Most important is this last key: Whatever it is that we do *has* to in some way enrich the lives of others. Whether it is designing clothes, rebuilding car engines, or becoming a child care provider, whatever we do will require us to be of service to others in some way. We humans are in the service business and part of our larger purpose on this earth is to serve each other. If our purpose does not somehow require us to assist other people in some way, whether directly or indirectly, then it cannot be our true purpose. Anything that does not help others is based on selfish desires. If you don't believe this to be true, ask anyone who has ever dealt drugs or chosen their purpose based solely upon greed.

We cannot sustain a commitment and maintain focus on something that doesn't touch our heart and soul.

Driven To Distraction

While it's true that other people or situations can lead us to lose focus, many of our biggest distractions come from within. Distracting ourselves with inconsequential activities is another way we can misuse the principle of focus. The following story explains how I was able to dramatically change my financial circumstances through the use of the SEPIA principle of focus.

For a very long time I believed that the level of my personal effectiveness could be measured by how busy I was on a daily basis. It didn't really matter what I focused my attention on...the important thing was keeping my day chock full of activity from the moment that I awoke to the minute my head hit the pillow. This was the only validation I needed to prove that I was actually doing something constructive with my life.

The fact that this frantic pace was overwhelming most of the time didn't stop me from putting more and more on my plate. My main focus was getting as much busy work done in the shortest amount of time possible. It's pretty safe to say that I performed most of these tasks haphazardly at best.

There was one thing however that I did choose to focus my attention on, and that was cleaning my apartment. Saturdays were my chosen day for this obsession, twelve hour chore marathons following on the heels of a forty hour work week. Had I approached these tasks differently, the laundry, grocery shopping and cleaning could have been handled in six hours, but my apartment couldn't be "surface clean" as my father used to call it. Everything in my home had to be cleaned with military precision. Floors couldn't just be mopped...they had to be clean enough to eat off. Kneeling on the parquet, armed with a scrub brush and bucket, I would attack the floor until the water ran clear. That wasn't enough either...the next step would be to get back down on my knees with a can of wood polish and buff the floor by hand until it shimmered in the sunlight. And heaven forbid if, during the course of picking up my children's room, I saw that their closet was a little out of order. Instead of throwing things back into their toy box, I would pull everything out and put it back in. It didn't matter that within a few days the closet would be disorganized all over again...if everything wasn't in its place, I would become irritable and short-tempered.

Maintaining an organized household is an important skill to master, and thorough cleaning is definitely needed on occasion. But I didn't just occasionally clean with such focus. Every Saturday for years, cleaning was a way for me to escape my feelings in the drudgery of housework. This entire mind numbing cleaning escapade was just another convenient distraction from yet another truth: I lacked any real self-fulfillment or sense of purpose.

Stuck In a Rut

There was only one other thing I would always find time for between the six loads of laundry and feverish toilet scrubbing. That was complaining. Complaining provided an outlet for my frustrations in life, and was my primary form of bonding with friends. It was a relatively easy indulgence, and didn't require anything more than a telephone line, a few hours, and a willing cohort. Complaining was the next best thing to an actual social life.

At the height of my obsession with cleaning, I was living paycheck to paycheck in a small rented apartment in the Bronx shortly after breaking up with Scott. My work as a secretary provided a steady but paltry income. The man I worked for, a former journalist turned sales executive was a charismatic and arrogant man given to inappropriate comments and temper tantrums. Every few weeks or so he would corner me in his office and regale me with some off-color story about his phenomenal sex drive. Needless to say, I didn't like going into his office alone.

My job consisted of small tasks like answering his phone lines and organizing his files. It was a long and uneventful day, but I was grateful to have healthcare benefits and a steady paycheck after years of financial uncertainty in the fashion business. At 5:00 p.m. sharp I would leave the office and rush home to pick up my children from the babysitter. After cooking dinner and helping with my son's homework, I would collapse into bed, only to get up and repeat the whole process over again.

Our financial situation was precarious to say the least. With Scott out of the home, I no longer had the benefit of the occasional income he provided. My salary was barely enough to support myself, let alone two young children, and I struggled to keep my family afloat. Every month was a nightmarish juggling act with the bills. One month the electric bill would be paid and the phone bill wasn't...the next month the phone bill would be paid but the cable bill wasn't. And there always seemed to be a fire to put out...my daughter would get an ear infection...my son's school would need a deposit for his tuition...my daughter's father would cancel his weekend visitation. Forget about nights out with friends...there was no way I could have afforded that. To do something simple like see a movie easily cost fifty dollars once childcare and transportation were figured in with the cost of my theatre ticket.

The way I lived wasn't unique by any means...in fact it is a typical single-parent nightmare. All around my bleak northern Bronx neighborhood were women just like me, many of them carrying much greater burdens and with much less money. The only thing that kept me going was the love I had for my two children...nothing more. This was not the life I had envisioned leading as a young girl. Hell, I hadn't planned on having any children until I was at least thirty-five, but here I was, twenty-seven years old, a single parent of two, and no help coming from any direction.

The Hamster Wheel

Work left me no respite from the frustration and tedium of my personal life. It too had become a monotonous chore. By the end of my first year of employment at the firm, my days at the office had settled into a routine in which I was able to compress the tasks of an eight hour workday in a three hour time frame. This left five hours for me to try and fill, but there is only so much internet surfing one can stand in a day.

One day I overheard another assistant complain that she didn't want to plan the office holiday party. For years this party had been the default responsibility of the CFO's assistant, and she had no interest or time to put into planning it. I approached her and offered to take over planning the event. It took her all of two minutes to agree, and with my boss's blessing I began planning my first special event.

Many people would be turned off by all of the work involved in event planning, but it fit my temperament to a tee. The multitasking I was used to as a parent, combined with my natural tendency to obsess over details, made it a very easy fit for my personality. Our holiday party turned out to be a huge success and I quickly became the go to person at the company for the coordination of all events.

For the first time in my life my passion was ignited for something other than a man, and my life's purpose became clear as day. Unfortunately, a full-time event planning position wasn't available at the company, so I continued to plod through my secretary's workday and plan the occasional event. My dissatisfaction with my work grew with each passing week as I fantasized about the large and glamorous events I could produce if only given a chance. Boredom became my predominant state of mind and I began to feel strangled by my surroundings.

And then my sister May Lai died.

Into Focus

The turning point in many of our lives often comes at a moment of profound crisis, when we finally realize with absolute clarity what is important to us. Armed with this knowledge, our actions from then on become extremely focused. For me this moment came when my younger sister died suddenly from a heroin overdose. The loss of one the most important people in my life brought into sharp focus how precious and fleeting life is. If the opportunity to become a full-time event planner wasn't there for me at my present job, then I was going to find another way to pursue my dream. I would no longer sit around and wait for someone to hand me my career. Once we have discovered our purpose, it becomes very challenging to continue doing work that doesn't inspire us.

So without any money saved or even a job lead, I quit my secretarial job and turned my attention toward making my dream happen. Perhaps if I had taken the time to map out what I would need in order to achieve my goal, I could have avoided spending the next two years bartending and temping while trying to hustle event planning work. But I didn't, and the next few years were spent slinging drinks and answering phones. The work was still uninspiring, but it didn't bother me because now I was actively searching for a way to break into the events industry. For two years I lived and breathed and dreamed nothing but events. Housework and cleaning became secondary to my passion for event planning and I spent every waking moment looking for any opportunity to further my goal.

Every decision I made was colored by the answer to the question: "Will this action move me closer to my dream of becoming an event planner?" As I became more and more focused on my goal, I began to block out any information that didn't support its achievement. I kept my ears open for any opportunity, no matter how small, to get my foot in the door.

Eventually I was able to secure a position at one of the largest nightclubs in New York City as an event coordinator, and my career began in earnest. Within weeks I was managing and selling events, learning every aspect of the business from the ground up.

This position provided invaluable work experience, but fell short of meeting my financial needs. Every month we slid further and further into debt. As I worked and reworked the household budget on Sunday afternoons it became clear that we were going to lose our apartment if I didn't double my income. We just couldn't stay afloat otherwise.

How the heck is this gonna happen? I wondered. *It's gonna take nothing short of a miracle!*

The Law of Attraction

One would think that doubling a salary overnight is a virtually impossible goal, but I believed it could happen *if I had a plan.* During a random conversation with an acquaintance, I learned that he and his partners were looking to hire an events director to open their new special events facility. I wasn't going to be the only person interviewing for the position. My competition would probably have much more experience than me, so I set out to create a plan that would at least give me a shot at the position.

For the first time in my life I turned my attention towards creating a plan of action that would change my circumstance. My plan focused on researching the competition in the neighborhood of the new facility and creating a marketing strategy. I had never done a marketing strategy before, but found a few examples on the internet and set about crafting one for the new event space. After a week of preparation I was ready for my interview.

The day of our meeting was a beautiful mild summer day, the kind of day that lifts my spirits the moment I see the sunshine. A soft warm breeze blew over me as I briskly walked to the interview. I had chosen to wear conservative black, something understated and elegant to boost my confidence. With long strides, I stepped into the air conditioned restaurant, and after spying the three partners in a corner booth, headed in their direction.

Sliding into the booth, I said hello. Nothing stood out as particularly noteworthy during the subsequent interview, and I couldn't tell how well I was doing in their eyes. The partners were very friendly and open but past experience has shown me that an amiable meeting doesn't always mean a job offer. At the end of the interview, I slid three large envelopes across the table, each stuffed with a marketing strategy.

"What's this?" one of them asked.

"I did some research on the competition in the neighborhood and came up with some strategies that I believe can help us meet the needs of our clients."

A small smile spread across each of their faces.

"Thanks, that's great. We'll let you know our decision in a few weeks."

Walking out of the interview and into the bright afternoon sun I was filled with a quiet sense of peace. I knew I had given the interview my best.

A few days, then a week, then another week went by with no word from the partners. I comforted myself with my thoughts: *Well, if they don't offer me the job, then it simply wasn't meant to be.* These words encouraged me on one level, but I was still disappointed that they hadn't called me back.

Almost three weeks passed. Just when I had given up on the position, I received a call from one of them offering me the job. The salary they offered me was double what I was making at the nightclub and on top of that I had an increase in title and responsibility!

After accepting the position I asked my new employer why they decided to offer the job to me.

"We offered you the position because not only did you impress us with your passion for event planning, but you took the time to research the competition and present us with a formal marketing strategy."

The time between discovering my purpose and choosing to focus on creating a plan of action was four years. I went from working as a corporate secretary to running a multimillion dollar special events facility, and I did it without a college degree or years of extensive training. Not only was I working in the field I had been dreaming of for years, but I was finally making enough money to take care of my children. All of this happened because I had discovered the truth about what I wanted to do for a living, accepted this information, took action, made a commitment, and focused on my goal.

Focus Summarized

It's important to learn how to focus our attention on what is most important to our existence if we are to fully embrace our power. Every action we take makes a statement about what we are focused on in the moment. When we are truly practicing this principle we will make decisions and choices in alignment with the achievement of our goals.

An empowered woman does not focus on her problems. She focuses on her opportunities. Instead of expending all her energy solving everyday problems, she chooses to focus much of her time on doing things to assist in achieving her long-range goals. We often busy ourselves with distractions when we're afraid to look at a larger issue. If we find ourselves engaging in repetitive behaviors like twelve hour cleaning marathons or endless venting about the problems in life, it's time to ask ourselves: "What am I trying to avoid focusing on by engaging in this behavior?" Sure, those files need to be organized and those clothes need to be ironed, but we shouldn't focus so much of our time on these activities that we don't leave any energy for long-term goals. Remember that we are the most important project in our life!

In life there are two kinds of people: The Predictors of the Inevitable and the Pursuers of the Possible. The Predictors of the Inevitable always expect the worst out of life, and direct their behaviors accordingly. They are defensive or reactive to their circumstances. Pursuers of the Possible see life as a fantastic journey and are always looking for ways to expand their level of awareness. One important difference between the two is their focus. If we always keep our focus on what is possible in life, we will be amazed at what we *will* achieve.

$\mathscr{F}$ AITH

You are Divinely Protected

"On a long journey of human life, faith is the best of companions; it is the best refreshment on the journey; and it is the greatest property."

~ Prince Gautama Siddharta, *founder of Buddhism*

The seventh SEPIA principle is *faith*. Next to life itself, faith is considered by many to be the greatest gift that we are given. It is what separates those who rise in triumph from the ashes of struggle from those who remain crawling on their hands and knees in discouragement. Throughout the centuries there have been many examples of faith uplifting us through the most difficult of circumstances. In his book "Man's Search for Meaning," the Viennese neurologist and psychiatrist Dr. Viktor Frankl observed faith in action during the time he spent living in the dreaded concentration camp at Auschwitz. He wrote, *"The prisoner who had lost faith in the future-his future was doomed. With his loss of belief in the future, he also lost his spiritual hold; he let himself decline and became subject to mental and physical decay...He simply gave up."* The lesson in his statement is simple: Without faith we will perish.

Very often, it is how much we lean on this principle during the times of great crises in our lives that gives us an accurate measure of our faith. Tragedy can help us find our humanity, but only if we have faith that everything that happens to us can help us evolve into a more loving and compassionate person. Without this belief, we will simply give up trying to move forward and resign ourselves to our current circumstances.

In the previous chapter we saw how important the principle of focus is in determining our personal purpose and achieving our goals. In this chapter we'll explore how our focus helps to determine the direction of our faith. We'll also see how it is possible, even probable, that our faith can grow in the most difficult of circumstances.

Faith Defined

The word "faith" has many different meanings, but only two will be used in this chapter. Religious affiliation is one of the most common uses of the word. Religious affiliation, or faith, is a tool that can help us develop a belief system and aligns us with a community of others who share our convictions. It's important to note that it's not necessary to belong to any particular religion in order to have faith. Faith can be developed independently, but within the framework of community we are supported and are able to support others in the search for a greater sense of meaning.

The second definition of the word faith is used when we possess specific beliefs that don't need proof or material evidence. Faith is an unshakeable belief that we are divinely protected and that there is meaning and purpose to our existence in this world. The reformer, Martin Luther, wrote about faith, *"Faith is a living, bold trust in God's grace, so certain of God's favor that it would risk death a thousand times trusting in it."*

Faith does not require supporting evidence. It is the very act of believing that matters...not what we believe in. We can even have faith while doubting if there truly is a God. For some people, God and faith *can* be mutually exclusive.

Although we cannot be taught *how* to have faith, we can develop it if we *choose* to do so. All that we need is the desire to develop our belief. Although the word God is used occasionally in this book, it is only used for the sake of simplicity. God. Jehovah. Universal Love. Higher Consciousness.

Yahweh. Allah. Buddha. Jesus Christ. Higher Power. All of these different terms refer to the same fundamental belief.

The Law of Polarity

Another universal truth is the Law of Polarity. Polarity means having two opposite attributes, such as the opposites of North and South or the opposites of male and female. The opposite of faith is fear. If we are not leading a life based upon the principle of faith, then we are living one based upon fear. We have already found that a fear based existence is a disempowered existence. Why then do so many of us not use this principle? Perhaps the main reason is disappointment. Let's explore this further.

Why Do We Lose Faith?

Disappointment is the feeling of dissatisfaction we have when our expectations are not realized. When we become disappointed it is because we have attached ourselves to the outcome of a situation. If we suffer enough disappointment we can become doubtful, and doubt nullifies faith.

It is harmful to allow doubt to creep into our mind for it carries with it the seeds of fear. Even a little doubt is enough to erode our faith.

The cure to disappointment is to remove our
attachment to the outcome of situations.

A survivor has faith only as long as things turn out the way they would like. When things don't, they use that as evidence that there is no God or that life is conspiring against them.

A contender understands that many unplanned things will occur in their life. They accept that everything that happens to them, regardless of whether or not it causes them happiness or pain, has the potential to help them evolve spiritually. They use this belief, or faith, to help them move towards their goals. A contender knows that without faith they cannot achieve anything.

Comparison Between Types

SURVIVOR	CONTENDER
• Is attached to the outcome of situations, inviting disappointment into their lives.	• Understands that all that happens in life is to help them grow. They do not place too much importance on the outcome of situations.

The Importance of Faith

Now that we have defined one of the main reasons why people lose faith, let's take a look at this in action. The following story illustrates how I learned to understand the sixth SEPIA principle of Faith after undergoing one of the most traumatic experiences in my life.

At the age of twenty four I had been fighting bulimia, an eating disorder characterized by binge eating large amounts of food and then purging it by vomiting, since I was seventeen years old. Like many people without health insurance, I didn't have the financial means to commit to treatment, but I wasn't really interested in treatment anyway. I only wanted to alleviate my actual binging and purging, not get to the root of *why* I had an eating disorder. That would have taken more time and energy than I was willing to give at that time in my life. Instead of seeing a psychiatrist, I decided to seek treatment from my *gynecologist*.

I had gone to see my gynecologist for my annual exam but had a secret mission: to get Prozac and Xanax. A national women's magazine had recently published an article on the antidepressant Prozac and was touting its effectiveness in treating bulimia. I was uncertain that my gynecologist would prescribe what I wanted if I told him about my eating disorder, so I decided to tell him that I was suffering from symptoms of depression and anxiety instead.

So what if I'm not being completely straight with him? What possible harm can this cause? It's just an antidepressant!

It wasn't a total lie...I really was depressed.

He asked no questions as he breezily scribbled the prescriptions I requested, as well as a heavy-duty sedative to help me sleep at night. I gave a huge sigh of relief as I walked out of his office.

Thank God I didn't have to bother with seeing a therapist. Fifty questions and more sessions? No thanks! That would have been such a pain!

It never occurred to me to ask whether any of these drugs could be harmful if I drank alcohol while taking them. I was just happy to have a solution for my eating disorder. Due to the restraints of his schedule, we were limited to only ten minutes of slightly embarrassed interaction, and he had no way of knowing I had a drinking problem. He made the very human error of judging a book by its cover.

By simply writing out the prescriptions without asking me any additional questions about my history of drinking or referring me to a mental health provider, he unwittingly gave me a loaded shotgun that would almost cost me my life.

Countdown to Destruction

It was an unusually busy period in my life at the time. My modeling career was finally taking off and although I had been living for several months in Milan, Italy, I returned briefly to the United States to move my permanent residence from Miami to New York. For part of the time I was in Europe, my son Christian had been cared for in Miami by Scott's mother. Since Scott and I had recently broken up, I packed up everything I owned and moved back to New York, a city we had lived in before. The move had taken place suddenly, and I hadn't yet had time to find an apartment of my own. Christian and I were going to have to stay at my friend Carol's apartment, at least until I could find my own place.

In New York the pace of my life was a bit slower than usual, consisting of occasional castings and bookings, caring for my son, and drinking alcohol late into the night. On one of these lazy days I got together with a former boyfriend named Ronald, a man I had known since I was nineteen years old. Ronald and I always made a point to hang out whenever I was in town. He was well known for only dating models and for a hard partying lifestyle funded by his very successful record label. His pallid complexion and protruding eyes had earned him the nickname "Gollum" from my sister May Lai, in honor of the character in the book series "The Lord of the Rings." It was a name we never called him to his face of course, but we sometimes chuckled behind his back.

. Once I settled into my friend Carol's apartment, Ronald and I met up at a trendy restaurant near his spacious downtown apartment. The restaurant was known less for its food than its stylish clientele, and had become a home away from home for him. Everyone in the place knew Ronald by name and I was tickled by the first-class treatment I always received when in his company.

It was late afternoon and the sun was still lingering overhead, warm rays of light washing over the half-moon green vinyl booth we sat in. A brown-skinned, lithe dancer/actor/model/waiter type came over take our orders.

"A pinot grigio...do you have Santa Margherita?" I asked.

Nodding his head, the waiter turned his attention to Ronald.

"And you? What are you drinking?"

"I'll have a Pellegrino, no ice."

This time it was my eyes that bulged.

"What! What do you mean *'Pellegrino'*? Why aren't you drinking? Are you sick?" I exclaimed.

"No, I'm not sick. I just quit drinking, okay? I don't want to get into it..."

"Okay, okay. That just means more for me!" I said, gulping my first glass halfway down.

Over the next few hours we chatted eagerly, catching up on what had been happening for the last few months since we last saw each other. The sun had dropped behind the buildings overlooking the restaurant, and the grey shadows of dusk were steadily moving in. It was by now almost 9:00 p.m., and I was ready to get the night really started.

"Hey, Brian just called me. Shakim is having a house party at his loft in Soho...you wanna go?" Ronald asked.

"Sure...that sounds like fun! Let's go!"

A Night like No Other

It was the year 1994, and the nightlife in Manhattan still oozed with the remnants of the over-the-top conspicuous consumption of the eighties. We piled into Ronald's chauffer-driven limousine and headed off into the night. Rolling down the windows, I felt the warm breeze of a balmy summer night flutter over my face. Stumbling in and out of the car, we stopped at one party after the next, from nightclub to loft, with Ronald working the room and me slamming back glass after glass of champagne.

By 3:00 a.m. I could barely stand. My eyes strained to keep in focus, but they only succeeded in staying mainly crossed together.

"Ronald...I wannnna go hoooome." I slurred.

Ignoring me, he continued to chat with another guest at the party.

"I'm seriousssssssss. Take me hooome." My words were becoming louder and more insistent.

"Hey man, I'll catch you later. Lemme get this one home, aight?"

We headed to back to his car and climbed in. Falling back into the buttery leather seat, my head rolled back on the headrest, glazed eyes half shut. In the distance I heard Ronald giving his driver instructions, but couldn't make out what he was saying. I faded in and out of consciousness.

I felt the car come to a stop, and flopped my head towards the window. Instead of pulling up to my building, we had stopped outside his. I was plastered, but I could still tell the difference between our residences.

"What're you doing? This isn't my aparrrtmint." I slurred.

"Come on...get out of the car. Come upstairs for a minute..."

Nodding my head, I stumbled into the lobby of his building, heels clattering across the marble floors.

The door to the elevator opened and we stepped inside. Ronald pressed the PH button, for his penthouse, and I leaned my back against the door, concentrating my attention on trying to stop the small compartment from spinning.

The doors slid open and we headed to his place.

Unlocking the door, he flung it open and said, "Go upstairs."

Teetering up the spiral staircase, I lurched through the kitchen and living room, finally flopping on the fluffy surface of Ronald's large bed. Within moments I was passed out, sprawled fully clothed on top of his bed.

It never occurred to me that there could be any danger. It had been years since we had been together, and I had made it very clear to him earlier that night (when I was still sober) that I was no longer sexually interested in him. In hindsight, going upstairs to a former lover's apartment while intoxicated wasn't such a smart idea, but I trusted him. As sleazy as he could be at times,

Ronald wasn't the type of man I ever thought would force himself on a woman. His wealth provided him with many willing sexual partners.

A False Sense of Security

Drifting in and out of consciousness, I opened my eyes groggily and saw Ronald walking towards me naked, wearing nothing but a condom. As he leaned over my body it suddenly dawned on me what he intended to do. Inside my mind I was panicking, but any signals my brain was sending to my body were short circuited by the champagne in my blood.

Climbing on top of me, his weight was heavy on my chest. I feebly pressed my hands against his shoulders and pushed, but my limbs couldn't respond with any strength to my mind's instructions.

"No, Ronald..." was all that I could manage to say.

Ignoring my protestations, he flipped me over onto my stomach and swiftly pulled down the bike shorts I had worn under my dress. Helpless to stop him, I lay flat on my stomach while he took my remaining shred of dignity.

Five foggy minutes later it was over, and I started to pass out again.

Nudging me awake, he told me to leave.

"You gotta go!" he urged, helping me towards the door. "Tommy will take you home. My girlfriend is gonna be calling me from London and you can't be here!"

"What girlfriend?" I slurred.

"Well, she's not really my girlfriend, but I hope that she will be soon..."

"Oh."

A Blur

Still sloppily drunk, I finally limped into Carol's apartment around 5:00 in the morning. Collapsing on the pullout sofa, I mercifully slept until awakening to the sound of the television at 11:00 a.m. *I was still drunk.*

My son was sitting on the bed next to me watching television. Carol was nowhere to be seen. I remembered that she had said she had to work that day, and I pulled my torso up on my elbows, hanging my head back far enough to touch the mattress.

Ugh! I feel like crap!

A sudden flash of memory burst to the forefront of my consciousness and the entire night came back to me in a rush. Numbly, I recalled what had happened to me the previous night.

I had been raped. I had gotten pathetically stinking drunk yet again and my so-called friend had raped me.

Horrified, I gazed into the cherubic face of my two year old son. Christian's eyes shone with such innocence, and I was filled with overwhelming feelings of sorrow and shame. He didn't deserve to have such a loser for a mother. He deserved so much better.

My shame unbridled all my emotions at once. I cracked. Memories of years and years of disappointment came flooding back in a storm.

I'm going to show them! They are all going to be so sorry for what they have done to me! They meaning Ronald, my parents… anyone and everyone that I felt had failed me over the years.

I lurched off the bed and went to the corner where my luggage was sitting. Rifling through my travel bag, I spied what I was looking for.

Yes. This is what I wanted. Sleeping pills.

Tilting the bottle, I shook it back and forth a few times, watching the capsules rattle around inside. I then strode to the kitchen and opened the refrigerator. It was empty, save for a few slices of American cheese, a box of cereal, and a large bottle of chardonnay. Bingo.

Whisking it off the shelf, I closed the refrigerator door and placed the bottle on the counter in front of me. Time slowed as I heard the sound of cartoons echoing from the living room. I emptied the entire contents of the bottle into my hand.

Eighteen sky blue capsules landed in my cupped palm. I fingered them for a minute and paused in a moment of indecision.

I'm such a loser. I don't even have the guts to kill myself! echoed my mind.

My determination returned, and I gripped the bottle of wine in one hand while placing three capsules at a time on my tongue with the other. Tipping my head way back, I washed them down with several large swigs of wine. After six gulps I had swallowed them all. Bottle trailing in hand, I stumbled back to the living room and sat down next to my son. Nuzzling his head with my own, I breathed the smell of his hair deeply through my nostrils. I wanted to remember his scent, this sweet Johnson's Baby Shampoo smell. Moving my head away, I brought the bottle of wine up to my lips and quickly finished its contents.

No Turning Back

For a moment I was awash with overwhelming feelings of remorse and briefly reconsidered.

Maybe I'm not ready to die! But how could I ever live this down? How could a mother ever explain this to her child? No! No way! There was no turning back now!

Pulling my son closer, I kissed him gently on his smooth golden forehead.

"Mommy loves you very much, you know that, don't you? I have to go away now, but Carol is going to be your Mommy, okay? Do you understand?"

Nodding yes, he never looked away from the Power Rangers program on the television set. *He has already moved on,* I thought bitterly, bursting into tears as I realized how my actions that day were going to damage my son for the rest of his life.

My rage welled over inside and spilled out in large angry tears on my chest.

How dare Ronald do what he did to me! It was his fault that this was happening! He needed to know that what he did was wrong and suffer for it too!

Picking up the phone, I dialed his number. His assistant answered the phone.

"Hello?"

"Sharon? It's Sil Lai. Put Ronald on the phone!"

"I'm sorry Sil Lai, but he is on another call right now..."

"I don't care what the hell he is doing! Get him on the phone!"

"Okay, let me see what I can do..." she said.

A few seconds later Ronald was on the line.

"What is it Sil Lai? What is it that can't wait?" he snapped.

"You raped me last night Ronald! You raped me and I want you to know that I'm killing myself and that it's your fault!"

"Whoa, whoa! Slow down! What are you talking about? I didn't rape you! Nothing happened..."

My voice shrieked. "Yes you did! I told you I didn't want to have sex with you and you did it anyway! YOU RAPED ME! It's my blood on your hands when I die, you freakin' rapist!"

"Calm down, calm down! It's just post-alcohol blues!"

"Don't tell me to calm down! It's too late! You're not getting away with this! I've already taken a bottle of sleeping pills!"

"What? You did what?" he exclaimed.

Screaming I replied, "I hope that you can live with yourself! I hope you know for the rest of your life that you made me kill myself!" and then slammed the phone down in his ear.

The pills were now starting to kick in and take effect. The phone would ring, and I would pick it up and drop it down into the cradle again and again. Everything was beginning to slow down, but the phone wouldn't stop ringing.

Stop freakin' calling Ronald! You're too late!

Briiing! Briing! Briing! Stoned out of my mind, it didn't occur to me to simply take it off the hook. After the fifth ring I lurched for the receiver and placed it to my ear. Instead of hearing Ronald's voice however, I was startled to hear my friend Carol's instead.

She sang into the phone, "Hi! How are you doing today? I didn't hear you come in last night."

"Leave me alone! Would everybody just leave me the hell alone?" I yelled, slamming the phone down into her ear.

The phone rang and rang, but this time I wouldn't pick up. The sound grated on my already exhausted nerves. Finally, after two minutes of continuous ringing I picked up the receiver.

"What is wrong with you? Why did you hang up on me?" she asked.

"Carooool," I wailed, "I can't do this anymore!"

"What can't you do anymore? What are you talking about?"

"This! Life! I'm no good at it!"

I told her what I had done.

She gasped out loud. "Oh my God! Stay there! I'm sending someone over to get you!"

She immediately called Jean, her estranged husband, and told him what I had done. He and his friend Zack dropped everything and jumped in a cab to rescue me.

Unbeknownst to us all, Ronald had instructed his assistant to come over and help as well. All three converged upon the apartment at the same time. Whisking me into a cab, Jean and Zack took me to the nearest hospital emergency room while Sharon stayed behind to look after my son until Carol got home. At 1:00 p.m. in the afternoon I was admitted to Bellevue Hospital's Emergency Room for acute alcohol and barbiturate poisoning.

In the Nick of Time

The next events all happened so quickly that I couldn't keep track of what was happening. I recall being moved onto a gurney in an open hallway and then wheeled into a dark room. A nurse held a container of thick grey liquid up to my lips.

"Drink." I was instructed by a blur in scrubs. Gagging, I did what I was told.

Wiping the drippings off the sides of my mouth with a napkin, the nurse stroked my hair and never left my side. Later I would discover that the chalky grey liquid had been activated charcoal. It had been too late to pump my stomach, and apparently charcoal is an action of last resort. After my release from the hospital I learned that if my friends had brought me in twenty minutes later I could not have been saved. I had barely escaped death.

Once the immediate threat to my life was over, it was time to be interviewed by the admitting psychiatrist, a thin young man with a dry demeanor. He began peppering me with questions about my background and I answered them as honestly as I could.

Why so many questions? I thought.

It was only about halfway through the interview that it dawned upon me why he was asking so many questions. He was going to commit me to the hospital psychiatric unit.

Holy crap! I hadn't taken this outcome into consideration when I tried to kill myself.

Backpedaling, I tried to talk my way out of being committed, but the psychiatrist wouldn't fall for it. Apparently I had blabbed all of the sordid details of my suicide attempt to the admitting physician.

"But I'm fine! Nothing is wrong with me. It was an accident!" I protested.

Looking me straight in the eyes, he said "Miss, you do realize that this was a very serious suicide attempt, don't you? You attempted to take your life in the presence of your son. You contacted your family members to say goodbye. I can't release you, and if you don't voluntarily commit yourself to the hospital we'll commit you ourselves."

Peering around the room, I looked for a way out. There were large orderlies stationed at every exit.

Giving that idea up, I asked "Can I call my lawyer?" He would know what to do.

The doctor handed me a phone and I dialed my attorney. I quickly told him where I was and what had happened.

"What should I do?" I asked.

"Sign yourself in. If you do it, you can sign yourself out, once the immediate threat has passed. If they do it, you'll have to petition the court to be released."

"Thanks for the advice." I answered stonily.

Damn! What the hell am I going to do now?

Hanging up the phone, I sighed and signed the commitment papers.

Lockdown

For five days I stayed in a low-security section of the hospital's psychiatric ward. I wasn't sure how long I was going to be held, but I desperately wanted to get out. One doesn't truly appreciate freedom until it's taken away.

God! I hope I'm not in here for long!

I missed my son and couldn't wait to get back to work. My boyfriend Mossimo was waiting for me back in Italy and I had bookings lined up for the fall.

I called Mossimo daily from the payphone located in the long hallway, calls that mainly involved me pleading with him to get me out of the hospital. He agreed to speak to my psychiatrist to see what he could arrange. The two of them spoke on the phone and Mossimo promised to make sure I would receive proper treatment if I were released. Maybe it was the fact that I didn't have health insurance, or maybe it was because Mossimo could be very convincing, but my doctor agreed to release me.

I signed myself out of the hospital one day before my twenty-fourth birthday and went back to Carol's to be with my son. Carol and I agreed that I was too emotionally exhausted to care for him for the time being, so I boarded a plane and headed back to Italy to spend the next month convalescing on a boat in the Mediterranean. I never received any follow up care, prescriptions, or psychiatric treatment. Mossimo never even sent me to see a psychiatrist, but he did throw away my Prozac when I wasn't looking. It was by the grace of God that I not only survived my suicide attempt, but didn't reattempt, after not receiving any follow up care.

All Is Not Lost

One may think that my actions on that mild summer day were that of a woman who had lost her faith, and to a certain extent it's true. I had lost faith in *myself*. After years of slipping and sliding through life, cutting corners and escaping serious consequences for my drinking, the ferryman had finally asked for his coin. Instead of seeing what had happened that night with Ronald as a wakeup call to quit drinking, I interpreted what had happened as proof that God had abandoned me.

The truth was that I didn't really want to die…I just didn't know how to stop living in such a destructive manner, and I didn't realize that my drinking was one of the primary reasons for my dramatic behavior. My disappointment in myself caused me to temporarily lose faith in believing that my life would ever get better.

Several months later, when I had finally quit drinking, I came to understand that my faith had never really left me. Once I sobered up, I realized that the problem had been with my mindset all along.

Shifting Perspectives

Where our faith is placed plays a huge role in determining the outcome of our life. It is essential that we have it pointed in a positive direction, for when our faith is negatively directed it can also work against us. A self-fulfilling prophecy is one example of how our faith can work for or against us.

A self-fulfilling prophecy is essentially the belief that whatever a person believes in will eventually become their reality. If we have faith that we will not overcome our issues then we won't, for our subconscious will direct our actions in manifesting this belief. Conversely, if we believe that nothing in life will keep us from realizing our goals, then we cannot fail. Self-fulfilling prophecy or faith…the term that we decide to use is entirely up to us, but in the end the results are the same, for our beliefs have an incredible impact on the outcome of our lives.

When doubt begins to gnaw away at the roots of our faith, we should challenge it by changing the negative thoughts poisoning our minds into positive thoughts. Adopting this principle will result in a change from: *I am never going to move out of this neighborhood* to *I am out of this neighborhood as soon as I get everything lined up! I am never going to get that promotion;* turns into *I will find a way to make my career aspirations happen, with or without a promotion!* There are no realistic goals that we cannot attain as long as we believe in our ability to achieve them.

Finding Faith Through Loss

The previous story in this chapter focused on how we can learn about our faith through the circumstances we undergo. Now let's explore how it's possible to discover the depth of our faith through the losses that we all suffer. The following story illustrates how I was able to reaffirm my faith and discover the true meaning of the principle.

My sister May Lai also struggled with her own drinking problem, but for years she never really faced any serious repercussions from it. Her circumstances changed quickly when she began dating a petty drug dealer with rock star ambitions named Ariel. With a pug nose and a long, lean body permanently bronzed from spending his days loitering on a north Florida beach, Ariel was a childhood boyfriend of my sister's with whom she had recently reunited. Ariel also happened to be hooked on heroin, and he soon introduced my sister to the drug. This didn't happen overnight of course. They had been dating for a few months, when one day she casually told me that she was considering trying the drug.

"Ariel wants me to try heroin…I think I'm going do it," she said, as flippantly as one would say "Where's the bathroom?" or "What do you think about my new hair color?"

"What the hell are you talking about May Lai? Are you kidding me?"

"I don't know…"

"Are you outta yer freakin' mind? You know you are going to get hooked, right? Tell me that you are going to be the one person who can beat the odds and become a recreational heroin user! It doesn't happen!"

I kept on berating her, on and on for several minutes, waiting to see if anything I said was sinking in. Her brow squinched together in a deep furrow and her jaw was tightly clenched, but I didn't let up. Finally, she flung herself around and started to storm off.

"I'm sorry I ever told you anything! Just leave me alone!" she yelled, leaving me standing alone on the sidewalk.

In retrospect, there were many other ways I could have approached the situation. I had hoped that my tough love approach would deter her from trying heroin, but it didn't. Years later I would wonder whether a different approach with her that day would have kept her from picking it up. Perhaps, if I had used compassion and understanding instead of belittling and shaming her, things would have been different.

To this day I don't know why she told me what she was planning to do. At the time I thought she told me because she wanted me to dissuade her from using heroin, but maybe she just wanted a witness to her self-destruction, or maybe she simply told me for shock value. I'll never know the answer.

Could Have Done Better

By the time May Lai picked up heroin I had been sober for a little over three years. Granted, my life was still a soap opera…drama was still my middle name. I was no longer modeling and raising two kids on my own while struggling to keep my daughter's father from creating too much trouble in our lives. Although I was now technically sober, I was focused on surviving from day to day. There was little joy or freedom in my life. Sobriety must have seemed *real* appealing to her, based upon my example. *Not.*

May Lai begrudgingly attended one recovery group meeting with me, but refused to go again. Funny how life is…now *I* was the person *she* couldn't identify with. Though I tried many different ways to coax her into treatment, she ignored everything I said and got high regardless. Nodding her head, she would smile sweetly at my suggestions and then do what she wanted to do anyway. Shoot up.

An active addict is an incredibly unreliable creature. Partying had taken its toll on May Lai's ability to show up for her modeling jobs (something she had never really been that good at even before heroin) and she was no longer working. It wasn't as if she really needed the income...a steady stream of money from her wealthy ex-boyfriend assured that she didn't have to work if she didn't want to. Since they had broken up, she had moved with a roommate named Jack into a squalid apartment one block from New York's epicenter of heroin addiction, Tompkins Square Park.

From first hand experience I know that anyone actively using drugs or alcohol has no idea how selfish and hurtful their actions are to the people who care about them. Everyone else is the problem...nobody gets them...they are so damned unique. For years I had no idea how my addictions had hurt the people who cared about me, and now it was my turn to watch someone else destroy herself through an addiction.

The entire situation was surreal. How could the little girl I had played Barbie with, the one I had taught how to put on makeup and fought with over coloring books, now be a *junkie*? It was an almost impossible concept to swallow. In *my* family? Come on...heroin addiction was something that happened to *other* peoples' families, families we saw on sappy made for TV movies. Yet it was true, my baby sister was now a junkie who *needed* a fix more than she needed her family, and there was nothing that I, or anyone else for that matter, could do about it.

A Life Forever Changed

I have always found it amazing how one simple decision can have an impact on our existence forever...how one choice can change the direction of the world as we know it. My sister made that choice on Monday, March 24, 1998. It was an unremarkable day, one filled with office work and child rearing. Nothing hinted of the agony that was crouched and waiting for me just one phone call away.

It was while I was reading my children the Dr. Seuss story *Green Eggs and Ham* that my telephone began to ring.

"Would you? Could you?" *Briiing!* "In a car?" *Briiing!*

Ignoring the sound of the phone, I continued to read.

"Eat them! Eat them, here they are!"

I finished the book and then kissed both my children goodnight on their soft foreheads. I smiled to myself, pleased to finally be able to enjoy my role as a mother. Scott was no longer in our home and our lives had become relatively peaceful.

The ringing started again. Closing their bedroom door behind me, I rushed over to the phone in the living room. Annoyed, I lifted the receiver to my ear and breathlessly answered.

"Hello?"

There was nothing but sobbing on the other end. Fear raced up my spine like a spider as I listened to the young woman's voice.

"Suh-suh Lai? It's Elena. May Lai...May Lai..."she stuttered.

Her crying had me so upset that I practically shouted into the phone.

"What happened? What is it?"

Elena began to ramble about the events of the night before.

"We were all at a party and then May Lai left around 5:00 in the morning to go pack for her trip to Florida and..."

"What are you trying to say? Don't do this to me...just say it! Where is my sister?"

"She's dead! I am sooooo sorry Sil Lai" she wailed. "Jack got home about an hour ago and found her dead in his bed." Her breathing was so ragged she could barely speak. A white flash of pain splashed across my chest. I had to speak to Jack.

"Is Jack at home?"

"Yeah, he's there with the police..."

"I gotta go Elena!" I said, and then clicked off the phone. Handset dangling, I walked into my bedroom, a few steps away, and stopped.

My hands were shaking uncontrollably as I dialed Jack's number.

A deep masculine voice answered the phone with a snappish "Hello?"

The words tumbled out of my mouth with incredible speed.

"My name is Sil Lai. May Lai is my sister! Someone just called my house and said she was dead and I want to talk to Jack! Where is he? Who are you?"

"Ma'am, I am a Detective with the New York City Police Department. Your sister..."

I didn't hear anything else. Sinking onto the edge of my bed, I dropped the phone in my lap, and turned my head up to the ceiling, letting out a shriek. One long piercing wail that rose from the pit of my stomach, scraped across the back of my throat and then echoed off the walls of my bedroom.

Picking up my phone again, I held it to my ear in time to hear him say "Ma'am, I need you to calm down...just calm down..."

I doubled over the edge of my bed, cradling the phone next to me and shrieked again and again.

"NO!" "NO!" "NO!" They were three short piercing shrieks punctuated with brief shallow breaths. Clutching the phone to my ear I hyperventilated while listening to the officer tell me how my baby sister's body had been discovered that evening lying in bed, dead from an apparent heroin overdose.

After he was finished, I asked to speak to Jack.

"Hey..." he said, coming onto the line.

"So you just got home tonight at 8:00? You didn't even stop in at all during the day?" I said, suspicion creeping into my voice.

Everyone was suspect, as far as I was concerned. Jack had been out with her the night before and May Lai had told me before that she occasionally did drugs with him. What if my sister had OD'd while with him and he had just bailed on her to save his own ass?

"No, I was out showing apartments all day. Our other roommate was here though. He was working from home and saw her lying in bed but thought she was only sleeping, so he just closed the door and left her alone."

I blew up.

"You're telling me that idiot didn't think there was anything strange about a grown woman sleeping for twelve hours in the middle of the afternoon? Jesus!"

Jack's other roommate had held my sister's life in his hand and didn't even know it. He had sat at his computer in the room next to the room she was in, while the last shallow breaths escaped from her lungs and her soul vanished from her body. He had chatted on his phone, eaten lunch, peed, and watched television while my sister lay dying in the next room.

I couldn't take hearing anything else.

"I'll call you back…I gotta call our parents." I said.

Going Through the Motions

The rest of the night I spent calling my entire family and telling them the horrible news. I finally fell into a fitful sleep around 4:00 a.m., only to wake up with a start three hours later. Opening my eyes, I briefly felt the bright sunlight streaming through the slats of the vinyl blinds hanging in front of my large bedroom window. Then the pain came smashing back, as I remembered the night before. Sobbing, I called my children's babysitter and made arrangements for them to spend the day at her house.

Once my children left I began to make the funeral arrangements. I don't know how I was able to do it…the part of me that was dying from the emotional pain shut down and God took over. That is the only explanation I had for being able to work despite my loss.

Days marched by and I kept on working…hashing out the details of the funeral. When the time came for me to select a coffin, I brought my friend Carol with me for support. Gripping her elbow, I walked through the funeral home in a daze blankly staring at the array of different caskets available.

Would she want a silver casket? Or brushed bronze? She always liked the color pink…maybe I should choose a copper one?

Never in a million years did I think I would be doing what I was doing. Overwhelmed with the number of choices, I finally selected a sleek copper-hued casket with ivory silk interior. It's strange to think that something as morbid as a casket can actually match a personality.

After retrieving her belongings from Jack's apartment, I sifted through May Lai's various battered suitcases for the clothes I thought *she* would want everyone to see her in the last time the light of day shone on her face. Arms wrapped tightly around my torso, hugging myself in the brisk cold wind moaning dolefully past us, I trudged around the large old cemetery in the Bronx, finally selecting a plot for her coffin.

The salesperson for the cemetery commented as I was leaving his office, "You are awfully young to have a responsibility this big." I simply nodded and walked out the door. May Lai's funeral fell on my shoulders, partly because no one else offered to step in and help, and partly because I was the only family she had in New York. It didn't matter that my family had placed this on me…if anyone had offered to help I would have pushed them away anyway.

The morning of the wake I got myself dressed and kissed my children goodbye, leaving them in the care of their sitter again. Riding down to the funeral home in the city, I stared out the car window and said nothing. My heart was as chilled as the air outside.

Walking up the steps to the viewing room I still didn't feel anything.

Maybe this isn't going to be as bad as I thought.

Looking back at Carol, who was following me up the stairs I said, "This is so strange, but I don't feel anything."

She simply responded "It's okay Sil Lai, everything is going to be okay."

I wondered what in the world she was talking about. *Everything is okay.*

Everything was okay for the next four seconds, but once my foot hit the landing at the top of the stairs, I could see my sister. Her body looked small and stiff, surrounded by the flowers in the room and the tufting of the casket. Suddenly, whatever had been holding me together for the past few days ripped apart and I doubled over. Legs buckling, I gripped my stomach and fell on one knee. Tears flooding my face, my brother Daniel gently lifted me up and carried me over to the coffin. Holding my shoulders, he half-carried and dragged me to her casket.

My tears clouded my vision…I couldn't see. Wiping them away, over and over, I strained to compose myself but it didn't work.

I can't take this…oh God, I can't take this. It hurts so much…please God…

I wanted to take my life and breathe it into her, to shake her and force her to open her eyes. My heart pleading, I wished as hard as I could, praying that God could hear me.

Wake up, baby! Wake up!

But she wasn't going to open her eyes. This was not sleep. She was gone…forever.

Lurching away from the coffin, I buried myself in my brother's arms. His arms were all that kept me from clawing at the curtains and flowers in the room. I wanted to bring everything down around me.

THIS IS NOT FAIR! I screamed silently.

Nothing was right…even the sun didn't have a right to shine that day. Not while my sister was lying dead in a coffin in this funeral home with tacky floral drapes. How could the world go on as if everything was normal when my life as I had known it had ended?

The Sound of Silence

After the funeral ended, I went home to my apartment and sat with my pain, suffering in wretched silence while my children quietly watched. Nothing can prepare us for the incredible sense of aloneness that occurs once the ceremonies around a death are over. The calls stop and life moves on while we stay stuck. Everyone just fades away to return to the simple routines of their lives while we struggle to make sense of the senseless, and battle the questions that circle in our mind.

Why did May Lai only use heroin for a year and die when so many addicts abuse the drug for decades and don't?

Why was I able to get sober but she couldn't?

Why did I survive my suicide attempt but she couldn't survive an accidental overdose?

Why did that idiot roommate of Jack's have to shut that door?

My faith in the goodness of life was seriously shaken. Just when I thought I had finally discovered my faith I had to suffer yet another loss.

Sometimes All We Have Is Acceptance

With time I eventually came to learn that I was never going to get a good answer to these questions. Yet somehow I was able to reclaim my faith out of the terrible loss of my sister. I still don't know why my sister had to die. I still don't know why I got sober and she didn't. I still don't know why I survived my suicide attempt and she didn't survive an accidental overdose. I still don't know why Jack's roommate shut the door. Still. Nine years later. And probably I never will.

166

What I do know now is that there is a higher purpose for me on this earth. I have that faith. I know that everything that occurs in my life is to help me evolve into a more loving and conscious person. Period. That is my faith.

Faith Summarized

Suffering is a part of life, but we don't have to allow our suffering to define us. There are lessons for us to learn from in even the most difficult of circumstances, if we seek to understand the lesson. Even if we don't look for the lesson, it may still come to us, for with time comes wisdom. The ancient Greek playwright Aeschylus wrote eons ago, *"He who learns must suffer. And even in our sleep, pain that cannot forget falls drop by drop upon the heart, and in our own despair, against our will, comes wisdom to us by the awful grace of God."*

With enough time knowledge will come. It may not happen today…or tomorrow…it may take years, but as long as that is our goal we will find it. Our perspective is the key to this process. If we believe that the lessons in our life are divine punishments designed to hurt us, then we will not be able to see the opportunity for growth.

Faith is a limitless principle which can be used to our advantage or disadvantage. Faith is not about religious rituals or about how much we donate to our church. It comes from a belief in the innate goodness of life itself. We should protect faith as one of our most cherished possessions. It is a principle that will lift and uphold us on our life's journey.

$\mathscr{L}$OVE

Continually Challenge & Expand Your Concept

"Love makes your soul crawl out from its hiding place."

~ Zora Neale Hurston

In the previous chapter we examined how painful circumstances can be used to help us find faith. After developing our faith, the next SEPIA principle for us to explore is *love*. Love has been written about through the ages and still continues to baffle the wisest among us. In writing this chapter I understand that any exploration of this principle will inevitably fall short in some respects. Love is simply too large a subject to be covered in twenty some pages. But within this chapter I hope to present at least a basic idea of what I have come to understand about love.

All of the SEPIA principles are needed in order to truly experience love. Before we can express love we must acknowledge and accept it. Next, we must take action and make a commitment to love. We must also focus on our commitment and actions, ensuring that we don't act in a manner contrary to the principle. Faith is a vital component of love, for without it we will not take the risk to open our hearts. Faith enables us to move forward into love freely and without fear. Finally, humility and charity need to be constantly utilized for love to truly blossom. Pride and ego damages our ability to love, and charity is our highest expression of the principle.

This chapter specifically deals with the definition of love and self-love. While the next chapter focuses on romantic love and relationships. The reason these components have been separated is because we must first understand the importance of self-love before moving into the realm of romantic love.

In this section we'll discuss how vitally important it is to our spirit and to those around us that we love ourselves. We'll also explore how our actions can only manifest one of two things: love or fear. Finally, we will look at how through loving discipline we can not only positively affect our own life but the lives of those around us.

What Is Love?

When the word love is mentioned, what is the first thing that comes to your mind? Do gentle thoughts of family bring a lingering smile or does it hearken to the feeling of a warm bond between friends? Does the word call forth the sense of a power greater than ourselves that watches over our every move, ensuring our protection from harm? Or does it evoke sentimental memories of romantic dinners complete with passionate kisses, flowers, and candlelight?

We all carry a basic concept of this principle around in our hearts, and that concept is the foundation of our relationships with others. It's important that we have a clear understanding of our version of this principle before we can begin to grow in this area of our life.

Love Defined

Love is traditionally defined as a strong, positive feeling of affection towards us or others, but this overly simplistic definition often creates confusion over the true nature of love. The late psychiatrist M. Scott Peck gave a beautiful definition of love in his classic book on psychology and spirituality, "The Road Less Traveled." He described love as *"The will to extend one's self for the purpose of nurturing one's own or another's spiritual growth."* Think about the ways in which the word is used today. It's very easy to get caught up using it in a casual way that is not truly reflective of the profound nature of this powerful word. When someone says, "I love money," or "He loves his job," they are not describing love. They are really saying that they enjoy and are attached to having that activity or object in their life. Using M. Scott Peck's definition, a feeling can only be love if it generates spiritual growth. Material things and activities are enjoyed in and of themselves, but they don't necessarily lead to our spiritual growth or anyone else's.

Love is a noun, but it's also a verb. I recall vividly hearing Oprah Winfrey say quite emphatically on her talk show a few years ago, *"La-dieees, how many times do I have to tell you, love is not a word, it's an action!"* Oprah was basically stating that saying we love ourselves (or anyone else for that matter) is not the same thing as actually doing it. How many times have we heard someone say they love us, even as they act in a non-loving manner? How many times have we said that we love ourselves, yet acted in ways that are self-destructive?

True love is not a feeling. It is a committed decision. When we truly love, we do so whether or not a loving feeling is present in our heart at any given moment. When we love ourselves, we won't act in a manner detrimental to our well being. Even when we're feeling down and out, we will not consciously choose to place ourselves in harm's way. Self-love doesn't mean walling ourselves off from the possibility of painful experiences, it just means that we'll thoughtfully consider whether or not the ramifications of our actions will help us to grow or not.

True love is an active principle and is motivated by the desire for spiritual growth.

Survivors tend to be extremely confused about the true meaning of love. Motivated by the belief that something is either missing or wrong with them, they desperately seek to find love outside of themselves. Most survivors believe they will be able to lead a happy and productive life once they find that special someone to love. This flawed perspective leads them further and further into a cycle of self-defeating and compulsive behaviors. What they are seeking is attachment, not love.

It's Not Love, It's Dependence

People who believe someone else can give them the love they need in order to be happy are acting like parasites. A parasite is dependent upon a host, and needs to take from another living being in order to survive.

An example of a parasitic relationship is that between a remora and a shark. Remoras are little fish that attach themselves by way of small suction cups to the underbelly of a shark. Once attached, they feed off the scraps of food that drift from the host's mouth. Remoras are lazy creatures. They can swim independently but usually don't, unless they are looking for a new host. A remora's entire life consists of finding hosts it can attach to so that it can get what it needs to survive.

Survivors live like remoras, moving about waiting to find a host they can attach to so they can try to satisfy their emotional or physical needs. What they don't realize is that while they may be able to get certain physical needs met through others, but they will never find the love that their spirit is truly seeking in this way. Contenders know that before they can love anyone else, they must love themselves. Contenders understand that love is a principle they must own before they can give it away. Their actions are motivated by a desire to either grow or to help others grow spiritually.

The Law of Correspondence states, *"As within, so without."* One of the greatest truths in this world is that we cannot receive love until we give it, and we cannot give it until we love ourselves first. Most people claim to love, but many people fail to ever learn how to truly love themselves, let alone another person. This is usually because of the misinformation they are given throughout their lives about the principle. Many believe that love just happens, but that is not true. Emotions can just "happen," but love is something that develops over time.

Four Different Types of Love

The Ancient Greeks gave the world timeless descriptions for love. They had many different versions of this principle, but the four we will focus on in this book are:

- Storge
- Philia
- Eros
- Agape

Storge

Storge is the kind of love shared between family members. Through the consistent loving between a parent and child, a child learns to love herself. If the child is treated with care and concern for their spiritual growth, she will grow to love herself in the same way. Unfortunately, because of ignorance about the true nature of love, and/or a lack of self-love, many parents fail to teach a child self-love. When a child is treated in unloving ways she grows up to believe she is inherently unlovable. A child who believes that she is unlovable will grow into an adult still manifesting a lack of self-love through outwardly destructive or self-destructive behavior. Anyone, be it a child or an adult, who is acting in a destructive manner, is simply manifesting a lack of self-love.

Philia

Philia is love between friends. It is the second type of love that we learn after the love of family, and it's usually learned during adolescence. This is the time when we learn to care for others in friendly, non-sexual ways. We spend time with friends of both sexes, bonding through mutual likes and dislikes, and looking out for each other's best interests. Philia is a very fundamental type of love. It is not one based upon the spirit, but upon shared interests.

Eros

Eros is romantic love. Like Philia, Eros is first expressed in adolescence, but unlike Philia, it always contains a sexual motivation. Eros is considered an immature love because it is based on lust. We don't even have to like someone in order to express this form of love. We simply have to be sexually attracted to them.

Agape

Agape is a spiritual love that embraces all of humanity. This form of love cares for others in an unconditional and selfless manner that is almost reverent. We become concerned with the spiritual and emotional growth of people other than ourselves, never consciously doing anything that will impede another's ability to pursue their spiritual growth. It is the most mature form of love.

Romance Is an Afterthought

Becoming self-empowered means learning to love ourselves first, humanity second and placing romance as an afterthought to our life. Romance as an *afterthought?* Yes, an afterthought! Society conditions us to look at intimate relationships as a goal in and of itself, but we will discover as we become increasingly self-empowered that finding a romantic partner will become less and less a focus of our lives. We'll begin to experience an out-flowing of love from our own heart and feel less need to fill ourselves up with the love of another. And here's the kicker: it is when we're not looking for someone else to fulfill us that we are most likely to discover romantic love! (We'll discuss this in greater detail in the next section on romantic relationships).

Why Don't We All Practice Love?

This may sound redundant, but the number one reason most of us don't love ourselves or those around us is because...you guessed it...fear. Fear is what makes us think we must attach ourselves to another person in order to emotionally survive. Fear is what makes us shrink our heart and express anger towards the world around us.

The opposite of love is fear. When we fear something, we cannot truly love it.

People say that love just is, but remember, love is an active principle. *Love is a choice that we make.* It takes courage and faith to love.

The smallest people in the world are those who have never made the effort to learn how to love themselves or others. Think about classic storybook characters like The Grinch, from Dr. Seuss' "How the Grinch Stole Christmas," or Charles Dickens' Ebenezer Scrooge, from his book "A Christmas Carol." Both characters were lonely creatures who could not love; both suffered from incredible bitterness, loneliness, and despair. They were only transformed when they opened their hearts and began to express love for themselves and others. But it wasn't the love of another that changed their lives. Instead, they both consciously challenged and expanded their concept of love and became concerned with the spiritual and emotional growth of the world around them. In return, they were rewarded with lives filled with joy and freedom. It is important to note that in both stories, they took action first, and only then did the reward come. This example is reflective of the truth of the principle that it is only through the act of loving of those around us that we truly love ourselves.

How Do We Learn To Truly Love?

We have established that self-love is the foundation of other types of love. The next question is, of course, how do we go about learning how to love ourselves? One of the first ways we can start loving ourselves is by walking away from those relationships which are not loving reflections of our spirit. We all need to learn to accept when an environment or relationship has ceased to be productive and to let go of it with dignity. Letting go of circumstances we have outgrown will be uncomfortable…it will most likely be very emotionally painful, but by embracing the pain that we are feeling *at the time it is occurring* we will be able to move through it much more quickly. Embracing emotional pain can be a liberating experience, and suffering is a sign that we are on our way to moving past our present situation.

Comparison Between Types

SURVIVOR	CONTENDER
• Believes that others can give them self-love.	• Knows that self-love comes from within.
• Thinks that love requires no effort.	• Understands that love is an action.
• Allows their fear to limit their ability to love.	• Has faith that by loving themselves they are able to love others and help them to grow spiritually.

The Importance of Self-Love

As we have seen, self-love is one of the most integral parts of self-empowerment. The following story illustrates how easy it is for someone to develop a distorted perception of the seventh SEPIA principle. It also describes how I was able to successfully challenge my long-held concept of what love is and to learn to truly care for myself.

For a very long time I placed little importance on developing any love in my life that was not directly related to courtship. This wasn't a conscious decision…it was something I did without any thought at all. I simply didn't have any interest in putting my energy into relationships that weren't romantically oriented. Driving this behavior was the belief that I would only have the foundation I needed in my life to succeed if I were in the right relationship. In a way I was very much like Dumbo the flying elephant.

In Disney's movie of the same name, Dumbo was an elephant with ears large enough to use for wings. The problem was that he was terrified of flying. A friend gave him a feather and told him that as long as he held it in his trunk he would be safe from harm, so he took his friend's well-meaning advice to heart and never attempted to fly without his feather. In a critical scene in the film, the feather slipped out of Dumbo's trunk while he was in mid-air, and because he believed he was powerless without it, he fell straight to earth with a crash.

A romantic relationship was my feather and my fear of living my life alone eventually led me to get involved in all sorts of destructive relationships. When they inevitably failed, I would emotionally crash, each time harder than the last time. The love that I was pursuing in others was a desperate attempt to fulfill my lack of self-love.

On an intellectual level I realized that my belief system was off base, but I held fast to my hope that Prince Charming was going to rescue me from my miserable existence. Society trains us from the time we are little girls that this sort of thing actually happens. Sleeping Beauty…Cinderella…Snow White. I read these and a whole host of other fairy tales as a small child, and like many little girls, I took them to heart. These tales whispered of a handsome and valiant prince who would sweep into the life of a forlorn young woman to rescue her from her tragic existence, and each man that I dated was another chance for me to make my fantasy come true. Of course, no man could fulfill my fantasies completely, and when it became clear that he was just another human being like the rest of us, I would discard the relationship.

For reasons still unclear, I believed that I was inherently unlovable. I thought that maybe if I were whiter, or shorter, or quieter, or smarter, maybe someone would be willing to love me. This belief may have stemmed from abandonment by my biological mother, or it could have come about because I never knew my biological father. Or maybe I was just born believing it. I have since realized that the reasons for my belief that I was unlovable are less important than understanding why I am lovable.

All the Wrong Places

As a child, there was nothing I wanted more than to be loved by my parents. Not just the "keeping a roof over our head and food in our belly" type of love I received, but the hugs and cuddles I didn't seem to get. I craved my parent's affection, but they were very uncomfortable with physical displays of love, and instead expressed their love in very practical ways. Basic clothing, a clean home, and three meals a day weren't enough for me...I wanted more.

As a child I believed that if I were good or helpful enough they would give me what I needed. At a young age I tried to earn their love by being indispensable around the house. At the age of four I would change my baby brother's diapers and babysit my younger sister, and by the age of ten I would shadow my stepmother in the kitchen and help her clean the house. None of my good actions earned me an overt display of love and acceptance, but my negative actions sure got me attention!

My parents' favorite form of punishment was to banish me to my room for weeks at a time, many times without any real discussion. When I started using alcohol at thirteen I pushed back...hard. I began to reject them as much as I felt they had rejected me. Once it became clear that they would never give me the love and acceptance I wanted, I began to actively seek it outside the home.

I discovered that boys were a way to get the affection I so desperately desired, and began to act out sexually by the time I was fourteen. In my quest for love I would sneak out of the house...waiting until it was late at night to rip the screens away from the windows so I could climb outside into the dark of night and into the waiting arms of a boy I barely knew. As I got older I stopped creeping out of the house and began to boldly stride out the front door, any time I pleased.

My parents tried to stop me from acting out on my sexual impulses by shaming me and placing harsh restrictions on my freedom, but they were never successful. Nothing could stop me from seeking self-love from others once I discovered that I could momentarily feel what I *thought* was love by sexually relating to boys.

Every tryst was a fix, a high, a momentary escape from the heartbreaking isolation that I felt at home and in school. It didn't matter that the boys didn't really care about me. Thirty minutes of passion gave me the feeling of being wanted, of being accepted, of being okay.

I didn't know that I had anything else to give other than sex. I had no idea how to connect on a level that didn't somehow involve the promise of or the actuality of a sexual connection. Lust and love were interchangeable to me.

Relationship After Relationship

Because of the warped way I used sexuality to try to meet my emotional needs, I carried a fear based belief that *all* men were incapable of controlling their erotic impulses and had ulterior motives in their friendships with women. This belief was simply a projection of my inability to relate to male friends in non-sexual ways, but I held the belief well into my early twenties. It wasn't until after my son was born that I was able to develop a friendship that finally opened me up to the principle of spiritual love.

Randy was a man I met through an ex-boyfriend. Tall, attractive, hard working, and single, he set many women's heart aflutter with his physical and spiritual beauty. He was a fervent Christian who dedicated much of his free time to helping others and attending church. Our friendship developed at a time in my life when I was active in the church. We spent many a Sunday afternoon together going to church or brunch. Sometimes we would just sit in the park and talk about God and religion for hours.

This friendship was the first time in my life I was able to experience a form of love between a man and woman that didn't have sexual overtones. Randy had made the decision to remain celibate until he was married, and he treated every woman he met with respect. His platonic expression of love allowed me to feel safe enough to challenge and expand my concept of love. He showed me that it was possible for men and women to care for one another without any hidden agendas.

Through his platonic expression of love, I came to believe that not all men were untrustworthy, and if just one man were capable of disciplining his behavior, then surely there must be others. Randy's self-discipline was inspiring, and slowly I began to develop feelings for him that were not strictly platonic. Finally, after two years of steady friendship I gathered the courage to confess my love to him.

In a very gentle, but firm voice he responded, "Sil Lai, you aren't in love with me. You are still sleeping with other people. You just think you are in love with me because I am probably your first male friend who hasn't tried to have sex with you."

"Randy, I swear that's not it! I really do love you! I can't explain it, but it's true!"

As much as I tried to convince him otherwise, he was not convinced by my assertions of love. His rebuff bruised my ego, but he was right. I would not have been able to love him, because I didn't love myself. Fortunately he was disciplined with his behavior and spared us both the pain of discovering through trial and error that I was incapable of truly loving him at that point in my life.

Since coming to a different understanding of love in my thirties, I've developed many friendships with men that are platonic. But before I could do so, I had to take action and work to purify my own spirit and intentions *first*, before I could expect another person to respond to me in kind.

Taking Action...With Love

Is love in action in your life? Do you take action with the people you love or do you choose to remain a passive participant? Deciding if we will love is not something that we need to ponder for any great length of time. Fear can grip our heart and prevent us from taking the action that we need to love ourselves and those around us.

A survivor allows the wounds from past experiences to dictate their potential for the future. A contender actively uses the principle of love in all that she does. She asks herself the question "Is what I am going to do adding to my/their spiritual growth, or will it take away from it instead?" She allows herself to be vulnerable and open to love. As we continue to follow the truth of our spirit, we will come to understand that there is a divine plan for all of us on this Earth. That plan includes those who we *choose* to love.

Learning to Love Through Loss

In the previous story in this chapter I described how my perception of others was transformed through the selfless love of another. In this story I share how I was able to discover how I was able to expand my concept of love through my relationship with my biological mother.

My birth mother left my siblings and I one day when I was four years old, never to return. We were left to be raised by the biological father of my younger siblings. From the day that she left until the day that I found her, twenty-two years later, I wondered why she had abandoned us. My thoughts were simple questions to which I could never fathom an answer.

Did she ever think of us?

Why had we never heard from her again?

Was she dead?

How could a mother abandon her children? It was an incredible idea to wrap your head around...and no matter how much I tried, I never could. At twenty-seven I finally stopped wondering and took action to try and get some answers.

At the onset of my search I asked my brother and sister if they wanted to see our mother again, but they were indifferent. It didn't seem to matter to them if they ever saw her again. In some ways this was understandable... my sister was under three years old and my brother was shy of one when she disappeared from our lives. They had been raised for most of their lives by our stepmother, the woman they considered their mother. For me it was different. Her image haunted my mind...fluttering memories of long thin fingers with crimson painted nails, a cigarette dangling from the tips. She was a part of me...and me of her. Aside from my brother and sister, no one in my family shared my blood. I wanted...no, I needed to see her again.

A Needle in a Haystack

Finding a person who has been missing for twenty-two years should be difficult. After all, there were decades separating me from the person I remembered...decades that could erase entire lives. In one of the most fortuitous events of my life, I was able to find our mother within two months of starting my search. It didn't cost me much to find her...in fact, all it cost me was a stamp and a book entitled, "How to Locate Anyone Anywhere Without Leaving Home." The book mentioned that one of the ways to locate a person is through the State Department of Motor Vehicles. The trouble was, I didn't know if she still used the same name or even what state she lived in. When I mentioned to my dad what I was trying to do, he looked up their divorce decree and read off the information listed on it. One of the items listed on the decree were their assets, which were negligible to say the least. The only asset my mother had put on the paper was her car, with year, make, and license plate number of the vehicle listed.

With just the license plate number of the car my mother owned in 1974 and her name at the time of the divorce, I wrote a letter containing this information to the State of California's DMV, and asked them to forward a letter I had written to her. It was a long shot for sure. I didn't know if she was even alive...let alone in the state of California, but I figured it was worth giving it a try.

One month later I received a phone call at my office.

"Good afternoon. This is Sil Lai speaking. How may I help you?" was my standard greeting.

I heard nothing but soft whimpers on the other side of the line.

"See You Lai?"

I froze. It had been twenty-two years, but I still knew my mother's voice. It had been almost a quarter century since she had left Hong Kong, but she still spoke with a slight Cantonese accent.

"Hello?" I asked.

"See You Lai, it's your mother, Daisy."

Twenty-two years of wondering disappeared in that moment as my heart leapt toward her with joy. And with that one brief sentence, my soul opened up.

Following that initial brief call, we began speaking regularly at night. For the first few weeks we would speak every night…both of us trying to condense two decades of living into three hour long conversations. Finally, after two weeks of talking on the phone, she decided to fly to New York to see us. May Lai and my brother Daniel flew to New York as well for the big reunion.

Looking into my mother's face for the first time in years, I finally saw what so many people take for granted every day: history. She was tall with an upright and aloof bearing and carried herself with a slightly nervous energy. Her laugh was like mine…loony and unrestrained. We had similar habits. The way our eyes froze when we were asked an uncomfortable question…our tendency to speak bluntly and directly…the way we opened public restroom doors by holding the top of the door with our left hand instead of using a paper towel to grip the doorknob like most people I know.

The most wonderful part of speaking with her face to face was simply watching the emotions dance across its rounded surface. Although I was now an adult, still trapped within me was the soul of a child who had lost her mother all those years ago. To have her back in my life was one of the greatest gifts in my life. My heart was awakened to an incredible sense of happiness.

Finally, I thought, *I am complete.*

My mother, or Daisy as she liked to be called, was brutally honest in disclosing the reasons she left all those years ago. With an impassive expression, she shared how frustrating it had been for her to lose track of us and how she had given up hope of ever seeing us again. Her marriage to our father was a stormy one and she remarried not long after the divorce. Twenty years later, she was still married to the same man.

Her candor was endearing. I trusted her and opened myself up completely to this stranger, my mother. The reason for her prolonged absence in our lives was of no consequence. It never occurred to me that perhaps there were other less obvious reasons why she stayed away so long, and I naively accepted her story at face value.

Playing Favorites

As time went by, a strange dynamic began developing between my mother and all of us. It was subtle at first…but quickly became obvious. It started with Daniel. I noticed that she was distancing herself from my brother and asked her why. Her response was strange, coming as it was from a woman who had just been reunited with her long lost children.

"Your brother is so hard to talk to," she said, "He never really has anything to say. He's just like his father."

"Yeah, Dan is an island unto himself," I agreed. "But he's nothing like Dad. He just needs time to get to know you before he opens up."

I left the subject alone after that…assuming that she would eventually work past her feelings. Secretly I suspected that the real motivation behind her behavior was that she felt she had been displaced in my brother's heart by our stepmother Julie.

Not long after that, my mother's calls to me became less frequent as well. Interestingly, when I asked if Daisy was still calling her, my sister said that they spoke all the time. I was a little hurt, but brushed those feelings aside; telling myself that they were just old sibling rivalry issues and nothing was different between my mother and me.

Your mind is playing tricks on you Sil Lai! You are just imagining things…

Then one day something happened that was so seemingly insignificant that it barely registered in my consciousness. Daisy and I had been having a conversation on the phone when it occurred. I don't recall the exact details, but at some point I made the mistake of telling her that although I hated the *way* in which our father had raised us, I respected him for at least putting a roof over my head and food in my stomach.

There was a deep silence on the other end of the phone for a moment, and then she changed the subject.

"Have you ever watched those talk show family reunions?' she asked.

"I've seen some, why?"

"You know, those shows never tell the stories about reunions that don't have happy endings. Did you know that most families that come together after years and years apart don't usually stay in touch afterwards?"

Red flags should have been waving in front of my eyes, but I was so wrapped up in my excitement that I couldn't see what was happening. I naively assumed that the reason she brought up the subject was because she was afraid of *us* rejecting *her*. It never occurred to me that she was getting ready to walk away from us again. In retrospect, if I had opened my eyes to the truth of the situation I could have seen it coming from a mile away.

For Whom the Bell Tolls

Daisy lived in southern California and because of the time difference between there and New York, we often spoke late at night. When my phone rang early one morning at 2 a.m., I wasn't particularly surprised to hear her voice.

"See-You Lai, I have to tell you something," she began, with slightly slurred speech. "I don't think we should talk to each other anymore."

Her words sent me rocketing up to an upright position in bed. I was instantly awake.

What did she just say to me?

An aching hollow feeling began to spread in my gut. My breath came in quick pants as I tried to absorb what she had just said. Hearing the slur in her voice gave me some comfort.

She's just drunk. She doesn't know what she's saying.

My father had told us a few stories about her drinking over the years, but I had just assumed that any problems she had with alcohol were in the past. Clearly that wasn't the case if she was dialing me in the middle of the night intoxicated.

Glancing over at my daughter asleep in my bed, I got out of bed and walked down the hall to my bathroom, shutting the door firmly behind me.

In low tones I responded to her statement. "What are you trying to say? Did I do something to offend you? If it was something I said, let's talk about it," my words came out as calmly as I could muster, with only a faint tremor in my voice.

I continued, "I'm sure we can work this out. It would be a shame to walk away from each other without giving our relationship…"

Abruptly she cut me off.

"You are controlling and bossy. You remind me of my sister Judy in Hong Kong. You are both alike: materialistic and so concerned about what you have."

I was dumbstruck as she continued, "I wouldn't choose you to be my friend! You just happen to be my daughter, but just because you are, doesn't mean we need to be in each other's lives. I don't think we should speak to each other anymore."

The words slipped out of her mouth with such ease, such icy precision, that they almost seemed rehearsed. As tipsy as she sounded when I first heard her on the phone, her apparent anger focused her speech with alarming intensity.

Tears welled up in my eyes and streamed down my cheeks. I couldn't believe what I was hearing.

For the next hour I questioned her resolve from many different angles, but she never wavered once. Her mind was made up and she was not going to change it.

In that hour my heart was shattered into a million little pieces. Part of me wanted to shout at her that she couldn't do this to me, but I knew there was no point. Her mind was made up. There was nothing I could do but accept what she had to say.

In a barely audible voice I whispered, "I'm sorry you feel this way, but I want you to know the door is always open if you change your mind."

The silence between us was deafening. After a moment of uncomfortable dead-air she finally responded.

"Uh, okay See-You Lai. Bye." And with those final four words she was gone.

It had taken twenty-two long years for me to find my mother and only seven brief months to lose her again. Never in my wildest dreams during those months did it occur to me that my mother would walk away from me a second time. As these thoughts struck my heart, I curled myself into a tight little ball on the rug on the bathroom floor. A lifetime of rejection began to spill out in low pitiable sobs that wracked my body. I cried the tears of a child who has lost her mother...of a woman who has lost her hope.

Why? Why? Why? I wailed.

What was so wrong with me that even my own mother would reject me? Twice!

For almost an hour I cried on the pale blue acrylic rug, face pressed against the soft surface. When the tears wouldn't flow any longer and my breathing had returned to normal, I dragged myself off the floor and back into my bed, nestled close to the warm and comforting body of my daughter.

Strangely, I found that in spite of my heartache I was filled with a sense of peace. It was as if God was with me in that small, five by nine room that dark morning. My mother was gone. She didn't want me now, and she never really had. Most importantly, there was nothing in the world that I could do about it. The truth was that I had opened myself up to loving her and she wasn't able to love me back. Her reasons for rejecting me were her own creation. She had abandoned me again, yet I was still standing. She couldn't allow herself to love me or my brother. But I still loved her. Nothing that she said to me that night changed that.

It was only by accepting her, with all of her limitations, that I could accept myself. By choosing to love her in spite of what she had done, I was showing self-love. Had I not opened up my heart entirely to her, I would not have been able to *emotionally* understand that her abandonment of me and my siblings as children had nothing to do with us. And although I didn't know it at the time, our reunion was a tremendous gift of love from my mother. I still loved her, although I had to let her go. My mother was a survivor and was allowing the ghosts of her past to dictate the outcome of her future. She was simply not willing to allow herself to be vulnerable and open herself up to love.

Love Summarized

We all desire to love and be loved, but who amongst us has the courage of spirit to allow ourselves to be vulnerable enough to risk it? *That* is the great Catch-22. In order to get the most out of life we have to be willing to allow life in. If we take the chance to be vulnerable with our hearts, what is the worst thing that could happen to us? We could be heartbroken...and we will live...and we will grow...and we will move on.

In order to truly love another, we must first learn self-love and after mastering self-love we can then move on to the platonic love of others. Next, we learn how to love romantically, and finally we learn to love others in a spiritual way. If we are to learn how to love others spiritually, we must control our desires. We never know how one act of self-restraint can change a person's entire outlook on life *for the better*. It takes self-discipline to do so, but the benefits to our spirit will far outweigh any momentary physical gratification we may derive from indulging in fleeting pleasures.

In the next chapter we'll continue our discussion on the principle of love, but focus on its romantic component. The act of loving those we care for requires us to make their happiness essential to our own. When we begin to actively love those around us in unselfish ways, we'll be ready to move on to engage in healthy intimate relationships.

$\mathscr{S}$IDEBAR

A Word on Romantic Relationships

"Spiritual relationship is far more precious than physical. Physical relationship divorced from spiritual is body without soul."

~ Mohandas Gandhi

A discussion on love would not be complete without talking about *romantic love* for relationships are the arenas that test our ability to love one another spiritually. Teilhard de Chardin, a nineteenth century philosopher and mystic observed, *"We are not human beings having a spiritual experience. We are spiritual beings having a human experience."* It is when we fail to acknowledge this that the simple struggle to connect intimately with another human being can become an epic disaster. Intimate relationships not based on a spiritual connection tend to very rocky because the foundation of the relationship is based upon externals or emotional needs, things which always change over time. This is not to say that a relationship with a spiritual foundation is a guarantee of lifelong partnership, as there are no guarantees in life. A strong spiritual connection *will* however provide a safe arena for two spirits to grow and expand. This deeper connection spares both parties from much of the routine discord that permeates most relationships, for the compassion and acceptance that arises from having a spiritual bond eliminates much of the selfishness and egocentricity prevalent in traditional partnerships.

Relationship Defined

"Relationship" is a subjective word, but in this book the term is used to define a committed romantic partnership. As so many of us have experienced, the issue of commitment within an intimate relationship can be exceptionally challenging. Though the reasons for this vary, many times it is clashing ideas about what exactly constitutes commitment and differing intimacy needs that is often at the root of conflict. Until these issues are explored, accepted, and then constructive action is taken to meet both partners' needs, conflict will remain at the core of the relationship.

More on Commitment

At its worst, this conflict can manifest in what is called a "commitmentphobic relationship." Many of us have had the painful experience of being in a relationship with a person who was ambivalent about being in a relationship with us. These relationships are often exciting, uncertain, and passionate… in short, dramatic. Relationships of this nature are not based upon a deeper spiritual connection, even if we feel as if this person is our "soul mate." They are based upon "how they make me feel."

It may be hard to accept, but all of our relationships are mirrors of our spirit. Whenever a commitmentphobic dynamic is occurring, there are *two* ambivalent partners, not one. Both have commitment issues, for people who are truly seeking love and commitment do not spend their time trying to create a relationship with a person who is not seeking to do the same. A relationship is like one coin…there are always two sides, but it is still one coin. The one running away from the relationship is just actively expressing their fear. The other partner is a passive participant, but stays in the relationship for exactly the same reason. Both are disempowered because they react to the relationship based upon their partner's actions or lack thereof.

Although we may feel as if we are a victim of our partner's conflicts, the truth is that if we choose to stay in a relationship with someone who is ambivalent about being in one, they are simply reflecting back to us our own issues with commitment.

You Are Not a Victim

People who have difficulty making romantic commitments often struggle with this issue in all areas of their life. If a person can't sustain a commitment in other areas, they will not be able to commit to those they love. This does not mean that they won't try...very often a person with commitment issues will actually make a commitment, but it is done with lots of room for flexibility. For instance, they commit to being in a relationship as long as the person lives in another city...or they commit to being in a relationship, but are rarely physically present because they are always working or traveling. The key thing to remember is that the fear of being smothered by another's emotional needs and being frightened of their own is what drives them to this sort of behavior. It is not a question of whether or not they love you. If they are running from you, it's probably because they do care. But their fear gets in the way of them actually being able to consistently show up in the relationship. If they have difficulty keeping dates or returning phone calls when they said they will, then that's usually a pretty good indication of their overall problem with emotional commitment.

These relationships, regardless of how painful or disappointing they may be, contain within them the spiritual lessons we need to learn in order to grow and evolve. We are not in these relationships by accident. We chose to be in them...no one held us hostage and forced us into them. If we're in them, there is something that our spirit is trying to learn. Recognizing that our relationships are vehicles for transformation and growth is one of the first steps that we can take to empowering ourselves.

Just because a romantic interaction does not become a committed relationship doesn't mean we are unworthy of being in a committed relationship, it simply means we need to move on so that we can allow a person into our lives who is ready for the same type of relationship we are.

If we are interested in creating committed and sustained intimate relationships, we can first address our own challenges with commitment. We can look for the ways that we struggle with this issue and begin to honor the commitments that we make. Once we successfully address this issue in other areas in our lives, it will eventually filter into all of our relationships.

Too Fast...Too Soon

One of the classic ways women get hooked into an unhealthy relationship is by moving too quickly into sexual activity with a new partner. Women naturally tend to bond through the sexual act. This isn't just my opinion...this has been substantiated through scientific research. During the act of sex our brains secrete the hormone oxytocin, the same hormone we secrete when we are nursing our children. Oxytocin creates a powerful need to bond for women, but for men it doesn't have the same effect. While men also release this hormone during sex, it is in such small doses that it doesn't really create an urge to bond to their sexual partners. This is why the act of sex won't, in and of itself, lead a man to make a commitment. For a woman however, oxytocin can trick our bodies into attaching to someone we barely know, placing us at risk of creating a relationship with someone who may be *completely* inappropriate for us.

It has been my experience that the best time to become sexually involved with a partner is after you are clear that you are both seeking the same type of relationship and are, more importantly, attuned to each other on a *spiritual level*.

If Not Now, When?

If both parties are attuned spiritually and desire the same type of relationship, for many is natural to want to take the next step and marry. But before doing this it's wise to exercise restraint in our actions. The reason for this, psychologists say, is because it takes time for the hormonal charge between two people to subside to a point at which they can objectively assess whether there is enough compatibility present to sustain a marriage. Experts vary on their estimates, but depending upon the individuals, this can happen anywhere between six to eighteen months.

Relationship experts say that one of the main reasons the divorce rate is so high is because many people marry while they are still in the honeymoon phase of their courtship. Many of us will spend more time researching a car before making a purchase decision than we will learning about a potential partner before committing to marriage.

The Importance of a Spiritual Bond

Without a spiritual foundation to a relationship, a partnership can be doomed from the start. The following story illustrates how easy it can be for our unmet dependency needs to drive us into an unhealthy relationship.

John and I met in Milan when we were both modeling for the same agency, and we reconnected not long after my sister had passed away. It was a very dark time in my life. I was still struggling to cope with her death and at the same time trying to adjust to being single again after breaking up with my daughter's father. Desperate for someone or something to lean on, John came along at just the right time. Given my history of bad relationships, he seemed like a safe choice. Scott and I had only been apart for a little over a year, and I was still terrified of being brutalized again. Cloaked in fear, I got involved with John more because of his externals than his internals, although I didn't see that at the time.

Like Scott, John was also a model, but that is where the similarities between them ended. While Scott was paranoid and controlling, John was easy going and uncomplicated. There was no undercurrent of jealousy or darkness to his personality...he was about as forthright as a person can be. We also shared an intense physical attraction for the other, and that fueled much of our relationship. Our short courtship was spent indulging our physical passion, which didn't give us much time to explore whether or not we shared any other interests. As far as we were concerned, we got along just fine.

John and I married despite the fact that I wasn't sure I was actually in love with him. My secret belief was that even if I wasn't, I could fall in love with him as time went by. There was no question in my mind that I cared for him a great deal. John was honorable and kind and he treated me and my children wonderfully. He was a hands-on father figure who would get on his hands and knees to play silly games with them daily. Every night he would sit and read a story to my daughter before bedtime. It wasn't until we attempted to build a life together that it became apparent how the decision to wed had been driven (at least by me) by emotional insecurity and physical attraction. But by then it was too late. We were already man and wife.

For all of his wonderful qualities I soon discovered that aside from tending to the children, John was unprepared for his new role as a husband. The beginning of our marriage was traditional in the sense that he earned the majority of the money, so he had the final say on decisions. Uncomfortable with his authority in our relationship, I slowly began to take away his power until eventually his role in our marriage became my consort and roommate. John was unhappy with this new arrangement and tried to push back, but I pushed back harder.

Although John could be bullheaded, I was even more so, and to save the peace in our marriage he completely abdicated the control of our lives to me. His reward for acquiescing was the loss of my respect for him because he had made the foolish mistake of actually letting me take control.

A Family Affair

Once my disillusionment set in, I emotionally distanced myself from John by using my career as an excuse. I aggressively pursued a career as an event planner, working long hours at the office. These sixty hour workweeks away from home weren't enough distance, however, and I started to look for other ways to extend my time away from him. Instead of facing the truth about my marriage, I buried myself in work and household projects. Emotionally restless, I began to dread coming home at night.

"Working late again?" His words grated on my nerves like fingernails dragged across a chalkboard every time we spoke.

"Yeah, things are crazy here. I'm gonna be home late. Don't wait up for me."

I began attending more and more functions in the evening just to escape having to spend time in my stultifying home environment. Too afraid to leave his emotional support completely behind, I chose the cowards way of coping and justified my actions by telling myself that I was staying in my marriage "for the sake of the children."

Walking the Line

As the gulf between us widened, my senses reawakened to the energy of the men outside my marriage. *It's just business! Damn! Stop being so insecure!* These were the words I would tell my husband when he questioned me yet again about my constant need to network late into the night. These events were always centered on business, but my true motivation was to see if one of these other men would be a more appropriate partner. The other men only served to further frustrate me about the state of my marriage, and to highlight my husband's supposed deficiencies.

The more time I spent in the company of others, the more I wanted out of my marriage. John simply couldn't compete with my fantasies of how much better my life would be if I had a more interesting and more powerful husband. The temptation to cheat was growing within me and I knew that if I wanted to keep my wedding vows I would have to do something about my marriage quick.

One month after September 11, 2001, I finally asked my husband to move out. For him the terrorist attacks made him realize how much he wanted our marriage to work, but for me, it spurred me into taking steps to end our relationship.

When we sat down to discuss our separation, I spent hours explaining to him all the reasons why we needed to end our relationship now before things broke down any further between us. I told him that I was finding other men attractive and wanted to explore other relationships. He *still* asked me to stay.

"You'll never find another man who will love you the way that I do, who accepts you and your past the way that I have."

He had hit a nerve. Part of me was afraid to leave my marriage because John was so "normal." *Normal* people like him didn't marry people like me. This play on my insecurity almost worked, but it didn't stop me from moving forward with our separation. I was too close to the edge of temptation with other men and never wanted to cheat on my husband, and I never did, at least sexually. When I look back now, I can see that all of those dinners and conversations with others were as much an infidelity as if I had slept with them. What was in my heart was what really mattered. *That* was where I committed my adultery.

The decision for us to divorce was one of hardest decisions I have ever had to make, for this choice impacted not only my husband and me, but also on my two children. They were going to pay for the decision that we made to marry after spending only seven months dating. Although I have no regrets for marrying John, I realize that we were horribly mismatched and that our bond was the emotional dependence we had for each other. There was no spiritual foundation to our relationship...only excessive need. In retrospect, my husband and I could have worked things out between us had I been willing. But I still had no capacity for commitment at that time in my life, and as a result or marriage was just another casualty of my own "commitmentphobia."

But What If...

Experience has shown me that the only romantic relationships which have a chance of lasting are the ones in which the parties involved have reasonably worked through their personal issues and have a strong spiritual connection. Careers, children, finances, and appearances always change, but the soul and the desire to grow never leaves us. Building our partnerships on emotions and sexual compatibility simply isn't enough. A relationship that can weather the storms of time must be based upon more than our physical and emotional being.

So what is a person to do if they are already in a relationship that doesn't appear to have a spiritual foundation? The action we take really depends upon how the relationship affects one's ability to pursue their truth and quest for self-empowerment. There are relationships in which it may not be readily apparent that the seeds of spiritual love have been sown even when they are present. We will recognize these relationships, for over time they will develop into an environment which nurtures the type of growth we need on the path toward enlightenment. These are the relationships that allow us to expand and push the boundaries of who we are once we begin the search for our truth. This is not to say that while we are changing things won't temporarily become more difficult between both partners, for change is in and of itself a challenging process. But in a spiritual partnership, your beloved will not limit you in your desire to evolve into all that you are meant to be.

And what action can we take with the relationships which are not a reflection of our highest selves? We can take the action we need to honor our spirits by removing ourselves. If we choose to stay in a relationship not aligned with our truth, we will eventually be forced into a situation where the action is taken for us. If our partner is not able to accompany us on our journey, then we need to accept this and move on. They may or may not understand, but the kindest thing we can ever do for all concerned is to leave an unhealthy relationship. Remaining dedicated to our personal truth is the most important thing in this life, for we cannot truly love anyone else if we do not honor ourselves.

Romantic Relationships Summarized

Without the element of spiritual love in our romantic relationships there will be so much fear and control in our partnerships that our healthy growth won't be able to take place. Love is an expansive principle and when we are in love we must allow our beloved to continue their spiritual evolution freely while in a relationship. If we do not allow them to expand to the fullest potential on an emotional and spiritual level, they will inevitably leave, for the human spirit is not meant to be caged, even by love.

Love always expands us and we are never the same after the experience of truly allowing ourselves to be known by another. In our intimate relationships, there is only one way for us to love: with our complete heart and spirit. Approached in any other way, it will fail by principle.

$\mathcal{H}$UMILITY

Exercise It at All Times

> *"Humility and success make great partners but rarely do they live together"*
>
> ~ Anonymous

Humility is the eighth of the SEPIA principles and is a trait that is essential in order for us to transform ourselves. Without it, our arrogance and pride will blind us to what we need to change. It is also a necessary part of relationships and relating to others, for we have the capacity to do ourselves and others considerable harm if we are not humble. In our drive to prove that there are no obstacles that we can achieve…that there are no obstacles we can't overcome, we often injure the very people we care about most.

In this chapter we will explore a few of the reasons why we may not use this principle, as well as explore some of the ways we can practically implement it in our lives. We will also discuss how the absence of humility can destroy whatever we have worked so hard to achieve.

Humility Defined

Humility is defined as *"the quality or condition of being humble; a modest opinion or estimate of one's own importance."* Humility is deferential behavior lacking in any arrogance, and while it is unselfconscious and discreet, it is not ignorant. Humility is in fact an extreme awareness of one's limitations.

To practice humility is to not compare ourselves to others…but to accept ourselves along with our limitations.

To be humble is to love the truth more than we love
ourselves or our ideas about who we think we are.

Humility is necessary for those of us seeking to transform our lives, because in order to accept the truth about ourselves, we must have the humility to be able to look within and make an honest assessment of our flaws.

Many people confuse humility with the word humiliation. Humiliation is a feeling of embarrassment or an instance in which we are caused to lose our self-respect. It occurs when we feel we have lost face with others. Although both words come from the same Latin root, humility is a virtue, while humiliation is not.

In his book "New Seeds of Contemplation," the Trappist monk and author Thomas Merton said, *"A humble man can do great things with an uncommon perfection because he is no longer concerned about incidentals, like his own interests and his own reputation, and therefore he no longer needs to waste his efforts defending them."* Humility requires that we recognize our gifts, yet don't identify with them to the point that we believe we are them. Thus, a gifted painter is not a brilliant painter but merely a person who paints brilliantly. A humble person does not do things to gain fame or glory, but to use their gifts to serve others.

Why Do We Avoid Humility?

In a world that values performance over content, humility is a concept that has become almost outdated in our society. It is the proud individual who often gets the most respect from those around them, and we are admonished from the time we are young children to "strive for high-self esteem." This attitude is reflective of the profound shift in our culture from being spirit-centered to man-centered.

Up until the last century or so the word pride had a very different meaning. Pride was considered the mother of all vices, the one from which all other sins sprang forth, and for very good reason. When we place too much of an emphasis on our self-importance it creates a blind spot in our ability to view our weaknesses of character. This flaw in perspective prohibits us from being able to accurately monitor our behavior, thus allowing less desirable personality traits to grow unchecked.

Three Reasons Why We Avoid Humility

Although there are many different reasons why we avoid humility, the three we will explore in this book are:

- Feelings of Inferiority
- Sense of Entitlement
- Success

Feelings of Inferiority

Prideful and arrogant behavior is often reflective of hidden feelings of inferiority, for at its root, a lack of humility often hides the craving for a sense of superiority over others. Envious of others, a prideful person masks their low self esteem through egotistical behavior. This sort of behavior indicates a need for greater recognition.

A survivor tries to mask feelings of inferiority by engaging in arrogant behavior and constantly compares herself to others. A contender does not define herself by what others have. She has no need to be superior to others and realistically assesses herself against a spiritual standard of behavior.

Sense of Entitlement

The term "sense of entitlement" is used to describe those who believe that the world owes them something. This mindset is completely lacking in humility, for the truth is that the world owes us nothing; and indeed if anything, we owe the world. Humble people are grateful for what they have and give of themselves to others. People with a sense of entitlement are never satisfied with what they have and always want more. Even when they do get what they want, they generally don't show any appreciation or acknowledge the effort that someone has gone through to help them.

While this behavior is perfectly normal for toddlers, it's completely unacceptable in adults. A sense of entitlement can be easily spotted by observing how a person speaks. If someone consistently complains and whines about the problems in her life yet does nothing to try and change her circumstances, she clearly feels a sense of entitlement. It's up to us to change our lives, and if we aren't willing to put in the work to do so, then we too are suffering from a sense of entitlement. Our life is *our* responsibility. The belief that someone else will do it for us is not only fantasy driven, but arrogant. If we hear ourselves habitually complaining and blaming others for our problems, we should ask ourselves what we have done to improve our situation.

A survivor is unwilling to take responsibility for the quality of their life because they believe they are entitled to a good life just because they exist. They aren't willing to make the effort to change, because they honestly believe that it is the responsibility of others to provide them with the life they desire. A survivor will complain and blame others for their problems and be unwilling to do the work to overcome the problems. They are chronically dissatisfied and unhappy because they always want more.

A contender knows that she is responsible for improving the quality of her life and doesn't have the expectation that others must do the work for her. A contender doesn't expect that the world should conform to her, and she is grateful for what she has earned.

Success

Success is a very broad term generally equated with power. Our culture breaks power down into five essential categories: influence, financial, intellectual, relational, and physical. The more categories a person wields power over, the more successful they are considered to be. But each category we conquer, no matter how enriching the experience may be, also gives us another opportunity to manifest a lack of humility.

Material or professional success is what many aspire to in life, and a few are blessed enough to achieve it. Unfortunately, many of these are ill-equipped to handle it. Success can create an environment that will allow us to live in any manner we choose. This environment can be very satisfying on many levels, yet it also provides greater opportunities for the creation of a vain and proud person, completely lacking in any real perspective. The more outwardly successful we are in the world, the easier it is for our pride to keep us from examining our weaknesses. This is what Jesus meant when he said in Mark 10:25, "It is easier for a camel to go through the eye of a needle than for a rich man to enter into the kingdom of God."

We may have all the freedom in the world, but we are still enslaved if we have become trapped in a world that no longer accurately reflects the truth of who we are. A survivor doesn't question their behavior or belief systems when they achieve success. They begin to believe in their own omnipotence and lose perspective on who they truly are.

A contender doesn't define themselves by the level of success they manifest in the world. Their assessment of themselves is based upon how well they are able to stay committed to living an honest and authentic spiritual life.

Comparison Between Types

SURVIVOR	CONTENDER
• Tries to cover up their feelings of inferiority by acting arrogant and proud.	• Acts humbly and accepts their humanity.
• Believes that they are entitled to whatever it is they desire in life.	• Works to earn the things they desire in life.
• Defines their worth by the level of their outward success.	• Defines their worth by the content of their character.

The Importance of Humility

Now that we have explored some of the reasons we don't use this principle, let's look at this behavior in action. The following story illustrates how easy it can be to destroy what we have, through a lack of the eighth SEPIA principle of Humility.

The most vivid memory I have of growing up was feeling alienated and different from the rest of my family. Over the years I have met many people who have expressed that they too felt like they didn't belong. Perhaps these were just the thoughts of those who needed a justification for breaking away from their families....or maybe these thoughts were legitimate in origin. Every family is unique in the way its members experience it, and while my feelings were not unique, my circumstances were. I *was* different from the rest of my family, although my parents did their best to convince me otherwise.

I was raised in a home by two parents biologically unrelated to me, but I was not adopted, at least in the sense that most people understand adoption to mean. My mother had married the man I call my dad after she became pregnant by another...a Black man. The story I was later told was that my dad had loved my mother so much that he had married her knowing that there was a possibility that the child she was carrying wasn't his. When I was born with light caramel skin and soft wavy hair there was still room for debate as to whether or not I was his biological child. My dad was half Italian so it was assumed that maybe his Italian genes were the reason for the hint of color to my skin. It was only upon the arrival of my sister May Lai that it became clear that there was a very distinct possibility that I wasn't his child. With alabaster skin and pin straight hair, it appeared that the stork had mixed up deliveries with their first baby. By the time my brother Daniel was born, there was no way to deny what had been ignored for the last three years. I was not my father's biological child.

My parent's marriage was an unstable one, marred with drinking and violence and their tempestuous union permanently disintegrated within a year of my brother's birth. In the divorce settlement, physical custody of the children was granted to my dad, something virtually unheard of in 1975. At thirty-one years old, our father struggled to work full-time as a mechanic and care for three small children. For many single-parents, dependable childcare is a common problem, and a parade of babysitters cycled in and out of our house. These were not licensed childcare providers or career nannies...they were anyone who needed a job and were willing to accept the low paying position that my father offered. The issue of dependable childcare was soon resolved when our father began dating one of our babysitters, a young woman thirteen years his junior. Within two years they were married and a young woman who was only thirteen years older than me became our new stepmother.

Our stepmother was tall, lean, and blue-eyed, in sharp contrast to my father's stocky and swarthy build. We were a motley looking crew, and family photos were always interesting, to say the least. A Mediterranean looking thirty-something man with his barely out of the teens Aryan bride, with three young Amerasian children under the age of eight hovering in the foreground, one of which was a cedar shade of brown.

Even though our family was a walking talking United Nations, within the four walls of our home there was never any mention of race, save my Dad's occasional tirades about "those Beaners jumping the border!" Nestled in the multicultural environment that was Anaheim, California in the mid-seventies, we lived in relative peace with our neighbors from around the globe: the Hawaiian family to the left of us, the Vietnamese one to our right, and the smattering of Mexican families who lived up our street. But I was in for a quick education on the differences in racial equality once we moved from Southern California to Central Florida in the spring of 1979.

A New Perspective

Our father said he chose Orlando as our new home because the real estate was so cheap and the weather was good. Well, he had the real estate part right at least. But there is nothing good, as far as I am concerned, about sweltering 90 degree plus weather with 100 percent humidity six months of the year. Once the decision was made to move, our home was packed up into dozens of brown cardboard boxes within weeks. Everything was loaded into my dad's old white Chevy work van and a small U-Haul trailer that was pulled behind the family car, a wood paneled AMC Pacer. The trip across country took nine days, two campsites, and several cheap hotels, but we eventually settled into a predominantly white town bordering northeast Orlando, named Winter Park.

At the time, Winter Park was best known for its orange groves and college music scene, courtesy of its liberal arts school, Rollins College. It was also a highly homogenous environment, with more than ninety percent of its inhabitants white. Out of the two hundred homes in our subdivision, there was only one other non-white family, the Quinones clan from Puerto Rico. The Quinones' household was headed by their mother, a woman who worked two jobs to support her family of five children. They also had the dreaded distinction of being not just the only Hispanic family in our development, but also the only single-parent home. The rest of the neighborhood shied away from them as well as us, the multicultural blue collar family.

In between Orlando and Winter Park lies the town of Eatonville. The nation's first incorporated Black Township after the Emancipation Proclamation, Eatonville had a rich history which included being the birthplace of the great African-American writer Zora Neale Hurston. With a history like that, one would think that Blacks would have an established foothold in the community, but that was far from the case. More than anything, the presence of an all-black town served to polarize Orlando even further. Most Blacks lived at one end of town and everyone else lived at the other. It was a strange setup, given the times, but it was one that wasn't questioned. This sort of division was just the way things were.

It was only after we moved to Florida that I became aware that for many, the color of my skin mattered. As a child in elementary school I was taunted on occasion by classmates, but by sixth grade the volume was turned up as I became singled out for ridicule by the children in my neighborhood. I was viciously bullied, with taunts of "Nigger, Chigger, Sand Nigger, Porch Monkey, Jungle Bunny, and Tar Baby," becoming a daily part of my life. My ethnically ambiguous appearance was a lightening rod for their racism.

"Nigger! Hey nigger! I'm talking to you, nigger. Why won't you look at me, nigger?"

My entire sixth and seventh grade years were spent ducking and dodging these attacks. Of course, I wasn't the only child being bullied. There were always a few of their own that they singled out as well, kids who were cursed with a difference, like the little girl with asthma or the boy with a limp. But the color of my skin was especially noteworthy to them, and served to distract them from teasing the girl with Coke bottle glasses whenever I showed up at the bus stop.

Although they were considered pariahs by the white majority, I secretly envied the other dark skinned children in my school. While the white children secretly whispered about the ugliness of their appearance, their various shades of brown skin and family ties created a unifying and safe environment for them at school. Quasi-brown, I drifted around the periphery of school society, never quite fitting into any particular group. There was no cultural identification for me with anyone…I wasn't Black, White or Hispanic…I was stuck in the category of Other at a time when Other didn't exist.

Although I would occasionally complain about it to my parents, I never shared with them the extent of the bullying. Being bullied was my secret shame and I took great pains to keep the depth of my suffering hidden. It horrified me to think that my parents would see me as weak.

"Can't you do something?" I would plead to my stepmother.

"Sil Lai, sticks and stones, remember?"

"I'm gonna hit them the next time they call me names!" I would exclaim.

"Oh no you won't! We're not gonna risk getting sued because you decided to hit someone for calling you a name. You better not fight anyone, or else you'll be very sorry you did!"

I was humiliated by my inability to fight back against their racism. My mother was wrong... words can bruise much deeper than a fist. They didn't understand the extent of the damage being done to me... the self-loathing and hatred that was growing inside me like a tumor. All for something I had no control over: the color of my skin. My pleas for help were ignored, and I slowly began to believe the hateful words of my peers. There was something wrong with me...I was ugly and defective and brown.

My parents never confronted the racism I was battling. I was on my own in a town that held contempt for anyone with melanin in their skin. As far as my parents were concerned it was a non-issue, for they couldn't even acknowledge that I was black. Instead, they hid the truth about my ethnicity from me until I was fourteen.

The Lie

My father had made the decision when I was very young to keep my paternity a secret. His decision was justified under the pretext of not wanting me to feel different from my siblings. The color of my skin was hard to rationalize however, and as I grew older I began to question why I was brown while my brother and sister were not. He explained away my skin color by telling me I was born in Hawaii, and was therefore a Hawaiian.

His explanation seemed perfectly reasonable when I was a very young child of four or five, but even then I sensed that something was not quite right. Our new extended family, courtesy of my stepmother, was disturbingly distant to me, while very receptive to my brother and sister. I figured they just didn't like me because my personality was annoying. It did strike me as odd that my stepmother's mother called prunes "nigger toes," but it didn't occur to me that the family's distance could have been because of my skin color.

As I grew older and my ability to reason increased, I would occasionally bring the subject of my race up to my dad. By now his explanation was losing steam. At the age of nine we would have conversations that went along these lines.

"Dad, if I was born in Hawaii that makes me a Hawaiian, right?"

"Yeah honey."

"So, May Lai and Dan are Californians then? But that isn't a race of people, is it? So how does that make me a *real* Hawaiian?"

"Do me a favor would you? Get me some pliers from the workbench."

I wasn't stupid…I knew something was wrong, but I couldn't get a straight answer from my parents about the elephant in the living room. My skin was the color of warm sepia while everyone else in the home, including my new stepsister, was pale. My hair was beginning to spin up into tight little curls and no one in the home knew what to do with it.

"Just pull it back!" was my stepmother's answer to my pleas for help with the tendrils which were beginning to twist out of control.

It was obvious to everyone else around us that something was off as well, and while their parents didn't come out and voice their questions, their children did.

May Lai and Dan were able to assimilate very easily into our new environment, but my experience was completely different. I was having far more difficulty making friends and could never understand why everyone had such a keen interest in my background.

"So what are you?"

"What am I?"

"Yeah, where are your parents from?"

"Um, well both my parents are from Syracuse…"

"That's not what I meant. I mean, are you Black, Puerto Rican, what are you?"

"Oh, no! I'm not Black! I'm Hawaiian."

"Oh, that's good. My parent's thought you were Black. Hawaiian huh?

That's so cool! I've always wanted to go to Hawaii!"

Drinking the Kool-Aid

In time even our family absorbed the message of hate in the environment around us. I shunned all of the children who were non-white in origin...the Hispanics, the Blacks...the Asians. Though there weren't a lot of them, all of my friends were white children who didn't acknowledge the color of my skin.

My siblings and I also began to use racial slurs (at least when my parents weren't around) and we openly flaunted our ignorance. It was while engaging in a particularly ugly session of hate with my sister the summer before I started high school that my father finally told me the truth about my ethnicity.

It was the summer of 1984, an otherwise uneventful time marked by days spent cavorting in our backyard swimming pool and riding bicycles around the neighborhood. Our stepmother, brother, and new little step-sister Julia weren't at home that afternoon. It was just May Lai and I entertaining each other while our dad tinkered around the garage on his newest hobby, a Harley Davidson Electra Glide motorcycle.

We were in the kitchen, seated at the wide wooden table, swapping dirty jokes back and forth. The source of our amusement was a book, a gross joke book that especially featured ethnic humor, an awful dime store book that only ignorant grade school children and drunken college frat boys read.

"Hey May Lai! How about this one? How many Pollacks does it take to change a light bulb?"

"That's a stupid one. Give me the book!"

I handed her the book and she picked out something equally offensive.

"How do you get a Nigger to stop jumping on a bed?"

"I don't know? How do you?"

"By putting Velcro on the ceiling!" We both cackled at the visual.

Just then our Dad strode into the kitchen. The look on his face was one of disgust...he must have been listening to our exchange from the garage only twenty feet from the kitchen.

"I don't know why you're laughing Sil Lai. You're one."

Both May Lai and I stopped laughing and stared at our father.

"What are you talking about?" I asked him.

"It's true. You're Black," he said, grabbing a cold Budweiser from the refrigerator and heading back into the garage.

May Lai and I were both silent. We looked awkwardly at each other and didn't say a word. I mean, what could we say? His words threw a sheet of ice water over my head, sobering me up from the laughter from a few minutes before. To hear my father tell me that he wasn't my father and that I was black meant I was a double outcast. I was ashamed, my face burning red with embarrassment.

Jumping out of my chair, I left my sister sitting at the table as I raced across the street to my best friend Cindy's house. Cindy was Michelle's younger sister. She and I had become close after Michelle moved on to older and faster friends.

Impatient for a response, I pressed the doorbell several times. Cindy's mother had very particular ideas about the way things should be, and I knew better than to ring it more than once. But I didn't care. I had to speak to someone before my head exploded.

Cindy's plump form filled the doorway as she approached the screen door.

"Hey! What's up?"

I blurted out "I'm Black! My Dad just told me that I was Black!"

"What? Come on inside!"

Sitting down on the muted floral comforter on her bed, I tearfully recounted what had just happened a few minutes before.

Cindy was unaffected. Pulling me close, she gave me a brief hug and said, "Don't worry. No one ever needs to know."

Nodding my head slowly, I thanked her for listening. Although the last thing in the world I wanted was to go home, I had to return for dinner. If I didn't, my stepmother, or worse, my father, would come over and get me.

I was angry. I hated my father. I hated my stepmother. I hated that they had been perpetuating a lie upon me for my entire life and now I had to reconcile my entire identity.

So this is why they never did anything about the bullying, I thought. *They knew what the kids were saying was true!*

Black Girl Lost

My sister and I never brought up what had happened that day in the kitchen again, but even if we never discussed it, she knew my shame. The way we acknowledged it to each other was by never using racial slurs again.

This event ruptured the gossamer thread that still bound me emotionally to my parents. My drinking career took off around the same time and not long after my dad's disclosure I began running away from home. At the time, my conscious motivation was to avoid the strict rules of my parents' household, but subconsciously I was running away from myself as well. The next three years were one big binge of boys, running away, fights with my parents, two week employment stints, and underage drinking at house parties and teen discos. I was a stray, a child who would disappear with anyone who held the promise of love and acceptance.

In time the frizzy haired skinny sepia toned girl became a curly haired caramel colored woman child. It amused me that the boys who had shunned me in grade school were now openly pursuing me and I reveled in the newfound attention. It was amazing how such an outcast could become so hotly desired. As confidence in my ability to attract a man increased, so did my fragile ego. Overnight I went from being a girl who could never look anyone in the eye to a young woman who never hesitated to throw herself into the spotlight. And as my self-assurance grew, so did my arrogance.

Kerosene on a Fire

My racially ambiguous appearance, so long a source of pain, now became a great asset. On more than one occasion I had been told, "You should be a model" by many of the adults and young people I knew. On a whim, I walked into a local modeling agency to see if a professional assessment of me would be the same. Apparently it was, for I was signed on the spot and within the week I was shooting a commercial for an Italian ice cream. The pay was more than I had ever earned while selling clothes or burgers at the mall, and the cluck cluck fawning of the various stylists and makeup artists boosted my ego even more. Almost immediately my attitude spun out of control and the clique of hard partying friends I had run with for the past few years began to shun me, disgusted by my conceited and contemptuous attitude. The loss of their friendship didn't matter much to me...they were quickly replaced by a series of twenty something boyfriends.

By seventeen I was a full-blown diva. Orlando was too small a town for a personality this big, so I set off to a bigger pond to try my luck. An opportunity came via a well-known New York photographer I had worked with on a job in Orlando.

At the shoot she casually said to me, "You should come to New York to model. You could work in that market."

"Really? You think so?"

"Yeah, I really do. My boyfriend and I will be out of town for the last two weeks of July. You can stay at my place while I'm gone and look for an apartment."

It took me about three seconds to make up my mind to go.

Bragging to everyone I knew, I told them how I had been "discovered" by a big-time New York City photographer who thought I was too good for such a small market. I didn't ask my dad for permission to leave. I simply booked a ticket and packed my bags.

Our family was in shambles at this point. Our stepmother was no longer living with us, having left my dad and taken my stepsister with her to California in early spring. May Lai had taken to running away from home and was currently living with her latest boyfriend in New Smyrna Beach. By now it was just my brother, Dad, and I left in the house, and I wasn't going to waste this opportunity to escape as well.

I headed off to New York City the day after my eighteenth birthday with $200.00 and a one-way plane ticket in my pocket. It was 1988, the real life time of Jay McInerney's "Bright Lights, Big City" and I was quickly swept up in a kaleidoscope of nightlife. My life was a constant parade of celebrities, limousines, champagne, and dancing until 6:00 a.m., followed by drunken breakfasts at all-night restaurants like Brasserie. We would stumble out of the restaurant clad in skintight black Betsy Johnson Lycra dresses and black patent leather Aigner heels to head back home in the early morning sunlight while everyone else was walking in suits on the way to work. The *walk of shame* we would call it, laughing at our own decadence.

These were exciting times, but the greatest part of moving to New York was that for the first time in my life I felt like I belonged. The city opened its arms to me and I fell gratefully into its embrace. What was most beautiful about this experience was discovering that the hatred I had been immersed in as a child in Orlando about the color of my skin was nothing but a lie. Everywhere I looked there were beautiful people of every color. In fact, I was surprised to find an entire subculture of ambitious and successful black people. These brothers and sisters accepted me with no questions. I was never asked, "What are you?" by my new family…there was a simple and unequivocal acceptance of me that had been missing from my entire previous existence.

Bonfire of the Vanities

Despite my new glamorous surroundings, I was still full of self-loathing and tried to mask it with increasingly haughty and self-centered behavior. Others' acceptance didn't change the way I really felt. I was a not a woman, but a doll who would decorate the rooms of a party or the arms of a man. Desperately afraid to lose the one thing that I felt I had going for me, I became completely obsessed with maintaining my appearance, spending hours at the gym or hundreds of dollars at a time on skin care and clothing that I couldn't afford. I was a slave to my vanity.

My modeling career was at best start and stop, given my fluctuations in weight and tendency to drink to excess. It did, however, provide me with plenty of access to the hottest parties in town with the black entertainment elite. A New York party girl is asked to be many things…available, attractive, and lots of fun. I was available and attractive for sure, but not really fun. My bitchy attitude caused me to lose many friends, but I kept it moving. With eight million people to choose from, I was always able to find another "fabulous" person to associate with.

Fortunately or unfortunately, depending on how one looks at it, I have never been a woman of moderation. As my ego continued to grow monstrously out of control, my modeling clients began to drop me because of my attitude. Never wildly successful to begin with, my bookings began to slow down and the bookers at my agencies stopped taking my calls. Of course I couldn't see that perhaps *I* was the cause for the downshift in my work. My lack of humility completely prevented it. *They* were the ones with the problems. *They* needed to adjust their attitudes, not me.

My career in fashion came crashing down around me in the summer of 1994. Blinded by my ego, I didn't see it coming. I had just worked on some of the biggest jobs of my career and was living the high life. My boyfriend Mossimo had asked me to move into his elegant home outside of Milan. On the surface, I was living a life that many dreamed of, yet it still wasn't good enough. I was embarrassed that he only had a Cigarette boat, not a yacht. I was angry that he didn't give me a large weekly allowance. I hated that he wouldn't allow me to bring my son to Italy to live with us. When he told me that I had to wait until the Christmas holidays to see my son, I abruptly terminated our relationship and returned home to be reunited with Scott in the States.

Soon thereafter I was pregnant and sleeping on a twin mattress on the floor of Scott's sister's apartment in the Bronx. The mattress was too small for the two of us, so Scott would take a pillow and prop it under the part of his arm that extended past the edge. We were so broke that there were times we had to count pennies from a change jar in order to buy food to eat.

This second pregnancy ended my career in fashion. Three months earlier I had been living on an estate outside Milan and vacationing on a half-million dollar boat off the Amalfi coast of Italy. Now I was pregnant and sleeping on a mattress on the floor of a two-bedroom apartment in the Bronx.

Lessons Hard Learned

Despite the drastic change in my circumstances, I still didn't understand how I had created my downfall. It took several years for me to realize that I was responsible for the mess I was in. It wasn't because of the color of my skin. It wasn't because of Scott, or my bookers, or my former clients. It wasn't even my parents or Ronald's fault. No, my problems were of my own design. I was the painter and my life the canvas. In order to begin to change my life, I had to accept that I was an arrogant and self-centered person, and then work on removing my overwhelming feelings of inferiority and overdeveloped sense of entitlement. I had to become willing to take a serious look at the flaws in my personality and take responsibility for changing what needed to be changed. Until I could not only acknowledge this but accept it and then take constructive action to change my behavior, I was doomed to continue to make the same mistakes over and over. That was the bottom line.

This understanding didn't come easily. By the time I was willing to humble myself, I had pretty much burned most of the bridges behind me. The beauty of empowering ourselves is that we no longer need to be a victim of ourselves or anyone else. By embracing the principle of humility, we give ourselves the freedom to learn and grow. Humility taught me that much of my arrogant behavior as a young woman was fueled by shame over the color of my skin. This arrogance was just one of the masks I wore to try to cover it up.

Today I strive to be right-sized. I do not consider myself above or below anyone else. I am just me...flawed and worthy of love. Someone told me once, *"Arrogance is just the front office of Shame Incorporated."* His words were so funny, yet true. It is clear to me today that whenever I start to behave in a self-righteous or "better than" manner, that is simply a sign that I am feeling ashamed or threatened.

How Do We Become Humble?

After all of this has been said, what actions can we practice to become more humble? We can begin by subjecting ourselves to the same level of scrutiny that we place on those around us. By redirecting our energy to focus on our own shortcomings, we take the focus off of what is wrong with the people we know and redirect it on what we need to change within ourselves. Whenever we find ourselves appraising the character defects of others, we can channel our thoughts in a more constructive direction.

There will be circumstances when this can be difficult to do, like when we are dealing with others in business, but even then we must be careful to focus on the situation at hand and not the overall character of the person. In essence we must "Love the sinner but hate the sin." It is challenging to do but we can stop the thought process when it starts.

Finally, we can help to keep humility in our lives by keeping an accounting of our darkest and innermost secrets and then confessing them to another person regularly. Find a person that we trust implicitly, be it a priest, pastor, counselor, or friend, and share the parts of our heart that bring us the most shame. When we take the risk to "tell on ourselves" by sharing our most private thoughts, we keep our egos in check and keep ourselves open to the trusted counsel of others. This is one of the ways that we can learn how to allow ourselves to be vulnerable with another person and start to break through the walls of shame that surround us when we hold secrets in our hearts. We are not meant to shoulder the burden alone.

It can be terrifying when we first take that step to open ourselves up in this way, but trust in this process. Allowing another to see our humanity will bring a sense of humbleness into our spirit and spur us on to greater overall success in life.

Humility Summarized

Humility helps us to separate our sense of personal worth from such things as social recognition, wealth, and physical appearance, for when we are humble we will not be concerned about how others respond to our status. Humility allows us to be free to pursue our truth in earnest for we will *respectfully* no longer care about what others' opinions of us are.

In the Bible, Luke 12:18 it is written, *"To whom much is given, much is expected,"* and we must always treat our successes with respect and remember that although we may have earned it, it is *not* a given. We should always remember that we have only been allowed to succeed in order to manifest our spiritual truth, which at the end of the day incorporates the virtue of grace.

We must take care to never elevate our self-importance too high or too low because of our circumstances. Our circumstances do not define who we are…the only thing that matters is following the truth of our spirit. Take care to cultivate humility in our heart so that we may always remain open to the truth of who we are.

CHAPTER *12*

$\mathscr{C}$HARITY
It's Not an Option

"Charity is the lovely marriage of gratitude and generosity; it is an
attitude more than an act, an opening of the heart more than an
opening of the wallet."

~ John Tye

The ninth and final SEPIA principle is *charity*. Truth gave us the awareness
to know what areas of ourselves and our lives we needed to change, for
we realized that we cannot transcend what we won't acknowledge exists.
Acceptance gave us the willingness to admit to ourselves on an emotional
level the facts of our lives into the very fiber of our being, which allows
us to use the next principle of action. Action allowed us to take the actual
physical steps to transform our lives, and commitment gave us the ability
to remain devoted to our goals. The principle of focus gave us the single-
mindedness needed to remain steadfast and uphold our commitment, while
the principle of faith enabled us to remain dedicated to our path, especially
when we are experiencing fear and doubt. Love is what nurtures and lifts
us up in this journey, warming the hearts and spirit of ourselves and others.
The principle of humility not only keeps us open and teachable, it also
keeps us from destroying all that we have accomplished so far. Charity is
the SEPIA principle that enables us to continue to maintain the practice of
all these principles.

To be self-empowered is to be a leader of example for those who still struggle with disempowerment. A contender has the ability to look beyond what they want and need and think of what it is that they can do for others. This last and final step in the SEPIA process is what enables us to take the power that we have claimed and use it to affect a positive change in the world.

In this chapter we will learn why the principle of charity is an important tool to maintaining self-empowerment. We will also talk about the physical and spiritual benefits to using this principle. Finally, we'll discuss how we can not only empower ourselves, but others through charity.

Charity Defined

Charity is a principle deeply rooted in Christian tradition, and originally had a meaning nearly identical to the Greek word agape - the spiritual love one has for God. In its most literal definition, charity is the spiritual love one has for humanity.

This beautiful principle has evolved into a slightly different meaning today, but the intent behind the concept is still the same: to show a spiritual love to others through selfless acts of giving. Charity is often expressed through the donation of financial gifts, but we can also practice this principle by giving of ourselves in emotional or spiritual ways.

Charity's basic purpose is to unite human beings in their relationship with God. It is a form of love and is therefore an active principle…it requires us to get actively involved in the process of loving our fellow human beings. Acts of charity are actions of self-love, and when we love ourselves, we will show love to others through the selfless giving of ourselves. Charity means literally *loving our neighbors as we love God,* and is the conscious will to do good to and for others, whether they deserve it or not. It is very easy to love those who love us, but it is very difficult to love those who don't love us, that is, unless we have charity.

Charity doesn't seek gratitude,
only more opportunities for expression.

Why Should We Practice Charity?

There are two benefits to practicing this very powerful principle. The first and obvious one is the benefit that charity brings to those who are being helped by the selfless acts of others. The second and less apparent benefit is to the individual who does the actual giving. Charity changes our beliefs about *abundance* and anchors us in a spirit of gratitude. This shift in attitude eliminates the belief that there is never enough to go around, for in order to give to others, we must believe that we possess something of value to share. When we are grateful, we are thankful for what we have, and when we are able to acknowledge what we have, we are able to conceive of sharing.

It is said that charity breeds virtue of spirit. Of course, this statement is based upon the assumption that we are emotionally involved in the act of giving. When it is not, and our intentions are impure, the act is not charitable. Part of the expression of true charity is being aware of our motivations. If our intention is pure, only then is it charity.

There are many ways we can use the principle of charity, and everyone has an ability to give. Even if we are not deemed "successful" by the measures of the outside world, we can always find creative ways to give to others. Among the various forms of this principle, time is equal with money. Time is available to everyone, regardless of status. If we have artistic ability then we can use it to teach another how to embrace that talent within them. If we are successful in business, we can mentor those seeking to learn the basics in our industry. Of course it goes without saying that if we possess abundant financial means we can willingly share our wealth with those who are in a less fortunate position.

There are many different ways we can show our love to others, and once we begin taking advantage of this in our lives, we will discover how much more we are empowered in our own lives because of this.

Three Reasons We Avoid Charity

Although there are many reasons why we avoid using the principle of charity, the three I have chosen to focus on are:

- Ungratefulness
- Selfishness
- Scarcity Mindset

Ungratefulness

When we are ungrateful, we are unappreciative, or not feeling or expressing gratitude. Ungratefulness is usually not a conscious act. Many times it is simply the result of having a short memory. It's easy to forget the things in our life that sustain us. It can be easy to forget to say "thank you," or "I really appreciate what you have done for me." The danger in being ungrateful lies in the fact that when we forget our blessings we are unlikely to appreciate what we have or to want to share with others. Once that occurs we risk developing a sense of entitlement.

How can we tell when we are being ungrateful? One way to tell is when we complain. It's possible to find a lesson or opportunity in everything that happens to us. Everything we receive, and I mean *everything*, can be received with a spirit of gratitude. This includes the things we perceive as bad.

Survivors are ungrateful. They don't recognize their blessings and have an attitude of entitlement. This mindset creates difficulty in sharing with others because nothing is ever good enough for them.

A contender is grateful for all that she has, and doesn't waste energy complaining about what she doesn't have. She is open to sharing with others because sharing is a natural outgrowth of the love she has for herself.

Selfishness

Selfishness is the mindset or practice of placing our own interests ahead of the interests of other people. It is the polar opposite of altruism, which refers to the care and concern of others. Whether it is consciously or unconsciously done is irrelevant; the end result is the same: destructiveness to self and others.

In all fairness, it is virtually impossible to perform an act without considering what the potential benefit could be to us. To do so would be unwise and foolhardy, as it is necessary to gauge the outcome of our actions in order to assess the benefit of expending our energy. While it is impossible to be completely unselfish, what determines our level of selfishness is the extent of our willingness to put aside our own desires and needs to help another. Selfless behavior is when we make a conscious choice to help another despite the fact that we could be doing something for ourselves in that moment.

Some people don't struggle with this at all…they naturally make room for the needs of others. But sometimes, if the intention is self-centered, what appears to be charity can be selfish as well. An example of this is when a mother refuses to allow her teenage child to drive, despite having a license. The mother's reasons may be noble; she loves her child and doesn't want to risk her daughter being injured in a car accident, or she wants to use the time together in the car to bond with her child. Regardless of the reasons, her underlying motivation is selfish, for she is not considering how her behavior is impacting her daughter's development. It is an unloving act because she is placing her desire for companionship or her fears for safety for her child ahead of her child's need to learn how to operate a car safely and independently. Her "selfless" action is selfish, for her motivations are based entirely upon her needs, not upon what they both need.

Survivors tend to place their own needs ahead of everyone else's. They have a difficult time sharing freely because they are overly concerned with what they will get out of what they give. Or they swing to the opposite extreme and devote themselves to meeting others needs because of their fear of losing control.

A contender seeks to find a balance between getting her needs and desires met and helping others to achieve theirs. She understands that in order to have balance in her life she must be willing to allow the needs of others to occasionally take precedence over her own. This mindset allows her to share and give freely give to others.

Scarcity Mindset

A scarcity mindset is one that looks at life in terms of what is missing or lacking. This is a mentality that focuses on what we don't have. Everything is viewed in absolutes, black and white. If we succeed, then someone else must fail, if someone gets married, that's one less potential mate for us. It's a mindset based on fear and originating from a lack of faith.

The scarcity mindset creates selfishness based on the fear that there aren't enough resources to go around. Resources can include anything…love, money, power, etc. Because of this belief, we can become ruthless in our quest to get what we want or keep what we have.

People with this mindset believe they are victims. Instead of recognizing that their thinking is scarcity based, they believe the reason they lack certain resources is because they are unlucky. The Law of Attraction states that if they believe this to be true, it will be true. Whatever we focus our attention on increases, either in our mind or in our actual physical reality.

Universal truth states that there is more than enough love, money, and power to go around. We live in an infinite universe, with unlimited potential. Once we truly accept this, we can change our mindset. We don't have to be frantic, anxious, or greedy because we are at peace with our own lives, which allows us to care about others.

The only scarcity that exists is the one is in our mind.

Scarcity is the prevailing mindset of the survivor. Because of the losses and problems they have faced in their lives, they have become fearful of never getting what they need or losing what they have. This fear based belief system prevents them from being open to giving to others and receiving the abundance of the universe.

A contender knows that there are enough resources in this world to meet her needs. Her belief allows her to express her faith in this abundance by giving freely to others. Her giving allows the flow of her giving energy to recycle back to her, over and over again.

Comparison Between Types

SURVIVOR	CONTENDER
• Is ungrateful for what they have and focuses on what they don't.	• Keeps the focus on what they have, which allows them to practice gratitude.
• Places their needs before anyone else's consistently and without any thought about others.	• Seeks to balance meeting their own and others' needs.

- Doesn't believe that their needs will be met, which causes them to desperately cling to their resources.

- Has belief in the abundance of life and gives freely of their resources.

Looking Back

Whether we are aware of it or not, we have all experienced charity. None of us has come to where we are at in our lives exclusively by our own means. There are countless people who have affected our lives along the way with sacrifices made for the benefit of our well-being. If we look deeply into our memory, it's easy to see the times we have received a form of charity from another when we were in need. Did someone give of their time when we needed help to pull off a project that was essential to our career? Did a friend or parent help us with money when we needed to cover the rent? Was there a teacher who took us under their wing to give us the extra instruction needed to pass a course? All of these forms of charity have helped to sustain us. Part of being self-empowered is recognizing the gifts we have been given and then seeking an opportunity to do the same for others.

The former Prime Minister of Great Britain, Sir Winston Churchill, summed this up well when he wrote, *"We make a living by what we get, but we make a life by what we give."*

The Importance of Charity

My personal experience with this principle while pregnant with my first child is a strong example of how acts of giving can change the course of a life. The following story illustrates my experience with the ninth SEPIA principle of Charity.

As a child I had no idea what charity was. My understanding was limited to what I heard through the media while growing up. Each year that annoying day would come when my siblings and I would turn on our television set and find to our dismay that the Tom & Jerry or Bugs Bunny cartoons we loved had been replaced with a six-hour fundraising marathon. These telethons were for institutions like Jerry Lewis' Muscular Dystrophy Telethon or the United Negro College Fund's annual pledge campaign. Charity to us was an older man in a suit and bowtie who gathered his famous friends once a year to plead with us, the common viewer, to part with our hard earned money so that the old man could help someone else.

Since we couldn't see any immediate benefit to giving away our limited funds, charity wasn't anything that anyone in our family ever concerned themselves with. It wasn't until I became pregnant with my first child that the importance of this principle became clear to me.

Opportunity of a Lifetime

At the age of nineteen I was kicked out of my most recent apartment by my roommate for not paying my share of the rent for several months and wearing her clothing without permission. With no money and nowhere else to turn, I asked my friend Carol if I could stay with her and her husband Jean. I crashed for a few weeks on their pullout couch and while they said that I could stay with them for as long as I needed, their small L-shaped studio apartment was barely large enough for them, let alone a third adult.

At this same time I had discovered to my horror that my most recent fling, a brief relationship with a man twenty years my senior named Keith, had resulted in an unplanned pregnancy. Keith was my first love. A well respected and successful record producer, he tried to help me stabilize my life by placing restrictions on my behavior. He wouldn't allow me to drink when we were together, and he pushed me into abandoning my job as a cocktail waitress to take up more respectable work as a temporary receptionist. Although he had pursued me off and on for a year, within two months of officially dating, our relationship was over. He apparently decided that to date me would require too much babysitting and hand-holding. I was devastated to say the least.

I discovered that I was pregnant the day after he broke up with me. Confused and scared, I asked my friends what I should do.

"Tell him. It's his responsibility too. You didn't end up pregnant by yourself!"

Although I was anxious about what his response would be, I got up the nerve to tell him two days later. When I told him over the phone, he had no immediate response to my announcement...there was nothing but silence on the other end.

"Well, what do we think we should do?" I prodded.

"What do you mean, 'what do I think we should do?' We? There is no we! We aren't together, and I have no reason to believe that child is mine!"

To say that I was hurt by his rejection is an understatement. Never did it occur to me that he would turn his back on me so harshly. Keith was a well respected adult member of society and a role model to many. He had also told me that he loved me, and I believed him. At nineteen, I was so naïve that I actually believed that a successful thirty-nine year old man would stand by the side of an alcoholic party-girl who was pregnant with his child. Stunned by his rejection, I pondered my next move. I was unemployed and sleeping on a friend's couch, which was definitely not the ideal circumstance to bring a child into.

After I explained to her what was going on, my sister May Lai offered to take me into the home that she shared with a boyfriend and some friends in Santa Barbara. Even though I knew she liked to party, it seemed a better option. There I would have my own room and some privacy. Besides, I was tired of New York and figured I could pull my life together without the temptation of nightlife hovering around me. Without any further thought, I packed up the few belongings I owned and boarded a plane to California.

A New Beginning

My seventeen year old sister's home was a large, airy space in downtown Santa Barbara that she shared with her boyfriend Eric and a couple of roommates. A small bungalow-style house with a red tile roof, it was within walking distance of the historic part of town. After living in New York for the past year and a half, the culture in Santa Barbara was a shock. Everyone wore colors and walked around in flip-flops...it was a hodge-podge of wealthy silver haired residents and artists in an enclave apparently made up of the leftovers from the latest Grateful Dead tour. City blocks consisted of a mix of elegant art galleries featuring local and national artists, and head shops where you could buy Jimi Hendrix posters and bong pipes. The city's vibrant arts culture was an interesting juxtaposition against the large number of Mexican immigrants who populated the outer lying areas of the city.

I had only been staying with my sister for three weeks when my welcome was yanked out from under me and for once it wasn't because of anything that

I had done. Eric was a sober alcoholic who had been in recovery for a few years. He didn't like the fact that May Lai drank as much as she did, and he tried to curtail her drinking by enforcing limits on what she could consume. May Lai resented his attempts to control her drinking, and unbeknownst to all of us was planning her escape. One day while Eric was at work she met a good looking young man downtown. He asked her if she wanted to go to a party in Los Angeles that night, and she agreed. Before any of us had realized what happened, May Lai not only went to the party, but moved in with him that next day! Eric was understandably angry and reacted by asking me to move out as well.

Within three weeks of arriving in Santa Barbara I was on the verge of homelessness...again. I was also suffering from terrible morning sickness that lasted all day, and wrestling with the decision of whether I should continue with my pregnancy. I had always figured that if I got pregnant, I would simply terminate the pregnancy. It didn't seem to be a big deal...I considered an abortion little more than a routine procedure. When I was actually faced with this situation however, it was a whole different story. Especially since I had feelings for the father. Keith wouldn't take my calls and I was broke, scared, and alone in a city where I knew no one. Eric had given me two weeks to find another place to live, and I had no idea what to do. I didn't have a job...I didn't have a car...and I didn't have any money to pay for rent.

An abortion is the only choice I really have, I thought sadly.

But the idea of destroying the part of Keith now growing inside of me was so painful it hurt my heart to think of it. Yet, what other option did I have?

Almost Doesn't Count

One of Eric's roommates named Sophia took an interest in my situation and offered to help. Sophia was ten years older than me and had moved to the States from Italy a decade earlier. Petite and possessing an abundant head of curly brown hair, she seemed the sympathetic ear I needed. After listening to what I had to say, she advised me to get an abortion. Although I was uncertain about her solution and scared about my future, I reluctantly agreed to let her take me to the local Planned Parenthood agency. Since no appointment was necessary we decided to go the next day.

That morning I was a jumble of nerves and confusion. Still ambivalent about this course of action, I dressed quickly and met Sophia at her truck. We drove the mile or so to the clinic in record speed and found ourselves within minutes in front of the building. As we pulled her small red pickup into the short driveway, I was shocked to find a small throng of protesters holding up various sized makeshift signs. Some of the signs were quite graphic. These images were haunting...alienesque photos of embryos and fetuses superimposed upon vividly colored posterboard and highlighted with glaring admonishments of the moral and spiritual repercussions of abortion.

As Sophia slowed down to enter the parking lot, a round woman clad in bright floral prints leaned toward my window. She extended two colorful pamphlets towards me.

"Get away from her!" Sophia exclaimed. "Sil Lai, don't take that..."

"Why not? I always wanted to see what these pro-lifers have been passing out."

Ignoring her direction, I took the pamphlets from the woman standing outside the door of the car and thanked her.

"God bless you," she said smiling, and turning away.

"Seriously Sil Lai...I don't think you should look at that..." Sophia continued.

Ignoring her, I opened the pamphlet and glanced at it. A steady stream of prose outlining the sacredness of life, and statistics about the developmental milestones of a fetus, stared me in the face. I looked at Sophia.

"Did you know an eleven week old fetus has fingernails and a heartbeat?" I asked.

"Sil Lai, those pamphlets are designed to get you to doubt..."

"To doubt my decision? They haven't done that...I have been unsure about what to do all along."

"Don't let this influence your decision..."

"This isn't my decision...this is your decision. I can't do this. I love Keith too much to do this...I just can't!"

"Look, it's not my choice, it's yours...I'm just trying to help you..."

"Well, thanks for helping me, but I've made up my mind. I'm keeping my baby."

Everyone was disappointed in my decision, most of all Keith. He hung up the phone on me when I told him what I had decided to do. If I had any doubt about his position before this call, it was crystal clear now. I was completely on my own.

Saved

I needed a plan…quick. My parents were of no assistance…my stepmother had remarried and her new husband wouldn't allow her to speak to me. My father and I didn't really speak much…he was busy creating a new life for himself with his latest girlfriend back home in Orlando. It actually never occurred to me to ask any of them for help anyway. Our relationship had never been good, and given the fact they had been so vocal about their desire for me to move out of their house while I was still living at home, I didn't think it was an option. The only thing left for me to do was to try and find some sort of social services agency that would help me through my pregnancy.

I spoke with a representative at the local welfare office and was dismayed to find that the State of California would only help if I had decided to abort or if I already had the baby. Moving on to the next logical step, I began flipping through the yellow pages and found several listings for counseling…specifically pregnancy counseling. Out of all the listings in the phone book, there were only two that offered counseling services to women who had chosen to continue with their pregnancy. Both were Christian based agencies, but I couldn't let that deter me from seeking their help. If the right-wingers were the only place that I could go for help, than so be it. Beggars can't be choosers. I chose one of the two centers to call and thought to myself, *Here goes nothing.*

A friendly woman answered the line. Giving her a brief overview of my circumstances, I told her I needed help. She told me she had an appointment available for that afternoon, and I was welcome to come and meet with her in person to discuss my options.

The counseling center was housed in an attractive Craftsman style home on the edge of the historic district of Santa Barbara. Its exterior was lined with gorgeous landscaping set off with a pair of lovely rocking chairs on the front porch. Pressing the doorbell, I waited a few moments before I heard footsteps approach the door. When it opened, I found myself looking into the eyes of a very thin faced, petite white woman. She introduced herself and extended her hand.

"Thank you so much for coming by. I'm Sally, the woman you spoke with on the phone earlier today."

Sally ushered me into cozy living area of the office. It was an interesting setup; clearly this had been someone's home in the past, but it had been completely renovated and was now an office. A periwinkle blue sofa featuring an array of floral style pillows beckoned. Sally motioned for me to sit down.

"So tell me why you are here today," she said.

Over the next twenty minutes I recounted the situation I was currently facing. She didn't say much, only interrupting me from time to time to nod her head and say "Uh-huh." Her presence was strangely calming. It was such a relief to be able to finally unburden to someone with experience in dealing with my situation, someone who could actually help. By the time I got to the part about the crisis surrounding my current living situation, she was staring at me intently.

"And my ex-boyfriend won't do anything to help me and he can!" I exclaimed. "He told me he loved me, but now he won't even talk to me!"

Sally began to tell me about the various services they offered, which included religious and pregnancy counseling.

"Well, do you know of anyone that can help me find a place to live?" I interjected. "I don't want to go back to New York and be around the same people as before, but I don't have anywhere else to go." I finished, hoping she would refer me to an agency that could help me find housing.

Sally paused for a moment and then took a deep breath. "I know we just met but you seem to be a really nice girl. Another teen mom named June is currently living in my house with me and my daughter, but there is another room you can stay in."

My eyes widened as I realized what she was saying. She continued, "I'd like to speak to June and make sure that she is okay with you coming to live with us. It shouldn't be a problem, but I want to run it by her just the same."

I was speechless. This woman was opening up her home to a complete stranger. I had never heard of this sort of thing happening back in Orlando or New York.

Tears welled up in my eyes. This woman was willing to do what my own parents weren't willing to do for me. I stood up, shook her hand and thanked her, and then walked the mile back to Eric's house to wait for her call. That night I could hardly sleep…so much was riding on what June said. The next morning she rang and said that June was fine with me staying with them. Within a week I was ensconced in my own bedroom in a beautiful home in the Montecito area of Santa Barbara, a home more beautiful than anything I had ever lived in before.

During this time, I spent my days lounging around her house, writing letters to Keith that I never sent, and sharing the responsibility of light household chores with June. Sunday's I spent in Sally's church, a small Presbyterian parish housed in a mission-style building not far from where she lived. I immersed myself in Christian life, even going away with the women in her church to an all-women's retreat for a weekend.

It was a very peaceful time, save the increasingly frequent arguments that June and I got into. June was a seventeen year old Mexican girl from a few towns away whose main aspiration was to get back to the life she led with her friends, a world where flannel shirts, heavy black eyeliner, and drag racing on desolate roads was the norm. Needless to say, my New York state of mind and its fascination with the lifestyles of the rich and famous clashed loudly with her mentality.

June and I were both young and headstrong, with very definite opinions on how things should be. We avoided each other whenever possible, and when we couldn't do that, we sniped at each other. After a few months Sally told me that I would have to find another place to stay. Our bickering had gotten to the point that it was unhealthy, and Sally was tired of playing referee.

In another stroke of luck, one of the members of Sally's church was also a supporter of the pro-life movement, a woman I had met at the women's retreat two months earlier. After discussing it with her husband and daughter, they invited me to stay in their home. They too lived in Montecito, in a rambling house in the foothills of the Santa Ynez Mountains. They welcomed me completely into their lives…taking me with them on day trips through the wine country and outings at their older children's homes. Their home, despite its spaciousness, only had two bedrooms, so they converted their dining room into a bedroom for me to live in. I spent the remainder of my pregnancy praying and reading the Bible, and attending secretarial school so I could learn basic office skills. My school expenses were covered by grants and student loans, and my nominal living expenses were paid for by social services.

Six months before I hadn't known what charity was, and now I was receiving it in every area of my life. Charity took a high-school dropout and teen mother out of uncertainty and gave me a chance to make a change in my life. More important than the food and shelter was the pure love these families showed me in my hour of need. Their willingness to give of themselves to an unknown young woman clearly demonstrated to me the magnificence of the human spirit.

It took almost fifteen years, but I finally understand how much I have been given by others over the years. This, coupled with my faith in the abundance of life, is what leads me to try to use every situation in life as an opportunity to give to others. Occasionally it is money, more often it is time. It doesn't take much to make a difference in the life of another person, but the effort that we make can change the direction of a life. Now, and only now, do I feel as if I have earned the right to say that I am self-empowered, for what use is power if we keep it all to ourselves?

A Final Thought

Perhaps nowhere has a greater description of charity been described than in Corinthians 1:13 in the Bible. The Apostle Paul wrote, *"If I speak in human and angelic tongues but do not have charity, I am a resounding gong or a clashing cymbal. And if I have the gift of prophecy and comprehend all mysteries and all knowledge; if I have all faith so as to move mountains but do not have charity, I am nothing. If I give away everything I own, and if I hand my body over so that I may boast but do not have charity, I gain nothing.*

Charity is patient, charity is kind. It is not jealous, is not pompous, it is not inflated, it is not rude, it does not seek its own interests, it is not quick-tempered, it does not brood over injury, it does not rejoice over wrongdoing but rejoices with the truth. It bears all things, believes all things, hopes all things, endures all things.

And now abideth faith, hope, and charity, these three; but the greatest of these is charity."

Charity Summarized

Charity helps to heal and fortify our spirit and the spirits of everyone we touch. It allows us to appreciate on a very deep level the gifts we have been given and changes our attitude from one of scarcity to one of abundance. Life is about attraction, and if we believe we are blessed with abundance we will be.

Charity opens our hearts and helps us to develop compassion for others while simultaneously empowering us with faith in the abundance of life. By giving selflessly to others, we learn to appreciate and value all that we possess. Through the principle of charity, people learn to manifest power not only for the good of their own lives but also the betterment of the existence of those around us. We can then take our rightful place as the empowered guides of our life journey.

AFTERWORD

"Authentic empowerment is the knowing that you are on purpose, doing God's work, peacefully and harmoniously."

~ Wayne Dyer

Self-empowerment is a beautiful journey that will transform the way you view yourself and interact with the world around you. The moment you chose to pursue your truth was the moment you took the first step to own your power and to create the life you have always dreamt of. Living consciously and authentically will bring your spirit the contentment of knowing that you are actively trying to be a part of the solution to the challenges you face.

Self-empowerment is a choice we will make every single day for the rest of our lives. The effort needed to change our lives is not small, and obstacles will pop up all along the way. At times we may believe that the path we have chosen is too difficult. We may believe we don't have the strength to continue pushing forward toward an authentic and empowered existence. The temptation to return to our old ways of thinking and behaving will be greatest when we are feeling tired and frustrated, and it is at these moments that we especially need to guard ourselves from old victim-based behavior and thought patterns.

But it is important to remember, at times like these, exactly what it is that we are actually tempted to return to. We need to play the tape through and ask ourselves why we chose to embark on this journey in the first place. Yes, the journey *will* be difficult, but things are difficult regardless of whether we choose to empower ourselves or to remain disempowered. These feelings of hopelessness will pass...and with their passing we'll find ourselves stronger and more determined than ever.

Self-empowerment is a unique gift, and we must guard against taking it for granted. The philosopher George Santayana said, *"Those who cannot remember the past are condemned to repeat it,"* and it is similarly true that those of us who take for granted what they have earned are condemned to lose it. Treasure your newfound perspective the way a mother cherishes a newborn child, and give thanks for release from a drama-filled way of life.

Self-empowerment is not just a way of thinking; it is an *active way of being.* It is not only a responsibility to ourselves, but to the people around us as well and whenever possible, we must share the joy that we have discovered with others. Robert Frost wrote the following poem in which he shared the process he went through when he embraced his truth:

The Road Not Taken

Two roads diverged in a yellow wood,
And sorry I could not travel both
And be one traveler, long I stood
And looked down one as far as I could
To where it bent in the undergrowth;

Then took the other, as just as fair,
And having perhaps the better claim,
Because it was grassy and wanted wear;
Though as for that the passing there
Had worn them really about the same,

And both that morning equally lay
In leaves no step had trodden black.
Oh, I kept the first for another day!
Yet knowing how way leads on to way,
I doubted if I should ever come back.

I shall be telling this with a sigh
Somewhere ages and ages hence:
Two roads diverged in a wood, and I –
I took the one less traveled by,
And that has made all the difference.

You are to be commended for taking the road less traveled, for it truly does make all the difference!

SEPIA BREAKTHROUGH WORKSHOPS

*Do you want to learn how to stop surviving and
start living an empowered and authentic life?*

Sil Lai Abrams conducts workshops for corporations,
nonprofit groups, and women's groups to help women
become aware of how they can empower themselves.

If you are interested in learning more about these
workshops or to invite Sil Lai Abrams to come speak
at your group, please write her at:

sillai@sepiaprocess.com

You may also visit her on the world wide web:
www.sepiaprocess.com.

sepia press publishing

NO MORE DRAMA

Nine Simple Steps to Transforming a Breakdown Into a Breakthrough

by Sil Lai Abrams

Stop surviving and start living!™

---

*Order your copy today and learn how to create
an **authentic**, **empowered**, and **drama-free** reality!*

NO MORE DRAMA WILL SHOW YOU HOW TO:

- *Identify the core beliefs that are preventing you from manifesting your dreams*
- *Take action to face your challenges*
- *Make and keep your commitments*
- *Eliminate a fear-based belief system*
- *Love and accept yourself and others*
- *Create healthy intimate relationships*
- *Develop an attitude of gratitude and humility*
- *Create a mindset of abundance!*

NO MORE DRAMA features the **SEPIA** process, a revolutionary new way of thinking that will help you stop surviving and start living! **SEPIA** stands for *Self Empowerment Principles In Action*. It is a nine-step method of self inquiry that enables you to challenge your disempowering beliefs and radically change your perspective on life, yourself, and others *permanently*.

Please make checks or money orders payable to Sepia LLC & mail to:
Sepia Press Publishing, 48 West 21st St., Ste.901, NY, NY 10010

BOOK ORDER FORM

☐ Yes! I want to order _____ copies of *No More Drama: Nine Simple Steps to Transforming a Breakdown Into a Breakthrough* ™ at **$15.95** each plus **$5.00** shipping for the first book, **$1.00** for each additional book. (NY State residents please add 8.625% sales tax.) Please allow up to two weeks for delivery.

Method of Payment ☐ Cash ☐ Visa ☐ American Express Total Amount: $ _____

☐ Check/M.O. ☐ MasterCard

Name _____

Address _____

Phone _____ Email _____

Credit Card # _____ Exp. date _____ CVV# _____

Signature _____

Orders of **5** or more books receive 20% off purchase price, a savings of **$3.19** each!